'*The Celestine Prophecy* homes in on the deepest, most
urgent search of our times, the search for meaning . . . this
is a book like no other'
Telegraph

The Celestine Prophecy: An Experiential Guide
'An extraordinary map for the evolutionary journey that
began in *The Celestine Prophecy*'
Michael Murphy, author of *The Future of the Body*

The Tenth Insight
'Spellbinding . . . A worthy sequel to his *Celestine*
masterpiece. James Redfield packs thrills, suspense
and spiritual wisdom into a book you cannot put
down. You must read *The Tenth Insight*!'
Brian Weiss, MD, author of *Many Lives, Many Masters*

The Celestine Vision
'The godfather of gurus is back . . . The style is clear
and engaging'
Express

The Secret of Shambhala
'Great storytelling . . . Read this book to get in touch with
the mysteries of great masters'
Deepak Chopra, author of *The Seven Spiritual Laws of Success*

God and the Evolving Universe
'Informative, thought-provoking and challenging'
Library Journal

Also by James Redfield

THE CELESTINE PROPHECY:
AN EXPERIENTIAL GUIDE
THE TENTH INSIGHT
THE TENTH INSIGHT: AN EXPERIENTIAL GUIDE
THE CELESTINE VISION
THE SECRET OF SHAMBHALA
GOD AND THE EVOLVING UNIVERSE

and published by Bantam Books

THE CELESTINE PROPHECY

An Adventure

James Redfield

BANTAM BOOKS

LONDON • TORONTO • SYDNEY • AUCKLAND • JOHANNESBURG

TRANSWORLD PUBLISHERS
61–63 Uxbridge Road, London W5 5SA
A Random House Group Company
www.transworldbooks.co.uk

THE CELESTINE PROPHECY
A BANTAM BOOK: 9780553409024

52

First published in Great Britain
in 1994 by Bantam Books
an imprint of Transworld Publishers
Bantam edition reissued 2009

Addresses for Random House Group Ltd companies outside the UK
can be found at: www.randomhouse.co.uk
The Random House Group Ltd Reg. No. 954009

The Random House Group Limited supports The Forest Stewardship
Council (FSC®), the leading international forest certification organisation.
Our books carrying the FSC label are printed on FSC® certified paper. FSC is
the only forest certification scheme endorsed by the leading environmental
organisations, including Greenpeace. Our paper procurement policy can be
found at www.randomhouse.co.uk/environment

Typeset in 11/14pt Palatino by
Falcon Oast Graphic Art Ltd.
Printed and bound by CPI Group (UK) Ltd, Croydon, CR0 4YY

MIX
Paper from
responsible sources
FSC® C016897

And those who have insight will shine brightly
like the brightness of the expanse of Heaven,
and those who lead the many to righteousness,
like the stars forever and ever.
But for you, Daniel, conceal these words and
seal up the book until the end of time. Many will
go back and forth, and knowledge will increase.

DANIEL 12:3–4

ACKNOWLEDGMENTS

So many people influenced this book that it would be impossible to mention them all. But I must say special thanks to Alan Shields, Jim Gamble, Mark Lafountain, Marc and Debra McElhaney, Dan Questenberry, B.J. Jones, Bobby Hudson, Joy and Bob Kwapien, Michael Ryce, author of the tape series 'Why is this happening to me again', and most of all, to my wife, Salle.

ACKNOWLEDGMENTS

CONTENTS

Author's Note

For half a century now, a new consciousness has been entering the human world, a new awareness that can only be called transcendent, spiritual. If you find yourself reading this book, then perhaps you already sense what is happening, already feel it inside.

It begins with a heightened perception of the way our lives move forward. We notice those chance events that occur at just the right moment, and bring forth just the right individuals, to suddenly send our lives in a new and important direction. Perhaps more than any other people in any other time, we intuit higher meaning in these mysterious happenings.

We know that life is really about a spiritual unfolding that is personal and enchanting – an unfolding that no science or philosophy or religion has yet fully clarified. And we know something else as well: we know that once we do understand what is happening, how to engage this elusive process and maximize its occurrence in our lives, human society will take a quantum leap into a whole new way of life – one that realizes the best of our tradition and creates a culture that has been the goal of history all along.

The following story is offered toward this new under-standing. If it touches you, if it crystallizes something that you perceive in life, then pass on what you see to another – for I think our new awareness of the spiritual is expand-ing in exactly this way, no longer through hype nor fad, but personally, through a kind of positive psychological contagion among people.

All that any of us have to do is suspend our doubts and distractions just long enough . . . and miraculously, this reality can be our own.

A Critical Mass

I drove up to the restaurant and parked, then leaned back in my seat to think for a moment. Charlene, I knew, would already be inside, waiting to talk with me. But why? I hadn't heard a word from her in six years. Why would she have shown up now, just when I had sequestered myself in the woods for a week?

I stepped out of the truck and walked toward the restaurant. Behind me, the last glow of a sunset sank in the west and cast highlights of golden amber across the wet parking lot. Everything had been drenched an hour earlier by a brief thunderstorm, and now the summer evening felt cool and renewed, and because of the fading light, almost surreal. A half moon hung overhead.

As I walked, old images of Charlene filled my mind. Was she still beautiful, intense? How would time have changed her? And what was I to think of this manuscript she had mentioned – this ancient artifact found in South America that she couldn't wait to tell me about?

'I have a two-hour layover at the airport,' she had said on the telephone. 'Can you meet me for dinner? You're going to love what this manuscript says – it's just your kind of mystery.'

My kind of mystery? What did she mean by that?

Inside, the restaurant was crowded. Several couples waited for tables. When I found the hostess, she told me Charlene had already been seated and directed me toward a terraced area above the main dining room.

I walked up the steps and became aware of a crowd of people surrounding one of the tables. The crowd included two policemen. Suddenly, the policemen turned and rushed past me and down the steps. As the rest of the people dispersed, I could see past them to the person who seemed to have been the center of attention – a woman, still seated at the table . . . Charlene!

I quickly walked up to her. 'Charlene, what's going on? Is anything wrong?'

She tossed her head back in mock exasperation and stood up, flashing her famous smile. I noticed that her hair was perhaps different, but her face was exactly as I remembered: small delicate features, wide mouth, huge blue eyes.

'You wouldn't believe it,' she said, pulling me into a friendly hug. 'I went to the rest room a few minutes ago and while I was gone, someone stole my briefcase.'

'What was in it?'

'Nothing of importance, just some books and magazines I was taking along for the trip. It's crazy. The people at the other tables told me someone just walked in, picked it up, and walked out. They gave the police a description and the officers said they would search the area.'

'Maybe I should help them look?'

'No, no. Let's forget about it. I don't have much time and I want to talk with you.'

I nodded and Charlene suggested we sit down. A waiter approached so we looked over the menu and gave him our order. Afterward, we spent ten or fifteen minutes chatting in general. I tried to underplay my self-imposed isolation but Charlene picked up on my vagueness. She leaned over and gave me that smile again.

'So what's *really* going on with you?' she asked.

I looked at her eyes, at the intense way she was looking at me. 'You want the whole story immediately, don't you?'

'Always,' she said.

'Well, the truth is, I'm taking some time for myself right now and staying at the lake. I've been working hard and I'm thinking about changing directions in my life.'

'I remember you talking about that lake. I thought you and your sister had to sell it.'

'Not yet, but the problem is property taxes. Because the land is so close to the city, the taxes keep increasing.'

She nodded. 'So what are you going to do next?'

'I don't know yet. Something different.'

She gave me an intriguing look. 'Sounds as if you're as restless as everyone else.'

'I suppose,' I said. 'Why do you ask?'

'It's in the Manuscript.'

There was silence as I returned her gaze.

'Tell me about this Manuscript,' I said.

She leaned back in her chair as if to gather her thoughts, then looked me in the eye again. 'I mentioned on the phone, I think, that I left the newspaper several years ago and joined a research firm that investigates cultural and demographic changes for the UN. My last assignment was in Peru.

'While I was there, completing some research at the University of Lima, I kept hearing rumors about an old manuscript that had been discovered – only no one could give me any of the details, not even at the departments of archaeology or anthropology. And when I contacted the government about it, they denied any knowledge whatsoever.

'One person told me that the government was actually working to suppress this document for some reason. Although, again, he had no direct knowledge.

'You know me,' she continued. 'I'm curious. When my assignment was over, I decided to stay around for a couple of days to see what I could find out. At first, every lead I pursued turned out to be another dead end, but then while I was eating lunch in a café outside of Lima, I noticed a priest watching me. After a few minutes, he walked over and admitted that he had heard me inquiring about the Manuscript earlier in the day. He wouldn't reveal his name but he agreed to answer all my questions.'

She hesitated for a moment, still looking at me intensely. 'He said the Manuscript dates back to about 600 BC. It predicts a massive transformation in human society.'

'Beginning when?' I asked.

'In the last decades of the twentieth century.'

'Now?!'

'Yes, now.'

'What kind of transformation is it supposed to be?' I asked.

She looked embarrassed for a moment, then with force

16

said, 'The priest told me it's a kind of renaissance in consciousness, occurring very slowly. It's not religious in nature, but it is spiritual. We're discovering something new about human life on this planet, about what our existence means, and according to the priest, this knowledge will alter human culture dramatically.'

She paused again, then added, 'The priest told me the Manuscript is divided into segments, or chapters, each devoted to a particular insight into life. The Manuscript predicts that in this time period human beings will begin to grasp these insights sequentially, one insight then another, as we move from where we are now to a completely spiritual culture on Earth.'

I shook my head and raised an eyebrow cynically. 'Do you really believe all this?'

'Well,' she said. 'I think . . .'

'Look around,' I interrupted, pointing at the crowd sitting in the room below us. 'This is the real world. Do you see anything changing out there?'

Just as I said that, an angry remark erupted from a table near the far wall, a remark I couldn't understand, but which was loud enough to hush the entire room. At first I thought the disturbance was another robbery, but then I realized it was only an argument. A woman appearing to be in her thirties was standing up and staring indignantly at a man seated across from her.

'No,' she yelled. 'The problem is that this relationship is not happening the way I wanted! Do you understand? It's not happening!' She composed herself, tossed her napkin on the table, and walked out.

Charlene and I stared at each other, shocked that the outburst had occurred at the very moment we were discussing the people below us. Finally Charlene nodded toward the table where the man remained alone and said, 'It's the real world that's changing.'

'How?' I asked, still off balance.

'The transformation is beginning with the First Insight, and according to the priest, this insight always surfaces unconsciously at first, as a profound sense of restlessness.'

'Restlessness?'

'Yes.'

'What are we looking for?'

'That's just it! At first we aren't sure. According to the Manuscript, we're beginning to glimpse an alternative kind of experience ... moments in our lives that feel different somehow, more intense and inspiring. But we don't know what this experience is or how to make it last, and when it ends we're left feeling dissatisfied and restless with a life that seems ordinary again.'

'You think this restlessness was behind the woman's anger?'

'Yes. She's just like the rest of us. We're all looking for more fulfillment in our lives, and we won't put up with anything that seems to bring us down. This restless searching is what's behind the "me-first" attitude that has characterized recent decades, and it's affecting everyone, from Wall Street to street gangs.'

She looked directly at me. 'And when it comes to relationships, we're so demanding that we're making them near impossible.'

Her remark brought back the memory of my last two relationships. Both had begun intensely and both within a year had failed. When I focused on Charlene again, she was waiting patiently.

'What exactly are we doing to our romantic relationships?' I asked.

'I talked with the priest a long time about this,' she replied. 'He said that when both partners in a relationship are overly demanding, when each expects the other to live in his or her world, to always be there to join in his or her chosen activities, an ego battle inevitably develops.'

What she said struck home. My last two relationships had indeed degenerated into power struggles. In both situations, we had found ourselves in a conflict of agendas. The pace had been too fast. We had too little time to co-ordinate our different ideas about what to do, where to go, what interests to pursue. In the end, the issue of who would lead, who would determine the direction for the day, had become an irresolvable difficulty.

'Because of this control battle,' Charlene continued, 'the Manuscript says we will find it very difficult to stay with the same person for any length of time.'

'That doesn't seem very spiritual,' I said.

'That's exactly what I told the priest,' she replied. 'He said to remember that while most of society's recent ills can be traced to this restlessness and searching, this problem is temporary, and will come to an end. We're finally becoming conscious of what we're actually looking for, of what this other, more fulfilling experience really is. When we grasp it fully, we'll have attained the First Insight.'

Our dinner arrived so we paused for several minutes as the waiter poured more wine, and to taste each other's food. When she reached across the table to take a bite of salmon from my plate, Charlene wrinkled her nose and giggled. I realized how easy it was to be with her.

'Okay,' I said. 'What is this experience we're looking for? What is the First Insight?'

She hesitated, as though unsure how to begin.

'This is hard to explain,' she said. 'But the priest put it this way. He said the First Insight occurs when we become conscious of the *coincidences* in our lives.'

She leaned toward me. 'Have you ever had a hunch or intuition concerning something you wanted to do? Some course you wanted to take in your life? And wondered how it might happen? And then, after you had half forgotten about it and focused on other things, you suddenly met someone or read something or went somewhere that led to the very opportunity you envisioned?

'Well,' she continued, 'according to the priest, these coincidences are happening more and more frequently and, when they do, they strike us as beyond what would be expected by pure chance. They feel destined, as though our lives had been guided by some unexplained force. The experience induces a feeling of mystery and excitement and, as a result, we feel more alive.

'The priest told me that this is the experience that we've glimpsed and that we're now trying to manifest all the time. More people every day are convinced that this mysterious movement is real and that it means something, that something else is going on beneath everyday life. This awareness is the First Insight.'

She looked at me expectantly, but I said nothing.

'Don't you see?' she asked. 'The First Insight is a reconsideration of the inherent mystery that surrounds our individual lives on this planet. We are experiencing these mysterious coincidences, and even though we don't understand them yet, we know they are real. We are sensing again, as in childhood, that there is another side of life that we have yet to discover, some other process operating behind the scenes.'

Charlene was leaning further toward me, gesturing with her hands as she spoke.

'You're really into this, aren't you?' I asked.

'I can remember a time,' she said, sternly, 'when you talked about these kinds of experiences.'

Her comment jolted me. She was right. There had been a period in my life when I had indeed experienced such coincidences and had even tried to understand them psychologically. Somewhere along the way, my view had changed. I had begun to regard such perceptions as immature and unrealistic for some reason, and I had stopped even noticing.

I looked directly at Charlene, then said defensively, 'I was probably reading Eastern Philosophy or Christian Mysticism at that time. That's what you remember. Anyway, what you're calling the First Insight has been written about many times, Charlene. What's different now? How is a perception of mysterious occurrences going to lead to a cultural transformation?'

Charlene looked down at the table for an instant and then back at me. 'Don't misunderstand,' she said. 'Certainly this consciousness has been experienced and described before. In fact, the priest made a point to say that the First Insight wasn't new. He said individuals have been aware of these unexplained coincidences throughout history, that this has been the perception behind many great attempts at philosophy and religion. But the difference now lies in the numbers. According to the priest, the transformation is occurring now because of the number of individuals having this awareness all at the same time.'

'What did he mean, exactly?' I asked.

'He told me the Manuscript says the number of people who are conscious of such coincidences would begin to grow dramatically in the sixth decade of the twentieth century. He said that this growth would continue until sometime near the beginning of the following century, when we would reach a specific level of such individuals – a level I think of as a critical mass.

'The Manuscript predicts,' she went on, 'that once we reach this critical mass, the entire culture will begin to take these coincidental experiences seriously. We will wonder, en masse, what mysterious process underlies human life on this planet. And it will be this question, asked at the same time by enough people, that will allow the other insights to also come into consciousness – because according to the Manuscript, when a sufficient number of individuals seriously question what's going on in life, we will begin to find out. The other insights will be revealed . . . one after the other.'

She paused to take a bite of food.

'And when we grasp the other insights,' I asked, 'then the culture will shift?'

'That's what the priest told me,' she said.

I looked at her for a moment, contemplating the idea of a critical mass, then said, 'You know, all this sounds awfully sophisticated for a Manuscript written in 600 BC.'

'I know,' she replied. 'I raised the question myself. But the priest assured me that the scholars who first trans-lated the Manuscript were absolutely convinced of its authenticity. Mainly because it was written in Aramaic,

22

the same language in which much of the Old Testament was written.'

'Aramaic in South America? How did it get there in 600 BC?'

'The priest didn't know.'

'Does his church support the Manuscript?' I asked.

'No,' she said. 'He told me that most of the clergy were bitterly trying to suppress the Manuscript. That's why he couldn't tell me his name. Apparently talking about it at all was very dangerous for him.'

'Did he say why most church officials were fighting against it?'

'Yes, because it challenges the completeness of their religion.'

'How?'

'I don't know exactly. He didn't discuss it much, but apparently the other insights extend some of the church's traditional ideas in a way that alarms the church elders, who think things are fine the way they are.'

'I see.'

'The priest did say,' Charlene went on, 'that he doesn't think the Manuscript undermines any of the church's principles. If anything, it clarifies exactly what is meant by these spiritual truths. He felt strongly that the church leaders would see this fact if they would try to see life as a mystery again and then proceed through the other insights.'

'Did he tell you how many insights there were?'

'No, but he did mention the Second Insight. He told me it is a more correct interpretation of recent history, one that further clarifies the transformation.'

'Did he elaborate on that?'

'No, he didn't have time. He said he had to leave to take care of some business. We agreed to meet back at his house that afternoon, but when I arrived he wasn't there. I waited three hours and he still didn't show up. Finally, I had to leave to catch my flight home.'

'You mean you weren't able to talk with him any more?'

'That's right. I never saw him again.'

'And you never received any confirmation about the Manuscript from the government?'

'None.'

'And how long ago did this take place?'

'About a month and a half.'

For several minutes we ate in silence. Finally Charlene looked up and asked, 'So what do you think?'

'I don't know,' I said. Part of me remained skeptical of the idea that human beings could really change. But another part of me was amazed to think that a Manuscript which spoke in these terms might actually exist.

'Did he show you a copy or anything?' I asked.

'No. All I have are my notes.'

Again we were silent.

'You know,' she said, 'I had thought you would be really excited by these ideas.'

I looked at her. 'I guess I need some proof that what this Manuscript says is true.'

She smiled broadly again.

'What?' I asked.

'That's exactly what I said, too.'

'To whom, the priest?'

'Yes.'

24

'What did he say?'

'He meant that our experience validates what the Manuscript says. When we truly reflect on how we feel inside, on how our lives are proceeding at this point in history, we can see that the ideas in the Manuscript make sense, that they ring true.' She hesitated. 'Does it make sense to you?'

I thought for a moment. Does it make sense? Is everyone as restless as me, and if so, does our restlessness result from the simple insight – the simple awareness built up for thirty years that there is really more to life than we know, more that we can experience?

'I'm not sure,' I finally said, 'I guess I need some time to think about it.'

I walked out to the garden beside the restaurant and stood behind a cedar bench facing the fountain. To my right I could see the pulsating lights at the airport and hear the roaring engines of a jet ready for take off.

'What beautiful flowers,' Charlene said from behind me. I turned to see her walking toward me along the walkway, admiring the rows of petunias and begonias which bordered the sitting area. She stood beside me and I put my arm around her. Memories flooded my mind. Years ago, when we had both lived in Charlottesville, Virginia, we had spent regular evenings together, talking. Most of our discussions were about academic theories and psychological growth. We had both been fascinated by the conversations and by each other. Yet it struck me how platonic our relationship had always been.

'I can't tell you,' she said, 'how nice it is to see you again.'

'I know,' I replied. 'Seeing you brings back a lot of memories.'

'I wonder why we didn't stay in touch?' she asked.

Her question took me back again. I recalled the last time I had seen Charlene. She was telling me good-bye at my car. At the time I felt full of new ideas and was departing for my home town to work with severely abused children. I thought I knew how such children could transcend the intense reactions, the obsessive acting out, that kept them from going on with their lives. But as time had progressed, my approach had failed. I had to admit my ignorance. How humans might liberate themselves from their pasts was still an enigma to me.

Looking back over the previous six years I now felt sure the experience had been worthwhile. Yet I also felt the urge to move on. But to where? To do what? I had thought of Charlene only a few times since she had helped me crystallize my ideas about childhood trauma, and now here she was again, back in my life – and our conversation felt just as exciting as before.

'I guess I got totally absorbed in my work,' I said.

'So did I,' she replied. 'At the paper it was one story after another. I didn't have time to look up. I forgot about everything else.'

I squeezed her shoulder. 'You know, Charlene, I had forgotten how well we talk together; our conversation seems so easy and spontaneous.'

Her eyes and smile confirmed my perception. 'I know,' she said, 'conversations with you give me so much energy.'

I was about to make another comment when Charlene stared past me toward the entrance to the restaurant. Her face grew anxious and pale.

'What's wrong?' I asked, turning to look in that direction. Several people were walking toward the parking lot, talking casually, but nothing seemed out of the ordinary. I turned to face Charlene again. She still appeared alarmed and confused.

'What is it?' I repeated.

'Over by the first row of cars – did you see that man in the gray shirt?'

I looked toward the parking lot again. Another group was exiting through the door. 'What man?'

'I guess he's not there now,' she said, straining to see.

She looked directly into my eyes. 'When the people at the other tables described the man who stole my brief-case, they said he had thinning hair and a beard, and wore a gray shirt. I think I just saw him over there by the cars . . . watching us.'

A knot of anxiety formed in my stomach. I told Charlene I would be right back and walked to the parking lot to look around, careful not to get too far away. I saw no one who fit the description.

When I returned to the bench, Charlene took a step closer to me and said softly, 'Do you suppose this person thinks I have a copy of the Manuscript? And that's why he took my briefcase? He's trying to get it back?'

'I don't know,' I said. 'But we're going to call the police again and tell them what you saw. I think they also ought to check out the passengers on your flight.'

We walked inside and called the police, and when they arrived we informed them of what had occurred. They spent twenty minutes checking each car, then explained that they could invest no more time. They did agree to check all the passengers boarding the plane Charlene would be on.

After the police had left, Charlene and I found ourselves standing alone again by the fountain.

'What were we talking about, anyway?' she asked. 'Before I saw that man?'

'We were talking about us,' I replied. 'Charlene, why did you think to contact me about all this?'

She gave me a perplexed look. 'When I was in Peru and the priest was telling me about the Manuscript, you kept popping into my mind.'

'Oh yeah?'

'I didn't think too much about it then,' she continued, 'but later, after I returned to Virginia, every time I would think of the Manuscript, I would think of you. I started to call several times but I always got distracted. Then, I received this assignment in Miami that I'm headed to now and discovered, after I had boarded the plane, that I had a layover here. When I landed I looked up your number. Your answering machine said to contact you at the lake only in an emergency, but I decided it would be okay to call.'

I looked at her for a moment, unsure of what to think. 'Of course,' I finally replied. 'I'm glad you did.'

Charlene glanced at her watch. 'It's getting late. I'd better get back to the airport.'

'I'll drive you,' I said.

We drove to the main terminal and walked toward the embarkation area. I watched carefully for anything unusual. When we arrived, the plane was already boarding and one of the policemen we had met was observing each passenger. When we approached him, he told us that he had observed everyone scheduled to board and no one fit the description of the thief.

We thanked him and after he had left, Charlene turned and smiled at me. 'I guess I'd better go,' she said, reaching out to hug my neck. 'Here are my numbers. Let's keep in touch this time.'

'Listen,' I said. 'I want you to be careful. If you see anything strange, call the police!'

'Don't worry about me,' she replied. 'I'll be fine.'

For an instant we looked deeply into each other's eyes.

'What are you going to do about this Manuscript?' I asked.

'I don't know. Listen for news reports about it, I guess.'

'What if it's suppressed?'

She gave me another of her full smiles. 'I knew it,' she said. 'You're hooked. I told you you'd love it. What are *you* going to do?'

I shrugged. 'See if I can find out more about it, probably.'

'Good. If you do, let me know.'

We said good-bye again and she walked away. I watched as she turned once and waved, then disappeared down the boarding corridor. I walked to my truck and drove back to the lake, stopping only for gas.

When I arrived, I walked out to the screened porch and sat in one of the rockers. The evening was loud with crickets and tree frogs and in the distance I could hear a whip-o-will. Across the lake, the moon had sunk lower in the west and sent a rippled line of reflection toward me on the water's surface.

The evening had been interesting, but I was still skeptical about the whole idea of a cultural transformation. Like many people, I had been caught up in the social idealism of the Sixties and Seventies, and even in the spiritual interests of the Eighties. But it was hard to judge what was really happening. What kind of new information could possibly alter the entire human world? It all sounded too idealistic and far-fetched. After all, humans had been alive on this planet for a long time. Why would we suddenly gain insight into existence now, at this late date? I gazed out at the water for a few more minutes, then turned off the lights and went into the bedroom to read.

The next morning I awoke suddenly with a dream still fresh in my mind. For a minute or two I stared at the bedroom ceiling, remembering it fully. I had been making my way through a forest searching for something. The forest was large and exceptionally beautiful.

In my quest I found myself in a number of situations in which I felt totally lost and bewildered, unable to decide how to proceed. Incredibly, at each of these moments, a person would appear out of nowhere as though by design to clarify where I needed to go next. I never became aware of the object of my search but the dream had left me feeling incredibly upbeat and confident.

I sat up and noticed a beam of sunlight coming through the window across the room. It sparkled with suspended dust particles. I walked over and pulled back the curtains. The day was radiant: blue sky, bright sunshine. A stiff breeze gently rocked the trees. The lake would be rippled and glistening this time of day, and the wind chilly against a swimmer's wet skin.

I walked outside and dived in. I surfaced and swam

out to the middle of the lake, turning on my back to look at the familiar mountains. The lake rested in a deep valley where three mountain ridges converged, a perfect lake site discovered by my grandfather in his youth.

It had now been a hundred years since he had first walked these ridges, a child explorer, a prodigy growing up in a world that was still wild with cougar and boar and Creek Indians that lived in primitive cabins up the north ridge. He had sworn at the time that one day he would live in this perfect valley with its massive old trees and seven springs, and finally he had – later to build a lake and a cabin and to take countless walks with a young grandson. I never quite understood my grandfather's fascination with this valley, but I had always tried to preserve the land, even when civilization encroached, then surrounded.

From the middle of the lake, I could see a particular rock outcropping near the crest of the north ridge. The day before, in the tradition of my grandfather, I had climbed to that overhang, trying to find some peace in the view and in the smells and in the way the wind whirled in the tree tops. And as I had sat up there, surveying the lake and the dense foliage in the valley below, I had slowly felt better, as if the energy and the perspective were dissolving some block in my mind A few hours later I had been talking with Charlene and hearing about the Manuscript.

I swam back and pulled myself up on the wooden pier in front of the cabin. I knew all this was too much to believe. I mean, here I was hiding out in these hills, feeling totally disenchanted with my life, when out of the blue, Charlene shows up and explains the cause of my restlessness – quoting some old manuscript that promises the secret of human existence.

Yet I also knew that Charlene's arrival was exactly the sort of coincidence of which the Manuscript spoke, one that seemed too unlikely to be a mere chance event. Could this ancient document be correct? Have we been slowly building, in spite of our denial and cynicism, a critical mass of people conscious of these coincidences? Were humans now in a position to understand this phenomenon and thus, finally, to understand the purpose behind life itself?

What, I wondered, would this new understanding be? Would the remaining Insights in the Manuscript tell us, as the priest had said?

I faced a decision. Because of the Manuscript I felt a new direction open in my life, a new point of interest. The question was what to do now? I could remain here or I could find a way to explore further. The issue of danger entered my mind. Who had stolen Charlene's briefcase? Was it someone working to suppress the Manuscript? How could I know?

I thought about the possible risk for a long time, but finally my mood of optimism prevailed. I decided not to worry. I would be careful and go slowly. I walked inside and called the travel agency with the largest ad in the yellow pages. The agent with whom I spoke said he could indeed arrange a trip to Peru. In fact, by chance, there was a cancellation I could fill – a flight with reservations already confirmed at a hotel in Lima. I could have the whole package at a discount, he said . . . if I could leave in three hours.

Three hours?

The Longer Now

After a frenzy of packing and a wild ride on the freeway, I arrived at the airport with just enough time to pick up my ticket and board the flight for Peru. As I walked into the plane's tail section and sat down in a window seat, fatigue swept over me.

I thought about a nap, but when I stretched out and closed my eyes, I found I couldn't relax. I suddenly felt nervous and ambivalent about the trip. Was it crazy to depart with no preparation? Where would I go in Peru? To whom would I talk?

The confidence I had experienced at the lake was quickly fading back into skepticism. Both the First Insight and the idea of a cultural transformation again seemed fanciful and unrealistic. And as I thought about it, the concept of a Second Insight seemed just as unlikely. How could a new historical perspective enhance our perception of these coincidences and keep them conscious in the public mind?

I stretched out further and took a deep breath. Maybe it would be a useless trip, I concluded, just a quick run to Peru and back. A waste of money perhaps but no real harm done.

The plane jerked forward and taxied out to the runway. I closed my eyes and felt a mild dizziness as the big jet reached the critical speed and lifted into a thick cloud cover. When we reached cruising altitude, I finally relaxed and drifted into sleep. Thirty or forty minutes later, a stretch of turbulence woke me up and I decided to go to the rest room.

As I made my way through the lounge area I noticed a tall man with round glasses standing near the window talking to a flight attendant. He glanced at me briefly, then continued speaking. He had dark brown hair and appeared to be about forty-five years old. For an instant I thought I recognized him, but after looking at his features closely, I concluded he was no one I knew. As I walked past I could hear part of the conversation.

'Thanks anyway,' the man said, 'I just thought since you travel to Peru so often that perhaps you had heard something about the Manuscript.' He turned away and walked toward the front of the plane.

I was dumbstruck. Was he speaking of the same Manuscript? I walked into the rest room and tried to decide what to do. Part of me wanted to forget about it. Probably he was talking about something else, some other book.

I returned to my seat and closed my eyes again, content to write off the incident, glad I didn't have to ask the man what he meant. But as I sat there, I thought about the excitement I had felt at the lake. What if this man actually had information about the Manuscript? What might happen then? If I didn't inquire, I would never know.

I wavered several more times in my mind, then finally stood up and walked toward the front of the plane, finding him about midway up the aisle. Directly behind him was an empty seat. I walked back and told an attendant I wanted to move, then gathered my things and took the seat. After a few minutes, I tapped him on the shoulder.

'Excuse me,' I said. 'I heard you mention a manuscript. Were you speaking of the one found in Peru?'

He looked surprised, then cautious. 'Yes, I was,' he said tentatively.

I introduced myself and explained that a friend had been in Peru recently and had informed me of the Manuscript's existence. He visibly relaxed and introduced himself as Wayne Dobson, an assistant professor of history from New York University.

As we spoke, I noticed a look of irritation coming from the gentleman sitting next to me. He had leaned back in his seat and was attempting to sleep.

'Have you seen the Manuscript?' I asked the professor.

'Parts of it,' he said. 'Have you?'

'No, but my friend told me about the First Insight.' The man beside me changed his position.

Dobson looked his way. 'Excuse me, sir. I know we're disturbing you. Would it be too much trouble for you to exchange seats with me?'

'No,' the man said. 'That would be preferable.'

We all stepped into the aisle and then I slid back into the window seat and Dobson sat beside me.

'Tell me what you heard concerning the First Insight,' Dobson said.

I paused for a moment, trying to sum up in my mind what I understood. 'I guess the First Insight is an awareness of the mysterious occurrences that change one's life, the feeling that some other process is operating.'

I felt absurd as I said it.

Dobson picked up on my discomfort. 'What do you think of that insight?' he asked.

'I don't know,' I said.

'It doesn't quite fit with our modern day common sense, does it? Wouldn't you feel better dismissing the whole idea and getting back to thinking about practical matters?'

I laughed and nodded affirmatively.

'Well, that's everyone's tendency. Even though we occasionally have the clear insight that something more is going on in life, our habitual way of thinking is to consider such ideas unknowable and then to shrug off the awareness altogether. That's why the Second Insight is necessary. Once we see the historical background to our awareness, it seems more valid.'

I nodded. 'Then as a historian you think the Manuscript's prediction of a global transformation is accurate?'

'Yes.'

'As a historian?'

'Yes! But you have to look at history in the correct way.' He took a deep breath. 'Believe me, I say this as one who has spent a lot of years studying and teaching history in the wrong way! I used to focus solely on the technological accomplishments of civilization and the great men who brought about this progress.'

'What's wrong with that approach?'

'Nothing, as far as it goes. But what's really important is the world view of each historical period, what the people were feeling and thinking. It took me a long time to understand that. History is supposed to provide a knowledge of the longer context within which our lives take place. History is not just the evolution of technology; it is the evolution of thought. By understanding the reality of the people who came before us, we can see why we look at the world the way we do, and what our contribution is toward further progress. We can pinpoint where we come in, so to speak, in the longer development of civilization, and that gives us a sense of where we are going.'

He paused, then added, 'The effect of the Second Insight is to provide exactly this kind of historical perspective, at least from the point of view of western thought. It places the Manuscript's predictions in a longer context that makes them seem not only plausible, but inevitable.'

I asked Dobson how many insights he had seen and he told me only the first two. He had found them, he said, after a rumor about the Manuscript prompted a short trip to Peru three weeks ago.

'Once I arrived in Peru,' he continued, 'I met a couple of people who confirmed the Manuscript's existence yet seemed scared to death to talk much about it. They said the government had gone a little loco and was making physical threats against anyone who had copies or dispersed information.'

His face turned serious. 'That made me nervous. But later a waiter at my hotel told me about a priest he knew who often spoke of the Manuscript. The waiter said the priest was trying to fight the government's effort to suppress the artifact. I couldn't resist going to a private dwelling where this priest supposedly spent most of his time.'

I must have looked surprised, because Dobson asked, 'What's wrong?'

'My friend,' I replied, 'the one who told me about the Manuscript, learned what she knew from a priest. He wouldn't give his name, but she talked with him once about the First Insight. She was scheduled to meet with him again but he never showed up.'

'It may have been the same man,' Dobson said. 'Because I couldn't find him either. The house was locked up and looked deserted.'

'You never saw him?'

'No, but I decided to look around. There was an old storage building in the back that was open and for some reason I decided to explore inside. Behind some trash, under a loose board in the wall, I found translations of the First and Second Insights.'

He looked at me knowingly.

'You just happened to find them?' I asked.

'Yes.'

'Did you bring the Insights with you on this trip?'

He shook his head. 'No. I decided to study them thoroughly and then leave them with some of my colleagues.'

'Could you give me a summary of the Second Insight?' I asked.

There was a long pause, then Dobson smiled and nodded. 'I guess that's why we're here.'

'The Second Insight,' he said, 'puts our current awareness into a longer historical perspective. After all, when the decade of the nineties is over, we'll be finishing up not only the twentieth century but a thousand year period of history as well. We'll be completing the entire second millennium. Before we in the west can understand where we are, and what is going to occur next, we must understand what has really been happening during this current thousand year period.'

'What does the Manuscript say exactly?' I asked.

'It says that at the close of the second millennium – that's now – we will be able to see that entire period of history as a whole, and we will identify a particular pre-occupation that developed during the later half of this millennium, in what has been called the Modern Age. Our awareness of the coincidences today represents a kind of awakening from this preoccupation.'

'What's the preoccupation?' I asked.

He gave me a mischievous half smile. 'Are you ready to relive the millennium?'

'Sure, tell me about it.'

'It's not enough for me to tell you about it. Remember what I said before: to understand history, you must grasp how your everyday view of the world developed, how it was created by the reality of the people who lived before you. It took a thousand years to evolve the modern way of looking at things, and to really understand where you are today, you must take yourself back to the year 1000 and then move forward through the entire millennium experientially, as though you actually lived through the whole period yourself in a single lifetime.'

'How do I do that?'

'I'll guide you through it.'

I hesitated for a moment, glancing out the window at

the land formations far below. Time was already beginning to feel different.

'I'll try,' I said finally.

'Okay,' he replied, 'imagine yourself being alive in the year one thousand, in what we have called the Middle Ages. The first thing you must understand is that the reality of this time is being defined by the powerful churchmen of the Christian church. Because of their position, these men hold great influence over the minds of the populace. And the world these churchmen describe as real is, above all, spiritual. They are creating a reality which places their idea about God's plan for mankind at the very center of life.

'Visualize this,' he continued. 'You find yourself in the class of your father – essentially peasant or aristocrat – and you know that you will always be confined to this class. But regardless of which class you're in, or the particular work that you do, you soon realize that social position is secondary to the spiritual reality of life as defined by the churchmen.

'Life is about passing a spiritual test, you discover. The churchmen explain that God has placed mankind at the center of his universe, surrounded by the entire cosmos, for one solitary purpose: to win or lose salvation. And in this trial you must correctly choose between two opposing forces: the force of God and the lurking temptations of the devil.

'But understand that you don't face this contest alone,' he continued. 'In fact, as a mere individual you aren't qualified to determine your status in this regard. This is the province of the churchmen; they are there to interpret the scriptures and to tell you every step of the way whether you are in accordance with God or whether you are being duped by Satan. If you follow their instructions, you are assured that a rewarding afterlife will follow. But if you fail to heed the course they prescribe, then, well . . . there is excommunication and certain damnation.'

Dobson looked at me intensely. 'The Manuscript says that the important thing to understand here is that every aspect of the Medieval world is defined in other-worldly terms. All the phenomena of life – from the chance thunderstorm or earthquake to the success of crops or the death of a loved one – is defined either as the will of God or as the malice of the devil. There is no concept of weather or geological forces or horticulture or disease. All that comes later. For now, you completely believe the churchmen; the world you take for granted operates solely by spiritual means.'

He stopped talking and looked at me. 'Are you there?'

'Yes, I can see that reality.'

'Well, imagine that reality now beginning to break down.'

'What do you mean?'

'The Medieval world view, your world view, begins to fall apart in the fourteenth and fifteenth centuries. First, you notice certain improprieties on the part of the churchmen themselves: secretly violating their vows of chastity, for example, or taking gratuities to look the other way when governmental officials violate scriptural laws.

'These improprieties alarm you because these churchmen hold themselves to be the only connection between yourself and God. Remember they are the only interpreters of the scriptures, the sole arbitrators of your salvation.

41

'Suddenly you are in the midst of an outright rebellion. A group led by Martin Luther is calling for a complete break from papal Christianity. The churchmen are corrupt, they say, demanding an end to the churchmen's reign over the minds of the people. New churches are being formed based on the idea that each person should be able to have access to the scriptures personally and to interpret them as they wish, with no middlemen.

'As you watch in disbelief, the rebellion succeeds. The churchmen begin to lose. For centuries these men defined reality, and now, before your eyes, they are losing their credibility. Consequently, the whole world is being thrown into question. The clear consensus about the nature of the universe and about humankind's purpose here, based as it was on the churchmen's description, is collapsing – leaving you and all the other humans in western culture in a very precarious place.

'After all, you have grown accustomed to having an authority in your life to define reality, and without that external direction you feel confused and lost. If the churchmen's description of reality and the reason for human existence is wrong, you ask, then what is right?'

He paused for a moment. 'Do you see the impact of this collapse on the people of that day?'

'I suppose it was somewhat unsettling,' I said.

'To say the least,' he replied. 'There was a tremendous upheaval. The old world view was being challenged everywhere. In fact, by the 1600s, astronomers had proved beyond a doubt that the sun and stars did not revolve around the Earth as maintained by the church. Clearly the Earth was only one small planet orbiting a minor sun in a galaxy that contained billions of such stars.'

He leaned toward me. 'This is important. Mankind has lost its place at the center of God's universe. See the effect this had? Now, when you watch the weather, or plants growing, or someone suddenly die, what you feel is an anxious bafflement. In the past, you might have said God was responsible, or the devil. But as the Medieval world view breaks down, that certainty goes with it. All the things you took for granted now need new definition, especially the nature of God and your relationship to God.

'With that awareness,' he went on, 'the Modern Age begins. There is a growing democratic spirit and a mass distrust of papal and royal authority. Definitions of the universe based on speculation or scriptural faith are no longer automatically accepted. In spite of the loss of certainty, we didn't want to risk some new group controlling our reality as the churchmen had. If you had been there you would have participated in the creation of a new mandate for science.'

'A what?'

He laughed. 'You would have looked out on this vast undefined universe and you would have thought, as did the thinkers of that day, that we needed a method of consensus-building, a way to systematically explore this new world of ours. And you would have called this new way of discovering reality the scientific method, which is nothing more than testing an idea about how the universe works, arriving afterward at some conclusion, and then offering this conclusion to others to see if they agree.

'Then,' he continued, 'you would have prepared explorers to go out into this new universe, each armed with the scientific method, and you would have given them their historic mission: Explore this place and find out how it works and what it means that we find ourselves alive here.

'You knew you had lost your certainty about a God-ruled universe and, because of that, your certainty about the nature of God himself. But you felt you had a method, a consensus-building process through which you could discover the nature of everything around you, including God, and including the true purpose of mankind's existence on the planet. So you sent these explorers out to find the true nature of your situation and to report back.'

He paused and looked at me.

'The Manuscript,' he said, 'says that at this point we began the preoccupation from which we are awakening now. We sent these explorers out to bring back a complete explanation of our existence, but because of the complexity of the universe they weren't able to return right away.'

'What was the preoccupation?'

'Put yourself in that time period again,' he said. 'When the scientific method couldn't bring back a new picture of God and of mankind's purpose on the planet, the lack of certainty and meaning affected western culture deeply. We needed something else to do until our questions were answered. Eventually we arrived at what seemed to be a very logical solution. We looked at each other and said: "Well, since our explorers have not yet returned with our true spiritual situation, why not settle into this new world of ours while we are waiting? We are certainly learning enough to manipulate this new world for our own benefit, so why not work in the meantime to raise

44

our standard of living, our sense of security in the world?"'

He looked at me and grinned. 'And that's what we did. Four centuries ago! We shook off our feeling of being lost by taking matters into our own hands, by focusing on conquering the Earth and using its resources to better our situation, and only now, as we approach the end of the millennium, can we see what happened. Our focus gradually became a preoccupation. We totally lost ourselves in creating a secular security, an economic security, to replace the spiritual one we had lost. The question of why we were alive, of what was actually going on here spiritually, was slowly pushed aside and repressed altogether.'

He looked at me intensely, then said, 'Working to establish a more comfortable style of survival has grown to feel complete in and of itself as a reason to live, and we've gradually, methodically, forgotten our original question ... We've forgotten that we still don't know what we're surviving for.'

Out the window, far below, I could see a large city. Judging from our flight-path, I suspected it was Orlando, Florida. I was struck by the geometric outline of streets and avenues, the planned and ordered configuration of what humans had built. I looked over at Dobson. His eyes were closed and he appeared to be asleep. For an hour he had told me more about the Second Insight, then our lunch had arrived and we had eaten and I had told him about Charlene and why I had decided to come to Peru. Afterward, I wanted only to gaze out at the cloud formations and consider what he had said.

'So what do you think?' he asked suddenly, looking sleepily over at me. 'Have you grasped the Second Insight?'

'I'm not sure.'

He nodded toward the other passengers. 'Do you feel as if you have a clearer perspective on the human world? Do you see how preoccupied everyone has been? This perspective explains a lot. How many people do you know who are obsessed with their work, who are type A or have stress related diseases and who can't slow down? They can't slow down because they use their routine to distract themselves, to reduce life to only its practical considerations. And they do this to avoid recalling how uncertain they are about why they live.

'The Second Insight extends our consciousness of historical time,' he added. 'It shows us how to observe culture not just from the perspective of our own lifetimes but from the perspective of a whole millennium. It reveals our preoccupation to us and so lifts us above it. You have just experienced this longer history. You now live in a *longer now*. When you look at the human world now, you should be able to clearly see this obsessiveness, the intense preoccupation with economic progress.'

'But what's wrong with that?' I protested. 'It's what made western civilization great.'

He laughed loudly. 'Of course, you're right. No one's saying it was wrong. In fact, the Manuscript says the pre-occupation was a necessary development, a stage in human evolution. Now, however, we've spent enough time settling into the world. It's time now to wake up from the preoccupation and reconsider our original question.

What's behind life on this planet? Why are we really here?'

I looked at him for a long time, then asked, 'Do you think the other insights explain this purpose?'

Dobson cocked his head. 'I think it's worth a look. I just hope no one destroys the rest of the Manuscript before we have a chance to find out.'

'How could the Peruvian government think they could destroy an important artifact and get away with it?' I asked.

'They would do it covertly,' he replied 'The official line is that the Manuscript doesn't exist at all.'

'I would think the scientific community would be up in arms.'

He looked at me with an expression of resolve. 'We are. That's why I'm returning to Peru. I represent ten prominent scientists, all of whom demand that the original Manuscript be made public. I sent a letter to the relevant department heads within the Peruvian government telling them that I was coming and that I expected cooperation.'

'I see. I wonder how they will respond.'

'Probably with denials. But at least it will be an official start.'

He turned away, deep in thought, and I stared out the window again. As I looked down, it dawned on me that the airplane on which we were riding contained within its technology four centuries of progress. We had learned much about manipulating the resources we had found on the Earth. How many people, I mused, how many generations did it take to create the products and the understanding that enabled this airplane to come into being? And how many spent their whole lives focused on one tiny aspect, one small step, without ever lifting their heads from that preoccupation?

Suddenly, in that instant, the span of history Dobson and I had been discussing seemed to integrate fully into my consciousness. I could see the millennium clearly, as though it was part of my own life history. A thousand years ago we had lived in a world where God and human spirituality were clearly defined. And then we had lost it, or better, we had decided there was more to the story. Accordingly, we had sent explorers out to discover the real truth and to report back, and when they had taken too long we had become preoccupied with a new, secular purpose, one of settling into the world, of making ourselves more comfortable.

And settle we had. We discovered that metallic ores could be melted down and fashioned into all kinds of gadgets. We invented sources of power, first steam then gas and electricity and fission. We systemized farming and mass production and now commanded huge stores of material goods and vast networks of distribution.

Propelling it all was the call to progress, the desire of the individual to provide his own security, his own purpose while he was waiting for the truth. We had decided to create a more comfortable and pleasurable life for ourselves and our children, and in a mere four hundred years our preoccupation had created a human world where all the comforts of life could now be produced. The problem was that our focused, obsessive drive to conquer nature and make ourselves more comfortable had left the natural systems of the planet polluted and on the verge of collapse. We couldn't go on this way.

Dobson was right. The Second Insight did make our new awareness seem inevitable. We were reaching a climax in our cultural purpose. We were accomplishing what we had collectively decided to do, and as this happened, our preoccupation was breaking down and we were waking up to something else. I could almost see the momentum of the Modern Age slowing as we approached the end of the millennium. A four hundred year old obsession had been completed. We had created the means of material security, and now we seemed to be ready – poised, in fact – to find out why we had done it.

In the faces of the passengers around me I could see evidence of the preoccupation, but also I thought I detected brief glimpses of awareness. How many, I wondered, had already noticed the coincidences?

The plane tilted forward and began its descent as the flight attendant announced that we would soon be landing in Lima.

I gave Dobson the name of my hotel and asked where he was staying. He gave me the name of his hotel and said it was only a couple of miles from mine.

'What is your plan?' I asked.

'I've been thinking about that,' he replied. 'The first thing, I guess, is to visit the American Embassy and tell them why I'm here, just for the record.'

'Good idea.'

'After that, I'm going to speak with as many Peruvian scientists as I can. The scientists at the University of Lima have already told me that they have no knowledge of the Manuscript, but there are other scientists who are working at various ruins who may be willing to talk. What about you? What are your plans?'

'I have none,' I replied. 'Do you mind if I tag along?'

'Not at all. I was going to suggest it.'

After the plane landed, we picked up our luggage and agreed to meet later at Dobson's hotel. I walked outside and hailed a taxi in the fading twilight. The air was dry and the wind very brisk.

As my cab drove away, I noticed another taxi pull out quickly behind us, then lag back in the traffic. It stayed with us through several turns and I could make out a lone figure in the back. A rush of nervousness filled my stomach. I asked the driver, who could speak English, not to go directly to the hotel, but to drive around for a while. I told him I was interested in sightseeing. He complied without comment. The taxi followed. What was this all about?

When we arrived at my hotel, I told the driver to stay in the car, then I opened my door and pretended to be paying the fare. The taxi following behind us pulled up to the curb some distance away and the man stepped out and walked slowly toward the hotel entrance.

I jumped back into the vehicle and shut the door, telling the cabbie to drive on. As we sped away, the man walked into the street and watched us until we were out of sight. I could see my driver's face in the rear view mirror. He was watching me closely, his expression tense. 'Sorry about this,' I said. 'I've decided to change accommodations.' I struggled to smile, then gave him the name of Dobson's hotel – although part of me wanted to go straight to the airport and take the first plane back to the States.

A half block short of our destination I had the driver pull over. 'Wait here,' I told him. 'I'll be right back.'

The streets were filled with people, mostly native Peruvians. But here and there I passed some Americans and Europeans. Something about seeing the tourists made me feel safer. When I was within fifty yards of the hotel, I stopped. Something wasn't right. Suddenly, as I watched, gunshots rang out and screams filled the air. The crowd in front of me flung themselves to the ground, opening up my view down the sidewalk. Dobson was running toward me, wild-eyed, panicked. Figures behind him pursued. One fired his gun into the air and ordered Dobson to halt.

As he ran closer, Dobson strained to focus, then recognized me. 'Run!' he yelled. 'For godsakes run!' I turned and ran down an alley in terror. Ahead was a vertical board fence, six feet high, blocking my way. When I reached it, I leaped as high as I could, catching the top of the boards with my hands and flinging my right leg over the top. As I pulled my left leg over and dropped to the other side I looked back down the alley. Dobson was running desperately. More shots were fired. He stumbled and fell.

I continued to run blindly, leaping piles of trash and stacks of cardboard boxes. For a moment I thought I heard footsteps behind me but I didn't dare look back. Ahead, the alley ran into the next street, which was also crowded with people, seemingly unalarmed. As I entered the street, I dared a glance to my rear, my heart pounding. No one was there. I walked hurriedly down the sidewalk to the right trying to fade into the crowd. Why did Dobson run? I asked myself. Was he killed?

'Wait a minute,' someone said in a loud whisper from behind my left shoulder. I started to run but he reached out and grabbed my arm. 'Please wait a minute,' he said again. 'I saw what happened. I'm trying to help you.'

'Who are you?' I asked, trembling.

'I'm Wilson James,' he said. 'I'll explain later. Right now we have to get off these streets.'

Something about his voice and demeanor calmed my panic, so I decided to follow him. We walked up the street and into a leather goods store. He nodded to a man behind the counter and led me into a musty spare room in the back. He shut the door and closed the curtains.

He was a man in his sixties, although he seemed much younger. A sparkle in his eyes or something. His skin was dark brown and his hair was black. He looked of Peruvian descent, but the English he spoke sounded almost American. He wore a bright blue T-shirt and jeans.

'You'll be safe here for a while,' he said. 'Why are they chasing you?'

I didn't respond.

'You're here about the Manuscript, aren't you?' he asked.

'How did you know that?'

'I guess the man with you was here for that reason, too?'

'Yes. His name is Dobson. How did you know there were two of us?'

'I have a room over the alley; I was looking out the window as they were chasing you.'

'Did they shoot Dobson?' I asked, terrified by what I might hear in reply.

'I don't know,' he said. 'I couldn't tell. But once I saw

52

you had escaped, I ran down the back steps to head you off. I thought perhaps I could help.'

'Why?'

For an instant he looked at me as though he was uncertain how to answer my question. Then his expression changed to one of warmth. 'You won't understand this, but I was standing there at the window and thoughts about an old friend came to me. He's dead now. He died because he thought people should know about the Manuscript. When I saw what was happening in the alley, I felt I should help you.'

He was right. I didn't understand. But I had the feeling he was being absolutely truthful with me. I was about to ask another question when he spoke again.

'We can talk about this later,' he said. 'I think we'd better move to a safer place.'

'Wait a minute, Wilson,' I said. 'I just want to find a way back to the States. How can I do this?'

'Call me Wil,' he replied. 'I don't think you should try the airport, not yet. If they're still looking for you they will be checking there. I have some friends who live out of town. They will hide you. There are several other ways out of the country you can choose. When you're ready they will show you where to go.'

He opened the door to the room and checked inside the shop, then walked outside and checked the street. When he returned, he motioned for me to follow. We walked down the street to a blue jeep that Wil pointed out. As we got in, I noticed that the back seat was carefully packed with foodstuffs and tents and satchels, as if for an extended trip.

We rode in silence. I leaned back in the passenger seat

and tried to think. My stomach was knotted with fear. I had never expected this. What if I had been arrested and thrown into a Peruvian jail, or killed outright? I had to size up my situation. I had no clothes, but I did have money and one credit card, and for some reason I trusted Wil.

'What had you and – who was it, Dobson? – done to get those people after you?' Wil asked suddenly.

'Nothing that I know of,' I replied. ' I met Dobson on the plane. He's a historian and he was coming down here to investigate the Manuscript officially. He represents a group of other scientists.'

Wil looked surprised. 'Did the government know he was coming?'

'Yes, he had written certain government officials that he wanted cooperation. I can't believe they tried to arrest him; he didn't even have his copies with him.'

'He has copies of the Manuscript?'

'Only of the first two insights.'

'I had no idea there were copies in the United States. Where did he get them?'

'On an earlier trip he was told a certain priest knew of the Manuscript. He couldn't find him but he found the copies hidden behind his house.'

Wil looked sad. 'Jose.'

'Who?' I asked.

'He was the friend I told you about, the one who was killed. He was adamant that as many people as possible hear about the Manuscript.'

'What happened to him?'

'He was murdered. We don't know by whom. His body was found in the forest miles from his house. But I have to think it was his enemies.'

54

'The government?'

'Certain people in the government or in the church.'

'His church would go that far?'

'Perhaps. The church is secretly against the Manuscript. There are a few priests who understand the document and advocate it covertly, but they must be very careful. Jose talked of it openly to anyone who wanted to know. I warned him for months before his death to be more subtle, to stop giving copies to anyone who came along. He told me he was doing what he knew he must.'

'When was the Manuscript first discovered?' I asked.

'It was first translated three years ago. But no one knows when it was first discovered. The original floated around for years, we think, among the Indians, until it was found by Jose. He alone managed to get it translated. Of course, once the church found out what the Manuscript said, they tried to suppress it totally. Now all we have are copies. We think they destroyed the original.'

Wil had driven east out of town and we were riding on a narrow two-lane road through a heavily irrigated area. We passed several small plank dwellings and then a large pasture with expensive fencing.

'Did Dobson tell you about the first two insights?' Wil asked.

'He told me about the Second Insight,' I replied. 'I have a friend who told me of the first. She talked to a priest at another time, to Jose, I guess.'

'Do you understand these two insights?'

'I think so.'

'Do you understand that chance encounters often have a deeper meaning?'

'It seems,' I said, 'like this whole trip has been one co-incidental event after another.'

'That begins to happen once you become alert and connected with the energy.'

'Connected?'

Wil smiled. 'That's something mentioned further in the Manuscript.'

'I'd like to hear about it,' I said.

'Let's talk about it later,' he said, indicating with a nod that he was turning the vehicle onto a gravel driveway. A hundred feet ahead was a modest wood frame house. Wil pulled up beneath a large tree to the right of the house and stopped.

'My friend works for the owner of a large farming estate who owns much of the land in this area,' he said, 'and provides this house. The man is very powerful and secretly supportive of the Manuscript. You'll be safe here.'

A porch light flicked on and a short squat man, who appeared to be a native Peruvian, rushed out, smiling broadly, and saying something enthusiastically in Spanish. When he reached the jeep, he patted Wil on the back through the open window and glanced pleasantly over at me. Wil asked him to speak in English, then intro-duced us.

'He needs a little help,' Wil said to the man. 'He wants to return to the States but he'll have to be very careful. I guess I'm going to leave him with you.'

The man was looking closely at Wil. 'You're about to go after the Ninth Insight again, aren't you?' he asked.

'Yes,' Wil said, getting out of the jeep.

I opened my door and walked around the vehicle. Wil

and his friend were strolling toward the house, having a conversation I couldn't hear.

As I walked up the man said, 'I will start the preparations,' then walked away. Wil turned to me.

'What did he mean,' I asked, 'when he questioned you about a Ninth Insight!'

'There is part of the Manuscript that has never been found. There were eight insights with the original text, but one more insight, the Ninth, was mentioned there. Many people have been searching for it.'

'Do you know where it is?'

'No, not really.'

'Then how are you going to find it?'

Wil smiled. 'The same way Jose found the original eight. The same way you found the first two, and then ran into me. If one can connect and build up enough energy, then coincidental events begin to happen consistently.'

'Tell me how to do that,' I said. 'Which insight is it?'

Wil looked at me as if assessing my level of understanding. 'How to connect is not just one insight; it's all of them. Remember in the Second Insight where it describes how explorers would be sent out into the world utilizing the scientific method to discover the meaning of human life on this planet? But they would not return right away?'

'Yes.'

'Well, the remainder of the insights represent the answers finally coming back. But they aren't just coming from institutional science. The answers I'm talking about are coming from many different areas of inquiry. The findings of physics, psychology, mysticism, and religion are all coming together into a new synthesis based on a perception of the coincidences.

'We're learning the details of what the coincidences mean, how they work, and as we do we're constructing a whole new view of life, insight by insight.'

'Then I want to hear about each insight,' I said. 'Can you explain them to me before you go?'

'I've found it doesn't work that way. You must discover each one of them in a different way.'

'How?'

'It just happens. It wouldn't work for me to just tell you. You might have the information about each of them but you wouldn't have the insights. You have to discover them in the course of your own life.'

We stared at each other in silence. Wil smiled. Talking with him made me feel incredibly alive.

'Why are you going after the Ninth Insight now?' I asked.

'It's the right time. I have been a guide here and I know the terrain and I understand all eight insights. When I was at my window over the alley, thinking of Jose, I had already decided to go north one more time. The Ninth Insight is out there. I know it. And I'm not getting any younger. Besides, I've envisioned myself finding it and achieving what it says. I know it is the most important of the insights. It puts all the others into perspective and gives us the true purpose of life.'

He paused suddenly, looking serious. 'I would have left thirty minutes earlier but I had this nagging feeling that I had forgotten something.' He paused again. 'That's precisely when *you* showed up.'

We looked at each other for a long time.

'You think I'm supposed to go with you?' I asked.

'What do you think?'

'I don't know,' I said, unsure of myself. I felt confused. The story of my Peruvian trip was flashing before my mind: Charlene, Dobson, now Wil. I had come to Peru because of a mild curiosity and now I found myself in hiding, an unwitting fugitive who didn't even know who his pursuers were. And the strangest thing of all was that at this moment, instead of being terrified, totally panicked, I found myself in a state of excitement. I should have been summoning all my wits and instincts to find a way home, but what I really wanted to do was to go with Wil – into what would undoubtedly be more danger.

As I considered my options, I realized that in reality I had no choice. The Second Insight had ended any possibility of going back to my old preoccupations. If I was going to stay aware, I had to go forward.

'I plan to spend the night,' Wil said. 'So you will have until tomorrow morning to decide.'

'I've already decided,' I told him. 'I want to go.'

A Matter of Energy

We rose at dawn and drove east all morning in virtual silence. Early on, Wil had mentioned that we would drive straight across the Andes into what he called the High Selva, an area consisting of forest-covered foothills and plateaus, but he had said little else.

I had asked him several questions about his background and about our destination, but he had politely put me off, indicating he wanted to concentrate on driving. Finally I had stopped talking altogether, and had focused instead on the scenery. The views from the mountain peaks were staggering.

About noon, when we had reached the last of the towering ridges, we stopped at an overlook to eat a lunch of sandwiches in the jeep, and to gaze out at the wide, barren valley ahead. On the other side of the valley were smaller foothills, green with plant life. As we ate, Wil said we would spend the night at the Viciente Lodge, an old nineteenth century estate which formerly belonged to the Spanish Catholic church. Viciente was now owned by a friend of his, he explained, and was operated as a resort specializing in business and scientific conferences.

With only that brief explanation, we departed and rode silently again. An hour later we arrived at Viciente, entering the property through a large iron and stone gate and proceeding northeast up a narrow gravel drive. Once more, I asked a few probing questions concerning Viciente and why we were here, but as he had done earlier, Wil brushed aside my inquiries, only this time he suggested outright that I focus on the landscape.

Immediately the beauty of Viciente touched me. We were surrounded by colorful pastures and orchards, and the grass seemed unusually green and healthy. It grew thickly even under the giant oaks that rose up every hundred feet or so throughout the pastures. Something about these huge trees seemed incredibly attractive, but I couldn't quite grasp what.

After about a mile the road bent east and up a slight rise. At the top of the knoll was the lodge, a large Spanish-style building constructed of hewn timbers and grey stone. The structure appeared to contain at least fifty rooms, and a large screened porch covered the entire south wall. The yard around the lodge was marked by more gigantic oaks and contained beds of exotic plants and walkways trimmed with dazzling flowers and ferns. Groups of people talked idly on the porch and among the trees.

As we got out of the vehicle, Wil lingered a moment and gazed out at the view. Beyond the lodge to the east, the land sloped gradually downward then flattened out into meadows and forests. Another range of foothills appeared bluish purple in the distance.

'I think I'll go in and make sure they have room for us,' Wil said. 'Why don't you spend some time looking around? You're going to like this place.'

'No kidding!' I said.

As he walked away, he turned and looked at me. 'Be sure to check out the research gardens. I'll see you at dinner time.'

Wil was obviously leaving me alone for some reason, but I didn't care why. I felt great and not the least bit apprehensive. Wil had already told me that because of the substantial tourist dollar Viciente brought into the country, the government had always taken a hands-off approach to the place, even though the Manuscript was often discussed here.

Several large trees and a winding path toward the south attracted me, so I walked that way. Once I reached the trees, I could see that the walkway proceeded through a small iron gate and down several tiers of stone steps to a meadow filled with wild flowers. In the distance was an orchard of some kind and a small creek and more forest land. At the gate I stopped and took several deep breaths, admiring the beauty below.

'It's certainly lovely, isn't it?' a voice from behind asked.

I turned quickly. A woman in her late thirties carrying a hiking pack stood behind me.

'It certainly is,' I said. 'I've never seen anything quite like it.'

For a moment we looked out at the open fields and at the cascading tropical plants in the terraced beds on each side of us, then I asked: 'Do you happen to know where the research gardens are?'

'Sure,' she said. 'I'm heading that way now. I'll show you.'

After introducing ourselves, we walked down the

steps and onto the well-worn path heading south. Her name was Sarah Lomer and she was sandy-haired and blue-eyed and could have been described as girlish except for her serious demeanor. We walked for several minutes in silence.

'Is this your first visit here?' she asked.

'Yes, it is,' I replied. 'I don't know much about the place.'

'Well, I've been here on and off for almost a year now so I can fill you in a bit. About twenty years ago this estate became popular as a sort of international scientific hangout. Various scientific organizations had their meetings here, biologists and physicists mainly. Then a few years ago . . .'

She hesitated for an instant and looked at me. 'Have you heard of the Manuscript that was discovered here in Peru?'

'Yes, I have,' I said. 'I've heard about the first two insights.' I wanted to tell her how fascinated I was with the document but I held back, wondering whether to trust her completely.

'I thought maybe that was the case,' she said. 'It looked as if you were picking up on the energy here.'

We were crossing a wooden bridge which traversed the creek. 'What energy?' I asked.

She stopped and leaned back against the railing of the bridge. 'Do you know anything about the Third Insight?'

'Nothing.'

'It describes a new understanding of the physical world. It says we humans will learn to perceive what was formerly an invisible type of energy. The lodge has become a gathering place for those scientists interested in studying and talking about this phenomenon.'

'Then scientists think this energy is real?' I asked.

She was turning to walk across the bridge. 'Only a few,' she said, 'and we take some heat for it.'

'You're a scientist, then?'

'I teach physics at a small college in Maine.'

'So why are some scientists disagreeing with you?'

She was silent for a moment, as if in thought. 'You have to understand the history of science,' she said, glancing at me as if to ask whether I wanted to get deeper into the subject. I nodded for her to proceed.

'Think about the Second Insight for a moment. After the fall of the medieval world view, we in the west suddenly became aware that we lived in a totally unknown universe. In attempting to understand the nature of this universe we knew we had to somehow separate fact from superstition. In this regard we scientists assumed a particular attitude known as scientific skepticism, which in effect demands solid evidence for any new assertion about how the world works. Before we would believe anything, we wanted evidence that could be seen and grabbed with the hands. Any idea that couldn't be proved in some physical way was systematically rejected.

'God knows,' she continued, 'this attitude served us well with the more obvious phenomena in nature, with objects such as rocks and bodies and trees, objects everyone can perceive no matter how skeptical they are. We quickly went out and named every part of the physical world, attempting to discover why the universe operated as it did. We finally concluded that everything that occurs in nature does so according to some natural law, that each event has a direct physical and understandable cause.' She smiled at me knowingly. 'You see, in many ways scientists have not been that different from others in our time period. We decided along with everyone else to master this place in which we found ourselves. The idea was to create an understanding of the universe that made the world seem safe and manageable, and the skeptical attitude kept us focused on concrete problems that would make our existence seem more secure.'

We had followed the meandering path from the bridge through a small meadow and into an area more densely covered with trees.

'With this attitude,' she went on, 'science systematically removed the uncertain and the esoteric from the world. We concluded, following the thinking of Isaac Newton, that the universe always operated in a predictable manner, like an enormous machine, because for a long time that's all it could be proved to be. Events which happened simultaneously to other events yet had no causal relationship were said to occur only by chance.

'Then, two investigations occurred which opened our eyes again to the mystery in the universe. Much has been written over the past several decades about the revolution in physics, but the changes really stem from two major findings, those of quantum mechanics and those of Albert Einstein.

'The whole of Einstein's life's work was to show that what we perceive as hard matter is mostly empty space with a pattern of energy running through it. This includes ourselves. And what quantum physics has shown is that when we look at these patterns of energy at smaller and smaller levels, startling results can be seen. Experiments have revealed that when you break apart small aspects of this energy, what we call elementary particles, and try to observe how they operate, the act of observation itself alters the results – as if these elementary particles are influenced by what the experimenter expects. This is true even if the particles must appear in places they couldn't possibly go, given the laws of the universe as we know them: two places at the same moment, forward or backward in time, that sort of thing.'

She stopped to face me again. 'In other words, the basic stuff of the universe, at its core, is looking like a kind of pure energy that is malleable to human intention and expectation in a way that defies our old mechanistic model of the universe – as though our expectation itself causes our energy to flow out into the world and affect other energy systems. Which, of course, is exactly what the Third Insight would lead us to believe.'

She shook her head. 'Unfortunately, most scientists don't take this idea seriously. They would rather remain skeptical, and wait to see if we can prove it.'

'Hey Sarah, here we are over here,' a voice called faintly from a distance. To the right about fifty yards through the trees, we could see someone waving.

Sarah looked at me. 'I need to go talk with those guys for a few minutes. I have a translation of the Third Insight with me, if you would like to pick out a spot and read some of it while I'm gone.'

'I sure would,' I said.

She pulled a folder from her pack, handed it to me, and walked away.

I took the folder and looked around for a place to sit

down. Here the forest floor was dense with small bushes and was slightly soggy, but to the east the land rose toward what looked like another knoll. I decided to walk in that direction in search of dry ground.

At the top of the rise I was awestruck. It was another spot of incredible beauty. The gnarled oaks were spaced about fifty feet apart and their wide limbs grew completely together at the top, creating a canopy overhead. On the forest floor grew broad-leafed tropical plants which stood four or five feet high and had leaves up to ten inches in width. These plants were interspersed with large ferns and bushes lush with white flowers. I picked out a dry place and sat down. I could smell the musty odor of the leaves and the fragrance of the blossoms.

I opened the folder and turned to the beginning of the translation. A brief introduction explained that the Third Insight brings a transformed understanding of the physical universe. Its words clearly echoed Sarah's summary. Sometime near the end of the second millennium, it predicted, humans would discover a new energy which formed the basis of and radiated outward from all things, including ourselves.

I pondered that idea for a moment, then read something that fascinated me: the Manuscript said the human perception of this energy first begins with a heightened sensitivity to beauty. As I thought about this, the sound of someone walking along the path below drew my attention. I saw Sarah at the exact moment she looked toward the knoll and spotted me.

'This place is great,' she said when she reached me. 'Have you come to the part about the perception of beauty yet?'

'Yes,' I said. 'But I'm not sure what that means.'

'Further in the Manuscript,' she said, 'it goes into more detail, but I'll explain it briefly. The perception of beauty is a kind of barometer telling each of us how close we are to actually perceiving the energy. This is clear because once you observe this energy, you realize it's on the same continuum as beauty.'

'You sound like you see it,' I said.

She looked at me without the slightest self-consciousness. 'Yes, I do, but the first thing I developed was a deeper appreciation of beauty.'

'But how does that work. Isn't beauty relative?'

She shook her head. 'The things that we perceive as beautiful may be different, but the actual characteristics we ascribe to beautiful objects are similar. Think about it. When something strikes us as beautiful, it displays more presence and sharpness of shape and vividness of color, doesn't it? It stands out. It shines. It seems almost iridescent compared to the dullness of other objects less attractive.'

I nodded.

'Look at this spot,' she continued. 'I know you are blown away by it because we all are. This place leaps out at you. The colors and shapes seem magnified. Well, the very next level of perception is to see an energy field hovering about everything.'

I must have looked bewildered because she laughed, then said very seriously, 'Perhaps we should walk on to the gardens. They're about a half mile farther south. I think you'll find them interesting.' I thanked her for taking the time to explain the Manuscript to me, a total stranger, and for showing me around Viciente. She shrugged her shoulders.

'You seem like a person friendly to what we're trying to do,' she said. 'And we all know we're involved in a public relations effort here. For this research to continue, we must get the word out in the United States and elsewhere. The local authorities don't seem to like us much.'

Suddenly a voice called out from behind: 'Excuse me, please!' We turned to see three men walking quickly up the path toward us. All appeared to be in their late forties and were dressed in stylish clothes.

'Would one of you tell me where the research gardens are?' the taller of the three asked.

'Could you tell me what your business here is?' Sarah asked in return.

'My colleagues and I have permission from the owner of this estate to examine the gardens and to speak with someone about the so-called research being conducted here. We are from the University of Peru.'

'Sounds as though you're not in agreement with our findings,' Sarah said smiling, obviously trying to lighten the situation.

'Absolutely not,' another of the men said. 'We think it is preposterous to claim that some mysterious energy can now be seen, when it has never been observed before.'

'Have you tried to see it?' Sarah queried.

The man ignored the question and asked again, 'Can you direct us to the gardens?'

'Of course,' Sarah said. 'About a hundred yards ahead you will see a path turning east. Take it and ahead maybe a quarter of a mile you'll run into them.'

'Thank you,' the tall man said as they hurried on their way.

'You sent them in the wrong direction,' I said.

'Not really,' she replied. 'There are other gardens in that area. And the people there are more prepared to talk with these kinds of skeptics. We get people like this through here occasionally, and not just scientists but curiosity seekers as well, people who can't begin to grasp what we're doing ... which points out the problem that exists in scientific understanding.'

'What do you mean?' I asked.

'As I said before, the old skeptical attitude was great when exploring the more visible and obvious phenomena in the universe, such as trees or sunshine or thunderstorms. But there is another group of observable phenomena, more subtle, that you can't study – in fact, you can't even tell they're there at all – unless you suspend or bracket your skepticism and try every way possible to perceive them. Once you can, then you return to your rigorous study.'

'Interesting,' I said.

Ahead the woods ended and I could see dozens of cultivated plots, each one growing a different type of plant. Most seemed to be food-bearing types: everything from bananas to spinach. At the eastern border of each crop was a wide gravel path which ran north to what appeared to be a public road. Three metal outbuildings were spaced along the path. Four or five people worked near each one.

'I see some friends of mine,' Sarah said, and pointed toward the closest building. 'Let's go over there. I'd like for you to meet them.'

Sarah introduced me to the three men and one woman, all of whom were involved in the research. The men spoke with me briefly then excused themselves to continue their work, but the woman, a biologist named Marjorie, seemed free to talk.

I caught Marjorie's eye. 'What exactly are you researching here?' I asked.

She appeared to be taken off guard, but smiled and finally answered. 'It's hard to know where to start,' she said. 'Are you familiar with the Manuscript?'

'The first sections of it,' I commented. 'I've just begun the Third Insight.'

'Well, that's what we're all about here. C'mon, I'll show you.' She motioned for me to follow her and we walked around the metal building to a plot of beans. I noticed they appeared to be exceptionally healthy, with no noticeable insect damage or dead leaves. The plants were growing in what appeared to be a highly humus, almost fluffy soil, and each plant was carefully spaced, the stems and leaves of one growing near but never touching those of the next.

She pointed to the closest plant. 'We've tried to look at these plants as total energy systems, and think of everything they need to flourish – soil, nutrients, moisture, light. What we have found is that the total ecosystem around each plant is really one living system, one organism. And the health of each of the parts impacts on the health of the whole.'

She hesitated, then said, 'The basic point is that once we started thinking about the energy relationships all around the plant then we started seeing amazing results. The plants in our studies were not particularly larger, but according to nutritional criteria, they were more potent.'

'How was that measured?'

'They contained more protein, carbohydrates, vitamins, minerals.'

She looked at me expectantly. 'But that wasn't the most amazing thing! We found that the plants which had the most direct human attention were even more potent.'

'What kind of attention?' I asked.

'You know,' she said, 'fiddling with the ground around them, checking them every day. That sort of thing. We set up an experiment with a control group: some getting special attention, others not, and the finding was confirmed. What's more,' she continued, 'we expanded the concept and had a researcher not just give them attention but to mentally ask them to grow stronger. The person would actually sit with them and focus all his attention and concern on their growth.'

'Did they grow stronger?'

'By significant amounts, and they also grew faster.'

'That's incredible.'

'Yes, it is . . .' Her voice trailed off as she watched an older man, appearing to be in his sixties, walk toward us.

'The gentleman approaching is a micro-nutritionist,' she said discreetly. 'He came down here about a year ago for the first time and immediately took a leave of absence from Washington State University. His name is Professor Hains. He's done some great studies.'

As he arrived, I was introduced. He was a strongly built man with black hair, gray streaks at his temples. After some prodding from Marjorie, the professor began to summarize his research. He was most interested, he told me, in the functioning of the body's organs as measured by highly sensitive blood tests, especially as this functioning related to the quality of food eaten.

He told me what interested him most were the results of a particular study which showed that while nutritionally rich plants of the kind grown at Viciente increased the body's efficiency dramatically, the increase was beyond what could be reasonably expected from the nutrients themselves as we understand how they work in human physiology. Something inherent in the structure of these plants created an effect not yet accounted for.

I looked at Marjorie, then asked, 'Then the focusing of attention on these plants gave them something that boosts human strength in return when they're eaten? Is this the energy mentioned in the Manuscript?'

Marjorie looked at the Professor. He gave me only a half smile. 'I don't know yet,' he said.

I asked him about his future research, and he explained that he wanted to duplicate the garden at Washington State and set up some long-term studies, to see if people eating these plants had more energy or were healthier over a longer period of time. As he spoke, I couldn't help glancing periodically at Marjorie. Suddenly she looked incredibly beautiful. Her body appeared long and slender, even under her baggy jeans and T-shirt. Her eyes and hair were dark brown, and her hair fell in tapered curls around her face.

I felt a powerful physical attraction. At the exact moment I became aware of this attraction, she turned her head, stared directly into my eyes, and backed away from me a step.

'I've got to meet someone,' she said. 'Maybe I'll see you later.' She told Hains good-bye, smiled coyly at me, and walked past the metal building and down the path.

After a few more minutes of discussion with the

professor, I wished him well and strolled back to where Sarah was standing. She was still talking intensely with one of the other researchers but she followed me with her eyes as I walked.

As I approached, the man she was with smiled, rearranged the notes on his clipboard and walked into the building.

'Find out anything?' Sarah asked.

'Yes,' I said, distractedly, 'it sounds like these folks are doing some interesting things.'

I was looking at the ground when she said, 'Where did Marjorie go?'

As I glanced up I could see she had an amused look on her face.

'She said she had to meet someone.'

'Did you turn her off?' she asked, smiling now.

I laughed. 'I guess I did. But I didn't say a thing.'

'You didn't have to,' she said. 'Marjorie could detect a change in your field. It was pretty obvious. I could see it all the way over here.'

'A change in my what?'

'In the energy field around your body. Most of us have learned to see them, at least in certain light. When a person has sexual thoughts the person's energy field sort of swirls about and actually propels out toward the person who's the object of the attraction.'

This struck me as totally fantastic, but before I could comment, we were distracted by several people coming out of the metal building.

'Time now for the energy projections,' Sarah said. 'You'll want to see this.'

We followed four young men, apparently students, to

a plot of corn. As we walked closer, I realized that the plot was made up of two separate sub-plots, each about ten feet square. The corn in one was about two feet high. In the other, the plants were less than fifteen inches. The four men walked to the plot containing the taller corn then sat down, each on one corner of the plot facing inward. On cue they all seemed to focus their eyes on the plants. The late afternoon sun shone from behind me, bathing the plot in soft, amber light, yet the woods beyond remained dark in the distance. The plot of corn and the students were silhouetted against the almost black background.

Sarah was standing beside me. 'This is perfect,' she said. 'Look! Can you see that?'

'What?'

'They're projecting their energy onto the plants.'

I stared intently at the scene but could detect nothing.

'I can't see anything,' I said.

'Squat down lower then,' Sarah said, 'and focus on the space between the people and the plants.'

For a moment I thought I saw a flicker of light, but I concluded it was just an after image, or my eyes playing tricks on me. I tried several more times to see something then gave up.

'I can't do it,' I said, standing.

Sarah patted me on the shoulder. 'Don't worry about it. The first time is the most difficult. It usually takes some experimenting with the way you focus your eyes.'

One of the meditators looked over at us and brought his index finger up to his lips, so we walked back toward the building.

'Are you going to be here at Viciente long?' Sarah asked.

'Probably not,' I said. 'The person I'm with is looking for the last part of the Manuscript.'

She looked surprised. 'I thought all of it had been located. Though I guess I wouldn't know. I've been so engrossed in the part that pertains to my work that I haven't read much of the rest.'

I instinctively reached for my pants pocket, suddenly uncertain where Sarah's translation was. It was rolled up in my back pocket.

'You know,' Sarah said. 'We've found two periods of the day most conducive to seeing energy fields. One is sunset. The other is sunrise. If you want, I'll meet you at dawn tomorrow and we'll try again.'

She reached out for the folder. 'That way,' she continued, 'I can make you a copy of this translation and you can take it with you.'

I pondered this suggestion for a few seconds, then decided it couldn't hurt.

'Why not?' I said. 'I'll have to check with my friend, though, and make sure we have enough time.' I smiled at her. 'What makes you think I can learn to see this stuff?'

'Call it a hunch.'

We agreed to meet on the hill at 6:00 A.M., and I started the one mile trek to the lodge alone. The sun had completely disappeared but its light still bathed the grey clouds along the horizon in hues of orange. The air was chilly but no wind blew.

At the lodge a line was forming in front of the serving bar in the huge dining room. Feeling hungry, I walked toward the head of the line to see what food was being served. Wil and Professor Hains were standing near the front, talking casually.

'Well,' Wil said, 'how did the afternoon go?'

'Great,' I said.

'This is William Hains,' Wil added.

'Yes,' I said, 'we met earlier.'

The professor nodded.

I mentioned my early morning rendezvous the next day. Wil saw no problem, as he wanted to find a couple of people he hadn't talked to yet, and didn't anticipate leaving before 9:00 A.M.

The line moved forward then and the people behind us invited me to join my friends. I stepped in beside the professor.

'So what do you make of what we're doing here?' Hains asked.

'I don't know,' I said. 'I'm trying to let it soak a little. The whole idea of energy fields is new to me.'

'The reality of it is new to everyone,' he said, 'but the interesting thing is that this energy is what science has always been looking for: some common stuff underlying all matter. Since Einstein particularly, physics has sought a unified field theory. I don't know if this is it or not but at the very least this Manuscript has stimulated some interesting research.'

'What would it take for science to accept this idea?' I asked.

'A way to measure it,' he said. 'The existence of this energy is not that foreign actually. Karate masters have talked about an underlying Chi energy responsible for their seemingly impossible stunts of breaking bricks with their hands and of being able to sit in one place unmoved with four men trying to push them over. And we've all seen athletes make spectacular moves, twisting, turning, hanging in the air in ways that defy gravity. It's all the result of this hidden energy that we have access to.

'Of course, it won't really be accepted until more people can actually see it themselves.'

'Have you ever observed it?' I asked.

'I've observed something,' he said. 'It really depends on what I've eaten.'

'How so?'

'Well, the people around here who readily see these energy fields eat mostly vegetables. And they usually eat only these highly potent plants they've grown themselves.'

He pointed ahead to the food bar. 'This is some of it, though thank goodness they serve some fish and fowl for old guys like me who are addicted to meat. But if I force myself to eat differently, yes, I can see something.'

I asked him why he didn't change his diet for longer periods of time.

'I don't know,' he said. 'Old habits die hard.'

The line moved forward and I ordered only vegetables. The three of us joined a larger table of guests and talked casually for an hour. Then Wil and I walked out to the jeep to remove our gear. 'Have you seen these energy fields?' I asked.

He smiled and nodded. 'My room is on the first floor,' he said. 'Yours is on the third. Room 306. You can pick your key up at the desk.'

The room had no phone, but a lodge attendant I saw in the hallway assured me someone would knock on my door at 5:00 A.M. sharp. I lay down and thought for a few minutes. The afternoon had been long and full, and I understood Wil's silence. He wanted me to experience the Third Insight in my own way.

The next thing I knew someone was banging on the door. I looked at my watch: 5:00 A.M. When the attendant knocked again I said, 'Thank you,' in a voice loud enough for him to hear, then rose and looked out the small frame window. The only sign of morning was a pale glow of light toward the east.

I walked down the hall and showered, then dressed quickly and went downstairs. The dining room was open and a surprising number of people were moving about. I ate only fruit and hurried outside.

Strands of fog drifted across the grounds and clung to the distant meadows. Songbirds called one another from the trees. As I walked away from the lodge, the very top of the sun breached the horizon toward the east. The color was spectacular. The sky was a deep blue above the bright peach horizon.

I arrived at the knoll fifteen minutes early so I sat down and leaned against the trunk of a large tree, fascinated by the web of gnarled branches growing out above my head. In a few minutes I heard someone walking toward me along the path and I looked that way, expecting to see Sarah. Instead I saw someone I didn't know, a man in his mid-forties. He left the path and walked my way without noticing me. When he was within ten feet he saw me with a start, which made me flinch also.

'Oh, hello,' he said in a rich Brooklyn accent. He was dressed in jeans and hiking boots and looked exceptionally fit and athletic. His hair was curly and receding.

I nodded.

'Sorry about walking up on you so suddenly,' he said.

'No problem.'

He told me his name was Phil Stone and I told him who I was and that I was waiting for a friend.

'You must be doing some research here,' I added.

'Not really,' he replied. 'I work for the University of Southern California. We're doing studies in another province on the rain forest depletion, but whenever I get the chance I drive over here and take a break. I like hanging out where the forests are so different.'

He looked around. 'Do you realize some of the trees here are close to five hundred years old? This is truly a virgin forest, a rare thing. Everything is in perfect balance: the larger trees filtering the sunlight, allowing a multitude of tropical plant life to thrive underneath. The plant life in a rain forest is old too, but it grows differently. It's basically jungle. This is more like what an old forest looks like in a temperate zone, such as in the United States.'

'I've never seen anything like this there,' I said.

'I know,' he said. 'Only a few remain. Most of the ones I know of were sold by the government to lumber interests, as though all they could see in a forest like this is board feet of lumber. Damn shame that anyone would mess with a place like this. Look at the energy.'

'You can see the energy here?' I asked.

He looked at me closely, as though deciding whether to elaborate.

'Yes, I can,' he said finally.

'Well, I haven't been able to,' I said. 'I tried yesterday when they were meditating with plants at the garden.'

'Oh, I couldn't see fields that large at first either,' he said. 'I had to start by looking at my fingers.'

'How do you mean?'

'Let's move over there,' he said, pointing to an area where the trees parted slightly and blue sky showed through overhead. 'I'll show you.'

When we arrived, he said, 'Lean back and touch the tips of your index fingers together. Keep the blue sky in the background. Now separate the tips about an inch and look at the area directly between them. What do you see?'

'Dust on the lens of my eye.'

'Ignore that,' he said. 'Take your eyes out of focus a little and move the tips closer, then further apart.'

As he talked I moved my fingers around, unsure what he meant by taking my eyes out of focus. I finally placed my gaze vaguely on the area between my fingers. Both finger-tips went slightly blurry, and as this happened I saw something like strands of smoke stretching between the tips.

'Good grief,' I said, and explained what I saw.

'That's it! That's it!' he said. 'Now just play with that a while.'

I touched all four fingers together, then my palms and forearms. In each case I continued to see streaks of energy between the body parts. I dropped my arms and looked at Phil.

'Oh, you want to see mine?' he asked. He stood up and stepped back a few feet, positioning his head and torso so the sky would be directly behind him. I tried for a few minutes but a noise behind us broke my concentration. I turned and saw Sarah.

Phil stepped forward and grinned broadly. 'Is this the person you've been waiting for?'

As Sarah approached, she too was smiling. 'Hey, I know you,' she said, pointing at Phil.

They embraced warmly, then Sarah looked at me and said, 'Sorry I'm late. My mental alarm didn't go off for some reason. But now I guess I know why. It gave you two a chance to talk. What have you been doing?'

'He just learned how to see the fields between his fingers,' Phil said.

Sarah looked at me. 'Last year Phil and I were up here at this very spot learning to do the same thing. ' She glanced at Phil. 'Let's put our backs together. Maybe he can see the energy between us.'

They stood back to back in front of me. I suggested they move closer and they stepped toward me until the space between us was about four feet. They were silhouetted against the sky, which was still a dark blue in that direction. To my surprise, the space between them looked lighter. It was yellow, or a yellowish pink.

'He sees it,' Phil said, reading my expression.

Sarah turned and grabbed Phil by the arm and they slowly stepped away from me so that their bodies were perhaps ten feet away. Surrounding their upper torsos was a whitish-pink field of energy.

'Okay,' Sarah said seriously. She had walked over and crouched down beside me. 'Now look at the scene here, the beauty.'

I was immediately awed by the shapes and forms around me. I seemed to be able to focus on each of the massive oaks in a total way, not merely on one part, but on the whole form at once. I was immediately struck by the unique shape and configuration of limbs each displayed. I looked from one to the other, turning all around.

Doing this somehow increased the feeling of presence each oak exuded to me, as though I was seeing them for the first time, or at least fully appreciating them for the first time.

Suddenly the tropical foliage underneath the huge trees attracted my attention; I again looked at the unique form each plant exhibited. I also noticed the way each type of plant grew together with others of its own kind in what struck me as little communities. For instance, the tall banana tree-type plants were often encircled by small philodendrons which themselves were poised among even smaller fern-like plants. When I looked at these mini-environments, I was again struck by their uniqueness of outline and presence.

Less than ten feet away, a particular foliage plant caught my eye. I had often owned just this type as a house plant, a particular variegated form of philodendron. Dark green, its foliage branched out to about four feet in diameter. The shape of this plant seemed perfectly healthy and vibrant.

'Yeah, focus on that one, but loosely,' Sarah said.

As I did so, I played with the focus of my eyes. At one point I tried to focus on the space six inches to one side of each physical part of the plant. Gradually I began to pick up glimpses of light, then with a single adjustment of my focus, I could see a bubble of white light encircling the plant.

'I'm seeing something now,' I said.

'Look around some,' Sarah said.

I stepped back in shock. Around each plant within my vision was a field of whitish light, visible, yet totally transparent, so that none of the plant's color or form was

83

obscured. I realized that what I was seeing was an extension of each plant's unique beauty. It was as though first I had seen the plants, then I had seen their uniqueness and presence, and then something had amplified in the pure beauty of their physical expression, at which time I had seen the energy fields.

'See if you can see this,' Sarah said. She sat down in front of me and faced the philodendron. A plume of the whitish light encircling her body erupted outward and engulfed the philodendron. The diameter of the plant's energy field, in turn, broadened by several feet.

'Damn!' I exclaimed, which provoked laughter between the two friends. Soon I was laughing myself, conscious of the peculiarity of what was happening, but feeling absolutely no uneasiness at seeing, quite readily, phenomena I had totally doubted minutes earlier. I realized that the perception of the fields, rather than evoking a surrealistic sensation, actually made the things about me seem more solid and real than before.

Yet at the same time, everything around me seemed different. The only reference I had for the experience was perhaps a movie which enhanced the color of a forest in order to make it seem mystical and enchanted. The plants, the leaves, the sky now all stood out with a presence and a slight shimmer that suggested life there, and perhaps consciousness, beyond our ordinary assumption. After seeing this, there would be no way to take a forest for granted again.

I looked at Phil. 'Sit down and put your energy on the philodendron,' I said. 'I'd like to compare.'

Phil appeared perplexed. 'I can't do it,' he said. 'I don't know why.'

I looked at Sarah.

'Some people can and some can't,' she said. 'We haven't figured it out. Marjorie has to screen her graduate students to see who can do it. A couple of psychologists are trying to correlate this ability with personality characteristics but so far no one knows.'

'Let me try it,' I said.

'Okay, go ahead,' Sarah replied.

I sat down again and faced the plant. Sarah and Phil stood at right angles to me.

'Okay, how do I begin?'

'Just focus your attention on the plant, as though to inflate it with your energy,' Sarah said.

I looked at the plant and imagined energy swelling up inside it, then after a few minutes I looked over at the two.

'Sorry,' Sarah said wryly, 'you're obviously not one of the chosen few.'

I shot a mock frown at Phil.

Angry voices from the path below interrupted our conversation. Through the trees we could see a group of men passing, talking harshly among themselves.

'Who are those people?' Phil asked, looking at Sarah.

'I don't know,' she said. 'More folks upset with what we're doing, I guess.'

I looked back at the forest around us. Everything appeared ordinary again.

'Hey, I can't see the energy fields anymore!'

'Some things bring you right down, don't they?' Sarah remarked.

Phil smiled and patted my shoulder. 'You can do it again anytime now. It's just like riding a bicycle. All you have to do is see the beauty and then extend from there.'

I suddenly remembered to check the time. The sun was much higher in the sky and a light mid-morning breeze swayed the trees. My watch showed 7:50 A.M.

'I guess I had better head back,' I said.

Sarah and Phil joined me. As we walked, I looked back at the wooded hillside. 'That's one beautiful place,' I said. 'Too bad there aren't more places like this in the States.'

'Once you see the energy fields in other areas,' Phil said, 'you'll realize just how dynamic this forest is. Look at these oaks. They are very rare in Peru, but they grow here at Viciente. A cut forest, especially one that's been stripped of hardwoods in order to grow pines for profit, has a very low energy field. And a city, except for the people, has a different kind of energy altogether.'

I tried to focus on the plants along the path, but the act of walking disrupted my concentration.

'You're sure I'll see these fields again?' I said.

'Absolutely,' Sarah replied. 'I've never heard of anyone failing to duplicate the experience once they've seen them initially. We had a research ophthalmologist come through here once and he got all excited after he learned to see the fields. Turned out he had been working with certain sight abnormalities, including forms of color blindness, and concluded that some people have what he called lazy receptors in their eyes. He had taught people how to see colors they'd never experienced before. According to him, seeing energy fields was just a matter of doing the same thing, of waking up other dormant receptors, something that everyone, theoretically, can do.'

'I wish I lived near a place like this,' I said.

'Don't we all,' Phil replied, then looked around me at Sarah. 'Is Dr Hains still here?'

'Yes,' Sarah said. 'He can't leave.'

Phil looked at me. 'Now there's a guy who's doing some interesting research on what this energy can do for you.'

'Yeah,' I said. 'I talked with him yesterday.'

'The last time I was here,' Phil continued, 'he was telling me about a study he would like to conduct in which he would look at the physical effects of merely being near certain high energy environments, such as that forest back there. He would use the same measurements of organ efficiency and output to see the effect.'

'Well, I already know the effect,' Sarah said. 'Whenever I drive into this estate, I begin to feel better. Everything is amplified. I seem stronger, I can think more clearly, and quickly. And the insights I have into all this and how it relates to my work in physics are amazing.'

'What are you working on?' I asked.

'So you remember me telling you about the perplexing experiments in particle physics, during which these little bits of atoms appeared wherever the scientists expected them to be?'

'Yes.'

'Well, I've tried to expand this idea a bit with some experiments of my own. Not to solve the problems those guys were working on in subatomic particles, but to explore questions I told you about before: To what extent does the physical universe as a whole – since it is made up of the same basic energy – respond to our expectations? To what extent do our expectations create all the things that happen to us?'

'The coincidences, you mean?'

'Yes, think of the events of your life. The old Newtonian idea is that nothing happens by chance, that one can make good decisions and be prepared, but that every event has its own line of causation independent of our attitude.

'After the recent discoveries of modern physics, we may legitimately ask if the universe is more dynamic than that. Perhaps the universe runs mechanistically as a basic operation, but then also subtly responds to the mental energy we project out into it. I mean, why not? If we can make plants grow faster, maybe we can make certain events come faster – or slower, depending on how we think.'

'Does the Manuscript talk about any of this?'

Sarah smiled at me. 'Of course, that's where we're getting these ideas.' She began to dig around in her pack as we walked, finally pulling out a folder.

'Here's your copy,' she said.

I glanced at it briefly and placed it in my pocket. We were crossing the bridge and I hesitated a moment, observing the colors and forms of the plants around me. I altered my focus and immediately saw the energy fields around everything in my view. Both Sarah and Phil had wide fields which seemed to be tinted yellow green, though Sarah's field occasionally flashed with a pinkish color.

Suddenly they both stopped and looked intently up the trail. Ahead about fifty feet, a man walked quickly toward us. A sensation of anxiety filled my stomach but I was determined to maintain my view of the energy. As he approached I recognized him; he was the taller of the scientists from the University of Peru who had asked for directions the day before. Around him I could detect a layer of red.

When he walked up to us he turned to Sarah and condescendingly said, 'You're a scientist, aren't you?'

'That's right,' Sarah replied.

'Then how can you tolerate this kind of science? I've seen these gardens and I can't believe the sloppiness. You people haven't controlled for anything. There could be many explanations for certain plants growing larger.'

'Controlling for everything is impossible, sir. We're looking for general tendencies.'

I could detect an edge growing in Sarah's voice.

'But postulating some newly visible energy that underlies the chemistry of living things – that's absurd. You have no proof.'

'Proof is what we're looking for.'

'But how can you postulate the existence of anything before you get some proof!'

The voices of both individuals sounded angry now, but I was only vaguely listening. What consumed my attention was the dynamics of their energy fields. When the discussion began, Phil and I had backed up a few feet, and Sarah and the taller man had squared off facing each other with a distance of about four feet between them. Immediately, both their energy fields had seemed to grow more dense and excited somehow, as though from an inner vibration. As the conversation progressed, their fields began to intermingle. When one of them made a point, his field would create a movement which seemed to suck at the other's field with what appeared to be a kind of vacuum maneuver. But then as the other person made his rebuttal the energy would move back in his direction. In terms of the dynamics of energy fields, winning the point seemed to mean capturing part of the opponent's field and pulling it into oneself.

'Besides,' Sarah was saying to the man, 'we have observed the phenomena we're trying to understand.'

The man gave Sarah a disdainful look. 'Then you are insane as well as incompetent,' he said, and walked away.

'You're a dinosaur,' Sarah shouted, which made Phil and me laugh. Sarah, however, was still tense.

'These people can make me angry,' Sarah said, as we resumed our walk along the path.

'Forget it,' Phil said. 'These kinds of people come around sometimes.'

'But why so many?' Sarah asked. 'And why right now?'

As we walked up to the lodge, I could see Wil at the jeep. The doors of the vehicle were open and gear was spread out on top of the hood. He saw me immediately and motioned for me to come over.

'Well, looks like I'm about to take off,' I said.

My comment broke a ten minute silence, which had begun when I had tried to explain what I had seen happen to Sarah's energy during the argument. Evidently, I had not put it very well, because my comments had provoked only blank stares, and had cast us all into a long period of self-absorption.

'It's been nice meeting you,' Sarah said, offering her hand.

Phil was looking toward the jeep. 'Is that Wil James?' he asked. 'Is he the guy you're traveling with?'

'Yes,' I said. 'Why?'

'I just wondered. I've seen him around. He knows the owner of this place and was one of the early group that first encouraged the research on energy fields here.'

'Come on up and meet him,' I said.

'No, I have to go,' he said. 'I'll see you around here later on. I know you won't be able to stay away.'

'No doubt,' I said.

Sarah interjected that she too needed to go, and that I could contact her through the lodge. I delayed them for a few more minutes, expressing my thanks for the lessons.

Sarah's expression grew serious. 'Seeing the energy – grasping this new way of perceiving the physical world – grows through a kind of contagion. We don't understand it, but when a person hangs out with others who see this energy, usually they begin to see it, too. So, go show it to someone else.'

I nodded and then hurried up to the jeep. Wil greeted me with a smile.

'Are you about ready?' I asked.

'Almost,' he said. 'How did the morning go?'

'Interesting,' I said. 'I've got a lot to talk to you about.'

'You'd better save it for now,' he said. 'We need to get out of here. Things are looking unfriendly.'

I walked closer to him. 'What's going on?' I asked.

'Nothing too serious,' he said. 'I'll explain later. Get your stuff.'

I walked into the lodge and picked up the few items I had left in my room. Wil had told me earlier there would be no charge, courtesy of the owner, so I walked down to the desk and handed the clerk my key and walked back outside to the jeep.

Wil was under the hood, checking something, and he slammed it closed as I walked up.

'Okay,' he said. 'Let's go.'

We drove out of the parking lot, then down the drive toward the main road. Several cars were leaving at the same time.

'So what's happening?' I asked Wil.

'A group of local officials,' he replied, 'along with some scientific types, have complained about the people associated with this conference center. They're not alleging that anything illegal is going on. Just that some of the folks hanging around here may be what they call undesirable, not legitimate scientists. These officials could cause a lot of trouble, and that could effectively put the lodge out of business.'

I looked at him blankly and he continued: 'You see, this lodge normally has several groups booked at any one time. Only a small number have anything to do with research associated with the Manuscript. The others are groups focused on their own disciplines who come down here for the beauty. If the officials get too ugly and create a negative climate, these groups will stop meeting here.'

'But I thought you said the local officials wouldn't tamper with the tourist money coming into Viciente?'

'I didn't think they would. Someone has them nervous about the Manuscript. Did anyone at the gardens understand what was occurring?'

'No, not really,' I said. 'They were just wondering why all of a sudden more angry people were around.'

Wil remained silent. We drove out the gate and turned southeast. A mile later we took another road which headed due east toward the mountain range in the distance.

'We'll be going right by the gardens,' Wil said after a while.

Ahead I saw the plots and the first metal building. As we came alongside, the door opened and I met eyes with the person coming out. It was Marjorie. She smiled and turned toward me as we passed, our gaze lingering for a long moment.

'Who was that?' Wil asked.

'A woman I met yesterday,' I answered.

He nodded, then changed the subject, 'Did you get a look at the Third Insight?'

'I was given a copy.'

Wil didn't reply, appearing to be lost in thought, so I pulled out the translation and found where I had stopped reading. From there, the Third Insight elaborated on the nature of beauty, describing this perception as the one through which humans would eventually learn to observe energy fields. Once this occurred, it said, then our understanding of the physical universe would quickly transform.

For instance, we would begin to eat more foods which were still alive with this energy, and we would become conscious that certain localities radiate more energy than others, the highest radiation coming from old natural environments, especially forests. I was about to read the final pages when Wil suddenly spoke.

'Tell me what you experienced back at the gardens,' he said.

As best as I could, I related in detail the events of the two days, including the people I had met. When I told him of the encounter with Marjorie, he looked at me and smiled.

'How much did you talk to these people about the other insights and how these insights relate to what they're doing in the gardens?' he asked.

'I didn't mention them at all,' I replied. 'I didn't trust them at first and later I just figured they knew more than me.'

'I think you could have given them some important information had you been perfectly honest with them.'

'What kind of information?'

He looked at me warmly. 'Only you know that.'

I was at a loss for words, so I looked out at the landscape. The terrain was growing increasingly hilly and rocky. Large granite outcrops overhung the road.

'What do you make of seeing Marjorie again as we passed the gardens?' Wil asked.

I started to say 'just a coincidence' but instead I said, 'I don't know. What do you think?'

'I don't think anything happens by coincidence. To me it means you two have unfinished business, something you needed to say to each other that you didn't.'

The idea intrigued me, but disturbed me as well. I had been accused all my life of remaining too distant, of asking questions but not expressing opinions or committing to a position. Why, I wondered, was this coming up again now?

I also noticed that I was beginning to feel differently. At Viciente I had felt adventurous and competent and now I was feeling what could only be called a growing depression, mixed with anxiety.

'Now you've made me depressed,' I said.

He laughed loudly, then replied, 'It wasn't me. It was the effect of leaving the Viciente estate. The energy of that place makes you high as a kite. Why do you think all these scientists began hanging around here years ago? They don't have a clue as to why they like it so much.' He turned to look directly at me. 'But we do, don't we?'

He checked the road, then looked at me again, his face full of regard. 'You have to crank up your own energy when you leave a place like that.'

I just looked at him, puzzled, and he gave me a reassuring smile. Afterward we were both silent for perhaps a mile when he said: 'Tell me more of what happened at the gardens.'

I continued the story. When I described actually seeing energy fields, he looked at me with amazement, but said nothing.

'Can you see these fields?' I asked.

He shot me a glance. 'Yes,' he said. 'Go on.'

I related the story without interruption until I came to Sarah's argument with the Peruvian scientist and the dynamics of their energy fields during the confrontation.

'What did Sarah and Phil say about that?' he asked.

'Nothing,' I said. 'They didn't seem to have a frame of reference for it.'

'I didn't think so,' Wil said. 'They're so fascinated with the Third Insight they haven't yet gone forward. How humans compete for energy is the Fourth Insight.'

'Compete for energy?' I asked.

He merely smiled, nodding toward the translation I was holding.

I picked up where I had left off. The text pointed clearly to the Fourth Insight. It said that eventually humans would see the universe as comprised of one dynamic energy, an energy that can sustain us and respond to our expectations. Yet we would also see that we have been disconnected from the larger source of this energy, that we have cut ourselves off and so have felt weak and insecure and lacking.

In the face of this deficit, we humans have always sought to increase our personal energy in the only manner we have known: by seeking to psychologically steal it from others – an unconscious competition that underlies all human conflict in the world.

The Struggle for Power

A pothole in the gravel road jolted the jeep and woke me up. I looked at my watch – 3:00 P.M. As I stretched and attempted to fully awaken, I felt a sharp pain in the small of my back.

The drive had been grueling. After leaving Viciente we had traveled the entire day, riding in several different directions as though Wil were looking for something he couldn't find. We had spent the night at a small inn where the beds were hard and lumpy and I had slept little. Now, after traveling hard for the second day in a row, I was ready to complain.

I looked over at Wil. He was focused on the road, and so intent and alert, that I decided not to interrupt him. He seemed to be in the same serious mood he had displayed several hours ago, when he had stopped the jeep and told me we needed to talk.

'Do you remember that I told you the insights had to be discovered one at a time?' he had asked.

'Yes.'

'Do you believe that each will indeed present itself?'

'Well, they have so far,' I said, half humorously.

Wil looked at me with a serious expression. 'Finding the Third Insight was easy. All we had to do was visit Viciente. But from now on, running across the other insights may be much more difficult.'

He paused for a moment then said, 'I think that we should go south to a small village near Quilabamba, a place called Cula. There is another virgin forest up there that I think you should see. But it is vitally important that you stay alert. Coincidences will occur regularly, but you have to notice them. Do you understand?'

I told him I thought I did and that I would keep what he said in mind. After that, the conversation had lapsed and I had fallen into a deep sleep – a sleep I now regretted because of what it had done to my back. I stretched again and Wil looked over at me.

'Where are we?' I asked.

'In the Andes again,' he said.

The hills had turned into high ridges and distant valleys. The vegetation was coarser now, the trees smaller and windblown. Inhaling deeply, I noticed the air was thinner, and cool.

'Better put on this jacket,' Wil said, pulling a brown cotton windbreaker from a bag. 'It'll be cold up here this afternoon.'

Ahead, as the road rounded a bend, we could see a narrow crossroads. On one side, near a white frame store and gas station, a vehicle was parked with the hood open. Tools lay on a cloth covering the fender. As we drove past, a blond man walked out of the store and glanced at us briefly. He was round faced and wore dark-rimmed glasses.

I looked at the man closely, my mind racing back five years.

'I know it wasn't him,' I said to Wil. 'But that guy looks just like a friend of mine I used to work with. I haven't thought of him in years.'

I noticed Wil was scrutinizing me.

'I told you to watch events closely,' he said. 'Let's go back and see if that fellow needs some help. He didn't look like a local.'

We found a place where the shoulders of the road were wide enough and turned around. When we returned to the store, the man was working on the engine. Wil pulled up to the pump and leaned out the window.

'Looks like you have trouble,' Wil said.

The man pushed his glasses back up on his nose, a habit my friend also shared.

'Yes,' he replied, 'I have lost my water pump.' The man appeared to be in his early forties and was of a slight build. His English was formal with a French accent.

Wil was quickly out of the vehicle, introducing us. The man offered me his hand with a smile that also looked familiar. His name was Chris Reneau.

'You sound French,' I said.

'I am,' he replied. 'But I teach psychology in Brazil. I am here in Peru seeking information about an archaeology crossroads artifact that has been found, a manuscript.'

I hesitated for a moment, unsure how much I should trust him.

'We're here for the same reason,' I finally said.

He looked at me with deep interest. 'What can you tell me about it?' he asked. 'Have you seen copies?'

Before I could reply, Wil walked out of the building, the

screen door slamming behind him. 'Great luck,' he said to me. 'The owner has a place where we can camp, and there's some hot food. We might as well stay for the night.' He turned and looked expectantly at Reneau. 'If you don't mind sharing your reservations.'

'No, no,' he said. 'I welcome the company. A new pump cannot be delivered here until tomorrow morning.'

While he and Wil began a conversation about the mechanics and reliability of Reneau's land cruiser, I leaned back against the jeep, feeling the warmth of the sun, and drifting into a pleasant reverie about the old friend Reneau had brought to mind. My friend had been wide-eyed and curious, very much like Reneau seemed, and a constant reader of books. I could almost recall the theories he liked, but time had obscured my recollection.

'Let's get our stuff down to the campsite,' Wil was saying, patting me on the back.

'Okay,' I said absently.

He opened the rear door and pulled out the tent and sleeping bags and loaded my arms, then grabbed a duffle bag full of extra clothing. Reneau was locking up his vehicle. We all walked past the store and down a course of steps. The ridge fell away steeply behind the building and we angled to the left along a narrow pathway. After twenty or thirty yards, we could hear water running, and further on we saw a stream cascading down the rocks. The air was cooler and I could smell the strong fragrance of mint.

Directly in front of us, the ground leveled out and the stream formed a pool about twenty-five feet in diameter. Someone had cleared a campsite and built a rock containment for a fire. Wood was stacked against a nearby tree.

'This is fine,' Wil said, and began unpacking his large

four man tent. Reneau spread his smaller tent to the right of Wil.

'Are you and Wil researchers?' Reneau asked me at one point. Wil had finished with the tent and had walked up to check on dinner.

'Wilson's a guide,' I said. 'I'm not doing much of anything right now.'

Reneau gave me a puzzled look.

I smiled and asked, 'Have you been able to see any parts of the Manuscript?'

'I have seen the First and Second Insights,' he said, stepping closer. 'And I'll tell you something. I think it is all happening just as the Manuscript says. We are changing our world view. I can see it in psychology.'

'What do you mean?'

He took a breath. 'My field is conflict, looking at why humans treat each other so violently. We've always known that this violence comes from the urge humans feel to control and dominate one another, but only recently have we studied this phenomenon from the inside, from the point of view of the individual's consciousness. We have asked what happens inside a human being that makes him want to control someone else. We have found that when an individual walks up to another person and engages in a conversation, which happens billions of times each day in the world, one of two things can happen. That individual can come away feeling strong or feeling weak, depending on what occurs in the interaction.'

I gave him a puzzled look and he appeared slightly embarrassed at having rushed into a long lecture on the subject. I asked him to go on.

101

'For this reason,' he added, 'we humans always seem to take a manipulative posture. No matter what the particulars of the situation, or the subject matter, we prepare ourselves to say whatever we must in order to prevail in the conversation. Each of us seeks to find some way to control and thus to remain on top in the encounter. If we are successful, if our viewpoint prevails, then rather than feel weak, we receive a psychological boost.

'In other words we humans seek to outwit and control each other not just because of some tangible goal in the outside world that we're trying to achieve, but because of a lift we get psychologically. This is the reason we see so many irrational conflicts in the world both at the individual level and at the level of nations.

'The consensus in my field is that this whole matter is now emerging into public consciousness. We humans are realizing how much we manipulate each other and consequently we're reevaluating our motivations. We're looking for another way to interact. I think this re-evaluation will be part of the new world view that the Manuscript speaks of.'

Our conversation was interrupted as Wil walked up. 'They're ready to serve us,' he said.

We hurried up the path and into the basement level of the building, the family's living quarters. We walked through the living room and into the dining area. On the table was a hot meal of stew, vegetables, and salad.

'Sit down. Sit down,' the proprietor was saying in English, pulling out chairs and rushing about. Behind him stood an older woman, apparently his wife, and a teenage girl of about fifteen.

102

While taking his seat, Wil accidently brushed his fork with an arm. It fell noisily to the floor. The man glared at the woman, who in turn spoke harshly to the young girl who had not yet moved to bring a new one. She hurried into the other room and returned holding a fork, then handed it tentatively to Wil. Her back was stooped and her hand shook slightly. My eyes met Reneau's from across the table.

'Enjoy the food,' the man said, handing me one of the dishes. For most of the meal Reneau and Wil talked casually about academic life, the challenges of teaching and publishing. The proprietor had left the room but the woman stood just inside the door.

As the woman and her daughter began serving individual dishes of pie the young girl's elbow hit my water glass, spilling the water on the table in front of me. The older woman rushed over in a rage, shouting at the girl in Spanish and pushing her out of the way.

'I am very sorry,' the woman said, wiping up the water. 'The girl is so clumsy.'

The young girl exploded, flinging the remaining pie at the woman, missing, and splattering pie and broken china across the middle of the table – just as the proprietor returned.

The old man shouted and the girl ran from the room.

'I'm sorry,' he said, hurrying to the table.

'It's no problem,' I replied. 'Don't be so hard on the girl.'

Wil was on his feet, figuring the bill, and we quickly left. Reneau had been quiet, but as we walked through the door and down the steps, he spoke.

'Did you see that girl?' he asked, looking at me. 'She is

a classic example of psychological violence. This is what the human need to control others leads to when taken to the extreme. The old man and woman are dominating the girl totally. Did you see how nervous and stooped she was?'

'Yes,' I said. 'But it appears she's fed up.'

'Exactly! Her parents have never let up. And from her point of view she has no choice but to lash out violently. It is the only way she can gain some control for herself. Unfortunately, when she grows up, because of this early trauma, she will think she has to seize control and dominate others with the same intensity. This characteristic will be deeply ingrained and will make her just as dominating as her parents are now, especially when she is around people who are vulnerable, such as children.

'In fact, this same trauma no doubt happened to her parents before her. They have to dominate now because of the way their parents dominated them. That's the means through which psychological violence is passed down from one generation to another.'

Reneau stopped suddenly. 'I need to get my sleeping bag out of the truck,' he said. 'I'll be down in a second.'

I nodded and Wil and I continued toward the campsite.

'You and Reneau have been talking a lot,' Wil remarked.

'Yes, we have,' I said.

He smiled. 'Actually Reneau has been doing most of the talking. You listen and answer direct questions but you don't offer much.'

'I'm interested in what he has to say,' I said, defensively.

Wil ignored my tone. 'Did you see the energy moving

between the members of that family? The man and woman were sucking the child's energy into themselves until she was almost dead.'

'I forgot to watch the energy flow,' I said.

'Well, don't you think Reneau would like to see it? What do you make of running into him in the first place?'

'I don't know.'

'Don't you think it has some meaning? We were driving down the road and you see someone who reminds you of an old friend and when we meet him he happens to also be looking for the Manuscript. Doesn't that sound beyond coincidence?'

'Yes.'

'Perhaps you met so that you could receive some information that will extend your journey here. And doesn't it follow that perhaps you have some information for him as well?'

'Yes, I guess so. What do you think I should tell him?'

Wil again looked at me with his characteristic warmth. 'The truth,' he said.

Before I could say anything else, Reneau came bounding down the path toward us.

'I brought a flashlight in case we need it later,' he said.

For the first time I became aware of the twilight and looked west. The sun had already set but the sky was still a bright orange. The few clouds in that direction carried a darker, reddish color. For an instant I thought I saw a whitish field of light around the plants in the foreground, but the image faded.

'Beautiful sunset,' I said, then noticed Wil had disappeared into his tent and Reneau was pulling his sleeping bag from its case.

'Yes, it is,' Reneau said distractedly without looking.

I walked over to where he was working.

He looked up and said, 'I didn't get to ask you; what insights have you seen?'

'The first two were only described to me,' I replied. 'But we just spent the last two days at the Viciente Lodge, near Satipo. While we were there, one of the people doing research gave me a copy of the Third Insight. It's pretty amazing.'

His eyes lit up. 'Do you have it with you?'

'Yes. Do you want to look at it?'

He jumped at the opportunity and took it into his tent to read. I found some matches and old newspaper and started the fire. After it was burning brightly, Wil crawled out of his tent.

'Where's Reneau?' he asked.

'He's reading the translation Sarah gave me,' I said.

Wil walked over and sat on a smooth log someone had placed near the fire area. I joined him. Darkness had finally descended and nothing could be seen except for the bare outline of the trees to our left, the dim lights from the station behind us, and a muted glow from Reneau's tent. The woods were alive with night sounds, some of which I had never heard before.

After about thirty minutes, Reneau emerged from his tent, the flashlight in his hand. He walked over and sat at my left. Wil was yawning.

'That insight is amazing,' he said. 'Could anyone there actually see those energy fields?'

I briefly told him of my experiences, beginning with our arrival and proceeding through the point where I actually saw fields myself.

He was silent for a minute, then he asked: 'They were actually doing experiments where they projected their own energy onto plants and affected the plant's growth?'

'It affected their nutritional potency, too,' I said.

'But the main insight is broader than that,' he commented, almost to himself. 'The Third Insight is that the universe on the whole is made up of this energy, and we can affect perhaps not only plants but other things as well, just by what we do with the energy that belongs to us, the part we can control.' He paused for a full minute. 'I wonder how we affect other people with our energy?'

Wil looked at me and smiled.

'I'll tell you what I saw,' I said. 'I witnessed an argument between two people, and their energies were doing really strange things.'

Reneau pushed up his glasses again. 'Tell me about that.'

Wil stood up at this point. 'I think I need to turn in,' he said. 'It's been a long day.'

We both said good night and Wil entered his tent. Afterward I described as best I could what Sarah and the other scientist had said to each other, emphasizing the action of their energy fields.

'Now wait a minute,' Reneau said. 'You saw their energies pulling at each other, trying to, say, capture each other as they argued?'

'That's right,' I said.

He was thoughtful for a few seconds. 'We must analyze this fully. We had two people arguing over who had the correct view of the situation, over who was right – each seeking to win out over the other, even to the point of invalidating the other's confidence and to outright name calling.'

Suddenly he looked up. 'Yes, this all makes sense!'

'What do you mean?' I said.

'The movement of this energy, if we can systematically observe it, is a way to understand what humans are receiving when we compete and argue and harm each other. When we control another human being we receive their energy. We fill up at the other's expense and the filling up is what motivates us. Look, I must learn how to see these energy fields. Where is this Viciente Lodge? How do I get there?'

I told him the general location but said he would have to ask Wil for specific directions.

'Yes. I'll do that tomorrow,' he said with commitment. 'For now I should get some sleep. I want to leave as early as possible.'

He said good night, then disappeared into his tent, leaving me alone with the crackling fire and the night sounds.

When I awoke, Wil was already out of the tent. I could smell the aroma of hot cereal. I slipped out of my sleeping bag and looked out through the tent flap. Wil was holding a pan over the fire. Reneau was nowhere to be seen, and his tent was gone.

'Where's Reneau?' I asked, climbing out and walking over to the fire.

'He's already packed up,' Wil said. 'He's up there working on his truck, getting ready so he can leave as soon as his part comes in.'

Wil handed me a bowl of oatmeal and we sat on one of the logs to eat.

'Did you two stay up late talking?' Wil asked.

'Not really,' I said. 'I told him all I knew.'

Just then we heard sounds from the path. Reneau was hurriedly walking down to us.

'I am all prepared,' he said. 'I must say good-bye.'

After several minutes of conversation, Reneau walked back up the steps and left. Wil and I took turns bathing and shaving in the station owner's bathroom, then we packed our gear, filled the vehicle with gas, and departed, heading north.

'How far is Cula?' I asked.

'We should be there before nightfall if we're lucky,' he said, then added, 'So what did you learn from Reneau?'

I looked closely at him. He seemed to be looking for a specific answer. 'I don't know,' I said.

'What conception did Reneau leave you with?'

'That we humans, although we are unconscious of it, have the tendency to control and dominate others. We want to win the energy that exists between people. It builds us up somehow, makes us feel better.'

Wil was looking straight ahead at the road. He looked as if he was suddenly thinking of something else.

'Why do you ask?' I inquired. 'Is this the Fourth Insight?'

He looked at me. 'Not quite. You have seen the energy flow between people. But I'm not sure you know how it feels when it happens to you.'

'Then tell me how it feels!' I said, growing exasperated. 'You accuse me of not talking! Getting information out of you is like pulling teeth! I've been trying for days to find out more about your past experiences with the Manuscript, and all you do is put me off.'

He laughed, then shot me a smile. 'We had a deal,

remember? I have a reason for being secretive. One of the insights concerns how to interpret the events of one's past life. It is a process of becoming clear about who you are, what you are here on this planet to do. I want to wait until we reach this insight before we discuss my background, okay?'

I smiled at his adventurous tone. 'Yeah, I guess.'

For the remainder of the morning we rode in silence. The day was sunny and the sky blue. Occasionally, as we proceeded higher into the mountains, thick clouds would float across our path, covering the windshield with moisture. Around noon, we pulled over at an overlook that afforded a spectacular view of the mountains and valleys to the east.

'Are you hungry?' Wil asked.

I nodded and he pulled two carefully wrapped sandwiches from a bag on the back seat. After he handed me one of them, he asked, 'What do you think about this view?'

'It's beautiful.'

He smiled slightly and stared at me, giving me the impression that he was observing my energy field. 'What are you doing?' I asked.

'Just looking,' he said. 'Mountain peaks are special places that can build energy in whomever sits on them. You look as though you have an affinity for mountain overlooks.'

I told Wil of my grandfather's valley and of the ridge overlooking the lake and how it had made me feel alert and energized the same day Charlene had arrived.

'Perhaps growing up there,' he said, 'prepared you for something here, now.'

I was about to ask him more about the energy that mountains provide when he added, 'When a virgin forest is on a mountain, the energy is amplified even more.'

'Is the virgin forest we're headed for on a mountain?' I asked.

'Look for yourself,' he said. 'You can see it.'

He pointed toward the east. Miles away, I could see two ridges which ran parallel to each other for what looked like several miles, then they converged, forming a V shape. In the space between the two ridges lay what looked like a small town, and at the vortex, the point where the two ridges met, the mountain rose sharply and butted off into a rocky summit. The summit appeared slightly higher than the ridge we were on and the area around its base seemed much greener, as though covered with lush foliage.

'That area of green?' I asked.

'Yes,' Wil said. 'It's like Viciente, yet more powerful and special.'

'How is it special?'

'It facilitates one of the other insights.'

'How?' I asked.

He started the jeep and pulled back onto the road. 'I'm betting,' he said, 'that you will find out.'

Neither of us said much more for an hour or so, then I drifted off to sleep. Sometime later Wil was shaking my arm.

'Wake up,' he said. 'We're coming into Cula.'

I sat up in the seat. Ahead of us, in a valley where two roads came together, was a small town. On both sides were the two ridges we had seen. The trees on the ridges seemed as large as those at Viciente and spectacularly green.

'I want to tell you something before we drive in there,' he said. 'In spite of the energy of this forest, this town is a lot less civilized than other areas of Peru. It's known as a place to get information about the Manuscript, but the last time I was here, it was full of greedy types who didn't feel the energy and didn't understand the insights. They merely wanted the money or recognition they might get by discovering the Ninth.'

I looked at the village. It consisted of four or five streets and avenues. Larger frame buildings lined the two main roads that crossed in the center of town, but the other streets were little more than alleyways lined by small dwellings. Parked at the cross-roads were perhaps a dozen off-the-road vehicles and trucks.

'Why are all these people here?' I asked.

He smiled daringly. 'Because it's one of the last places to get gas and supplies before going deeper into the mountains.'

He started the jeep and drove slowly into town, then stopped in front of one of the larger buildings. I couldn't read the Spanish signs but from the products in the window I presumed it was a grocery and hardware.

'Wait here for a minute,' he said. 'I want to go in for a few things.'

I nodded and Wil disappeared inside. As I looked around, a truck pulled up across the street and several people got out. One was a dark-haired woman in a fatigue jacket. To my amazement, I realized it was Marjorie. She and a young man in his early twenties crossed the street and walked right in front of me.

I opened my door and got out. 'Marjorie,' I yelled.

She stopped and looked around, then saw me and smiled. 'Hello,' she said. As she began to walk toward me, the young man grabbed her arm.

'Robert told us not to talk with anyone,' he said very softly, trying not to let me overhear.

'It's okay,' she said, 'I know this person. Go on in.'

He looked at me skeptically, then backed away and went into the store. I tried then, in a stuttering way, to explain what had happened between us at the gardens. She laughed, and told me Sarah had related everything to her. She was about to say something else when Wil walked out with a handful of supplies.

I introduced them, and we all talked for a few minutes as Wil placed the supplies in the back of the jeep.

'I have an idea,' Wil said. 'Let's get something else to eat across the street.'

I looked over at what appeared to be a small café. 'Sounds good to me,' I said.

'I don't know,' Marjorie said. 'I need to leave soon. My ride.'

'Where are you going?' I asked.

'Back to the west a couple of miles. I've come up to visit a group studying the Manuscript.'

'We can take you back later, after dinner,' Wil commented.

'Well, I guess that will be okay.'

Wil looked at me, 'I have one more thing to pick up. You two go ahead and order and I'll order something when I get there. I'll only be a few minutes.'

We agreed, and Marjorie and I waited as several trucks passed. Wil walked down the street to the south.

Suddenly the young man with whom Marjorie had arrived walked out of the store and confronted us again.

'Where are you going?' he said, holding her arm.

'This is a friend of mine,' she replied. 'We're going to eat and then he can run me back later.'

'Look, you can't trust anyone up here. You know Robert wouldn't approve.'

'It's okay,' she said.

'I want you to come with me, now!'

I took his arm and pulled it off Marjorie. 'You heard what she told you,' I said. He stepped back and looked at me, suddenly appearing very timid. He turned and walked back into the store.

'Let's go,' I said.

We walked across the street and into the small diner. The eating area consisted of one room and just eight tables and was permeated with the smell of grease and smoke. I spotted an unoccupied table on the left. As we walked over, several people glanced up at us for an instant, then returned to what they were doing.

The waitress spoke only Spanish, but Marjorie knew the language well and ordered for us both. Afterward, Marjorie looked at me warmly.

I grinned at her. 'Who is that guy you were with?'

'That's Kenny,' she said. 'I don't know what's wrong with him. Thanks for helping.'

She was looking directly into my eyes, and her comment made me feel wonderful. 'How did you get connected with that group?' I asked.

'Robert Jensen is an archaeologist. He's formed a group to study the Manuscript and to search for the Ninth

Insight. He came by Viciente a few weeks back, then again a couple of days ago . . . I . . .'

'What?' I asked.

'Well, I was in a relationship at Viciente that I wanted to get away from. Then I met Robert and he was so charming and what he was doing seemed so interesting. He convinced me that our research at the gardens would be enhanced by the Ninth Insight, and that he was on his way to find it. He said searching for this insight would be the most exciting thing he has ever done, and when he offered me a place on his team for a few months I decided to accept . . .' She paused again and looked down at the table. She appeared uncomfortable so I changed the subject.

'How many of the insights have you read?'

'Only the one I saw at Viciente. Robert has some others but he believes people have to rid themselves of their traditional beliefs before they can understand them. He says he would rather they learn the key concepts from him.'

I must have frowned because she added: 'You don't like that much, do you?'

'It sounds suspicious,' I said.

She looked at me intensely again. 'I wondered about it too. Maybe when you take me back, you can talk with him and tell me what you think.'

The waitress arrived and brought our food, and as she was walking away, I saw Wil come in the door. He walked quickly to our table.

'I've got to meet some people about a mile north of here,' he said. 'I'll be gone about two hours. Take the jeep and take Marjorie back. I'm riding with someone else.' He shot me a smile. 'We can meet back here.'

The thought came to me to tell him about Robert Jensen but I decided against it.

'Okay,' I said.

He looked at Marjorie. 'Nice to have met you. Wish I had time to stay and talk.'

She looked at him with her coy expression. 'Maybe some other time.'

He nodded, handed me the keys, and walked away.

Marjorie ate for a few minutes, then said, 'He seems like a man with a purpose. How did you meet him?'

I told her in detail of my experiences upon first arriving in Peru. As I talked, she listened intently. So intently, in fact, that I found myself telling the story with great ease and expressing the dramatic turns and episodes with insight and true flair. She seemed spell-bound, hanging on every word.

'Goodness,' she said at one point, 'do you think you're in danger?'

'No, I don't think so,' I said. 'Not this far from Lima.'

She was still looking at me expectantly, so while we finished eating I briefly summarized the events at Viciente up to the point where Sarah and I had arrived at the gardens.

'That's where I met you,' I said, 'and you ran off.'

'Oh, it wasn't like that,' she said. 'I just didn't know you, and when I saw your feelings, I thought it was best to leave.'

'Well, I apologize,' I said chuckling, 'for letting my energy get out of hand.'

She looked at her watch. 'I guess I should be getting back. They'll be wondering about me.'

I left enough money for the bill and we walked outside to Wil's jeep. The night was chilly and we could see a trace of our breath. As we got in, she said, 'Head back north on this road. I'll tell you when to turn.'

I nodded, and made a quick u-turn in the street and headed that way.

'Tell me more about this farm we're going to,' I said.

'I think Robert rents it. Apparently his group has been using it for a long time while he has studied the insights. Since I've been there everyone has been assembling supplies, and readying the vehicles, things like that. Some of his men seem very rough.'

'Why did he invite you along?' I asked.

'He said he wanted a person who could help interpret the last insight, once we found it. At least that's what he said back at Viciente. Here he has only talked about supplies and helping to prepare for the trip.'

'Where is he planning to go?'

'I don't know,' she replied. 'He never answers me when I ask.'

After about a mile and a half, she pointed out a turn to the left onto a narrow, rocky road. It meandered up a ridge and down into a flat valley. Ahead was a farmhouse made of rough planking. Behind it were several barns and outbuildings. Three llamas peered at us from a fenced pasture.

As we slowed to a stop, several people walked around the vehicle and stared without smiling. I noticed a gas powered, electric generator humming at the side of the house. Then the door opened and a tall, dark-haired man with strong, lean features walked toward us.

'That's Robert,' Marjorie said.

117

'Good,' I said, still feeling strong and confident.

We got out as Jensen walked up to us. He looked at Marjorie.

'I was worried about you,' he said. 'I understand you ran into a friend.'

I introduced myself and he shook my hand firmly.

'I'm Robert Jensen,' he said. 'Glad you two are all right. Come in.'

Inside several people busied themselves with supplies. One carried a tent and camping gear toward the back. Through the dining room, I noticed two Peruvian women in the kitchen, packing food. Jensen sat in one of the chairs in the living room and directed us to two others.

'Why did you say you were glad we were all right?' I asked.

He bent toward me and asked in a sincere tone, 'How long have you been in this area?'

'Only since this afternoon.'

'Then you couldn't know how dangerous it is here. People are disappearing. Have you heard of the Manuscript, of the missing Ninth Insight?'

'Yes, I have. In fact . . .'

'Then you need to know what's going on,' he interrupted. 'The search for the last insight is getting ugly. There are dangerous people involved in this.'

'Who?' I asked.

'People who don't care about the archaeological value of this discovery at all. People who just want the insight for their own purposes.'

A huge man with a beard and paunch interrupted the

conversation and showed Jensen a list. They discussed something briefly in Spanish.

Jensen looked at me again. 'Are you here to find the missing insight too?' he asked. 'Do you have any idea what you're getting into?'

I felt awkward and had difficulty expressing myself. 'Well . . . I'm mainly interested in finding out more about the entire Manuscript. I haven't seen that much of it yet.'

He straightened in his chair, then said: 'Do you realize that the Manuscript is a state artifact and that copies of it have been made illegal except by permit?'

'Yes, but some scientists disagree with that. They feel the government is suppressing new . . .'

'Don't you think the nation of Peru has the right to control its own archaeological treasures? Does the government know that you're in this country?'

I didn't know what to say – the surge of anxiety in my stomach was back.

'Look, don't get me wrong,' he said, smiling. 'I'm on your side. If you have some sort of academic support from outside the country, then tell me. But I get the feeling you're just floating around.'

'Something like that,' I said.

I noticed Marjorie's focus had shifted from me to Jensen. 'What do you think he should do?' she asked.

Jensen stood up and smiled. 'I could perhaps work you into a position with us here. We need more people. Where we are going is relatively safe, I think. And you could find some avenues home along the way if things didn't work out.'

He looked at me closely. 'But you'll have to be willing to do exactly as I say, every step of the way.'

I glanced over at Marjorie. She was still looking at Jensen. I felt confused. Perhaps I should consider Jensen's offer, I thought. If he was in good standing with the government then this might be the only opportunity I had for a legitimate way back to the States. Perhaps I had been fooling myself. Perhaps Jensen was right and I was in way over my head.

'I think you should consider what Robert is saying,' Marjorie commented. 'It's too frightening out there alone.'

Though I knew she might be correct, I still had faith in Wil, in what we were doing. I wanted to express this thought but when I tried to speak, I found I couldn't formulate the words. I could no longer think clearly.

Suddenly the large man walked into the room again and looked out the window. Jensen was quickly up and looking, then he turned to Marjorie and in a casual tone said, 'Someone is coming. Go ask Kenny to come up here, please.'

She nodded and left. Through the window I could see truck lights approaching. The vehicle parked just outside the fence, fifty feet away.

Jensen opened the door and as he did, I heard my name mentioned outside.

'Who is that?' I asked.

Jensen looked at me sharply. 'Be very quiet,' he said. He and the large man walked outside and pulled the door closed. Through the window I could see a lone figure silhouetted behind the truck's lights. My first impulse was to stay inside. Jensen's assessment of my situation had filled me with foreboding. But something about the person by the truck seemed familiar. I opened the door and walked outside. As soon as Jensen saw me, he quickly turned and walked my way.

'What are you doing? Go back inside.'

Above the generator I thought I heard my name again.

'Go back inside, now!' Jensen said. 'It could be a trap.' He was standing directly in front of me, blocking my view of the vehicle. 'Go back inside now!'

I felt totally confused and panicked, unable to make a decision. Then the figure behind the lights walked closer and I could see his form around Jensen's body. Distinctly I heard: '. . . come here, I need to talk with you!' Then as the figure approached, my head cleared and I realized that it was Wil. I rushed past Jensen.

'What was wrong with you?' Wil asked quickly. 'We need to get out of here.'

'But what about Marjorie?' I asked.

'We can't do anything about her right now,' Wil said. 'We'd better leave.'

We started to walk away when Jensen called out. 'You'd better stay here. You won't make it.'

I glanced back.

Wil stopped and looked at me, giving me a choice to stay or go.

'Let's go,' I said.

We passed the truck in which Wil had arrived and I noticed two other men had been waiting in the front seat. When we got to Wil's jeep, he asked me for the keys and we drove away. The truck with Wil's friends followed.

Wil turned and looked at me. 'Jensen told me you had decided to stay with his group. What was going on?'

'How do you know his name?' I stammered.

'I just heard all about this guy,' Wil replied. 'He works

for the Peruvian government. He's a real archaeologist, but he's committed to keeping the whole thing secret in return for exclusive rights to study the Manuscript, only he wasn't supposed to go looking for the missing insight. Apparently he's decided to violate that agreement. He is rumored to be leaving soon in pursuit of the Ninth.

'When I learned he was the person Marjorie was with, I thought I'd better get down here. What did he say to you?'

'He told me I was in danger and that I should join up with him and that he'd help me leave the country if that's what I wanted.'

Wil shook his head. 'He really had you hooked.'

'What do you mean?'

'You should have seen your energy field. It was flowing almost totally into his.'

'I don't understand.'

'Think back to Sarah's argument with the scientist at Viciente . . . If you had witnessed one of them winning, convincing the other that he was correct, then you would have seen the loser's energy flowing into the winner's, leaving the loser feeling drained and weak and somewhat confused – the way the girl in the Peruvian family appeared and the way,' he smiled, 'that you look now.'

'You saw that happening to me?' I asked.

'Yes,' he replied. 'And it was extremely difficult for you to stop his control of you and to pull yourself away. I thought for a minute you weren't going to do it.'

'Jesus,' I said. 'That guy must really be evil.'

'Not really,' he said. 'He's probably only half aware of what he's doing. He thinks he's right to control the situation, and no doubt he learned a long time ago that he could control successfully by following a certain strategy. He first pretends to be your friend, then he finds something wrong with what you're doing, in your case that you were in danger. In effect, he subtly undermines your confidence in your own path until you begin to identify with him. As soon as that happens, he has you.'

Wil looked directly at me. 'This is only one of many strategies people use to con others out of their energy. You'll learn about the remaining ways later, in the Sixth Insight.'

I wasn't listening; my thoughts were on Marjorie. I didn't like leaving her there.

'Do you think we should try to get Marjorie?' I asked.

'Not now,' he said. 'I don't think she's in any danger. We can drive out tomorrow, as we leave, and try to talk to her.'

We were silent for a few minutes, then Wil asked: 'Do you understand what I said about Jensen not realizing what he was doing? He's no different from most people. He just does what makes him feel the strongest.'

'No, I don't think I understand.'

Wil looked thoughtful. 'All this is still unconscious in most people. All we know is that we feel weak and when we control others we feel better. What we don't realize is that this sense of feeling better costs the other person. It is their energy that we have stolen. Most people go through their lives in a constant hunt for someone else's energy.'

He looked at me with a twinkle in his eye. 'Although occasionally it works differently. We meet someone who at least for a little while will voluntarily send us their energy.'

123

'What are you getting at?'

'Think back to when you and Marjorie were eating together at the restaurant in town and I walked in.'

'Okay.'

'I don't know what you two were talking about but obviously her energy was pouring into you. When I walked in, I could see it clearly. Tell me, how did you feel during that time?'

'I felt good,' I said. 'In fact, the experiences and concepts I was relating seemed crystal clear to me. I could express myself easily. But what does that mean?'

He smiled. 'Occasionally, another person will voluntarily want us to define their situation for them, giving us their energy outright, the way Marjorie did with you. It makes us feel empowered, but you'll see that this gift doesn't usually last. Most people – Marjorie included – aren't strong enough to keep giving energy. That's why most relationships eventually turn into power struggles. Humans link up energy and then fight over who is going to control it. And the loser always pays the price.'

He stopped abruptly and looked at me. 'Do you get the Fourth Insight? Think about what has happened to you. You observed that energy flows between people and wondered what it meant, and then we ran into Reneau, who told you that psychologists were already searching for some reason humans sought to control each other.

'All that was demonstrated with the Peruvian family. You saw clearly that dominating another makes the dominator feel powerful and knowledgeable, but it sucks the vital energy out of those who are being dominated. It makes no difference if we tell ourselves that we are doing it for the person's own good, or that they are our children, and therefore we should be in control all the time. The damage still occurs.

'Next, you ran into Jensen and got a taste of what this actually feels like. You saw that when someone is dominating you psychically, they actually take your mind away. It was not as if you lost some intellectual debate with Jensen. You didn't have the energy or mental clarity to debate with. All your mental power was going to Jensen. Unfortunately this kind of psychic violence happens all the time throughout human culture, often by otherwise well-meaning people.'

I just nodded. Wil had summarized my experience exactly.

'Try to integrate the Fourth Insight fully,' Wil continued. 'See how it fits together with what you already know. The Third Insight showed you that the physical world is actually a vast system of energy. And now the Fourth points out that for a long time we humans have been unconsciously competing for the only part of this energy we have been open to: the part that flows between people. This is what human conflict has always been about, at every level: from all the petty conflict in families and employment settings to wars between nations. It's the result of feeling insecure and weak and having to steal someone else's energy to feel okay.'

'Wait a minute,' I protested. 'Some wars had to be fought. They were right.'

'Of course,' Wil replied. 'But the only reason that any conflict can't be immediately settled is that one side is holding on to an irrational position, for energy purposes.'

Wil appeared to remember something. Reaching into a

satchel, he pulled out a bundle of papers clipped together.

'I almost forgot!' he said. 'I found a copy of the Fourth Insight.'

He handed me the copy and said nothing else, looking straight ahead as he drove.

I picked up the small flashlight Wil kept on the floorboard and for the next twenty minutes read the short document. Understanding the Fourth Insight, it said, is a matter of seeing the human world as a vast competition for energy and thus for power.

Yet, once humans understand their struggle, the insight continued, we would immediately begin to transcend this conflict. We would begin to break free from the competition over mere human energy . . . because we would finally be able to receive our energy from another source.

I looked at Wil. 'What's the other source?' I asked.

He smiled, but said nothing.

The Message of the Mystics

The next morning I awoke as soon as I heard Wil stirring. We had spent the night at a house belonging to one of his friends, and Wil was sitting up in a cot across the room, dressing quickly. It was still dark outside.

'Let's get packed,' he whispered.

We gathered our clothes and made several trips out to the jeep with some extra supplies Wil had bought. The center of town was only a few hundred yards away, but few lights penetrated the darkness. Dawn was but a streak of lighter sky toward the east. Other than a few birds signaling the impending morning, there were no sounds.

When we finished, I stayed with the jeep while Wil spoke briefly with his friend, who stood sleepily on the porch while we completed our packing. Suddenly we heard noise at the crossroads. We could see the lights of three trucks as they drove into the center of the town and stopped.

'That could be Jensen,' Wil said. 'Let's walk over there and see what they're doing, but carefully.'

We made our way across several streets and into an

alley that entered the main road about a hundred feet from the trucks. Two of the vehicles were being filled with fuel and the other was parked in front of the store. Four or five people stood nearby. I saw Marjorie walk out of the store and place something in the truck there, then walk casually toward us, gazing into the adjacent shops.

'Walk over there and see if you can get her to come with us,' Wil whispered. 'I'll wait for you here.'

I slipped around the corner and as I walked toward her I was horrified. Behind her, in front of the store, I noticed for the first time that several of Jensen's men carried automatic weapons. A few moments later my fright intensified. In the street across from me armed soldiers crouched low and slowly approached Jensen's group.

At the exact time Marjorie saw me, Jensen's men saw the others and scattered. A burst of machine gun fire filled the air. Marjorie looked at me with terror in her eyes. I rushed forward and grabbed her. We ducked into the next alley. More shots were being fired amid angry shouting in Spanish. We tripped over a pile of empty cartons and fell, our faces almost touching.

'Let's go!' I said, jumping to my feet. She struggled up, then pulled me down again, nodding ahead to the end of the alley. Two men with weapons were hiding with their backs to us, looking down the next street. We froze. Finally, the men raced across the street to the wooded area beyond.

I knew we had to get back to the house of Wilson's friend, to the jeep. I was sure Wil would go there. We crept carefully to the next street. Angry shouting and gunfire could be heard toward the right, but we could see no one. I looked left; nothing there either –

no sign of Wil. I figured he had run ahead of us.

'Let's run across to the woods,' I said to Marjorie, who was now alert and looking determined. 'Then,' I continued, 'we'll stay along the edge of the woods and bear left. The jeep is parked in that direction.'

'Okay,' she said.

We crossed the street quickly and made our way to within a hundred feet or so of the house. The jeep was still there but we could see no movement anywhere. As we prepared to dash across the last street to the house, a military vehicle turned a corner to our left and proceeded slowly toward the dwelling. Simultaneously, Wil ran across the yard, started the jeep, and sped away in the opposite direction. The vehicle pursued.

'Damn!' I said.

'What'll we do now?' Marjorie asked, panic returning to her face.

More shots were being fired in the streets behind us, closer this time. Ahead, the forest thickened and inclined up the ridge which towered over the town and ran north and south. It was the same ridge that I had seen from the overlook earlier.

'Let's get to the top,' I said. 'Hurry!'

We climbed several hundred yards up the ridge.

At an overlook, we stopped and looked back toward the town. Military vehicles seemed to be pouring into the crossroads and numerous soldiers were conducting what seemed to be a house to house search. Below us, at the base of the ridge, I could hear muffled voices.

We rushed further up the mountain. All we could do now was run.

* * *

We followed the ridge north all morning stopping only to crouch down when a vehicle traveled along the ridge parallel to us on our left. Most of the traffic was the same sort of steel-gray military jeep we had seen before, but occasionally a civilian vehicle would pass. Ironically, the road provided a lone landmark and point of security against the wilderness all around us.

Ahead the two ridges grew closer together and more steeply sloped. Jagged outcroppings of rock protected the valley floor between. Suddenly, from the north we saw a jeep like Wil's approach, then turn quickly onto a side road which looped down into the valley.

'That looks like Wil,' I said, straining to see.

'Let's get down there,' Marjorie said.

'Wait a minute. What if it's a trap? What if they've captured him and are using the jeep to lure us out?'

Her face fell.

'You stay here,' I said. 'I'll go down there and you watch me. If everything's okay, then I'll motion for you to follow.'

Reluctantly she agreed, and I started down the steep mountain toward the spot where the jeep had parked. Through the foliage I could vaguely see someone get out of the vehicle, but couldn't see who it was. Holding onto small bushes and trees, I worked my way between the outcroppings, occasionally sliding down in the thick humus.

Finally, the vehicle was directly across from me on the opposite slope, perhaps a hundred yards away. The driver, leaning against a rear fender, was still obscured. I moved to my right to get a better look. It was Wil. I rushed further to my right and felt myself slide. At the

130

last minute, I reached for a tree trunk and pulled myself back up. My stomach twisted with fright, below me was a sheer drop-off of thirty feet or more. I had barely avoided killing myself.

Still holding the tree, I stood up and tried to gain Wil's attention. He was surveying the ridge above my head and then his eyes dropped and he looked right at me. He jerked up and walked toward me in the bushes. I pointed down to the steep gorge.

He surveyed the valley floor, then called to me. 'I don't see a way across,' he said. 'You'll have to move down the valley and cross there.'

I nodded and was about to signal Marjorie when I heard a vehicle approaching in the distance. Wil jumped into his jeep and sped back toward the main road. I hurried up the hill. I could see Marjorie through the foliage, walking toward me.

Suddenly from the area behind her came loud shouts in Spanish and the sounds of people running. Marjorie hid below a rock overhang. I changed directions, running as quietly as I could to the left. As I ran, I searched for a view of Marjorie through the trees. Just as I caught sight of her, she screamed loudly as two soldiers grabbed her arms and forced her to stand.

I continued to run up the slope, keeping low, her look of panic frozen in my mind. Once at the top of the ridge, I headed north again, my heart pounding with terror and panic.

After running more than a mile, I stopped and listened. I could hear no movement or talking behind me. Lying flat on my back, I tried to relax and think clearly, but the awful specter of Marjorie's capture was overwhelming.

Why did I ask her to remain on the ridge alone? What should I do now?

I sat up and took a deep breath, and gazed over at the road on the other ridge. I had seen no traffic while I was running. Again I listened intently: nothing except the usual forest sounds. Slowly I began to calm down. After all, Marjorie had only been captured. She was guilty of nothing except running from gunfire. Probably she would be detained only until her identity as a legitimate scientist could be established.

Once more I headed north, my back aching slightly. I felt dirty and tired, and pangs of hunger erupted in my stomach. For two hours I walked without thinking and without seeing anyone.

Then, from the slope to my right I heard sounds of running. I froze and listened again but the sounds had stopped. Here the trees were larger, shielding the ground below from the sun, thinning the underbrush. I could see fifty or sixty yards. Nothing moved. I walked past a large boulder on my right and several trees, stepping as softly as possible. Three other massive outcroppings lay along my path and I moved past two of them. Still no movement. I walked around the third boulder. Twigs cracked behind me. I turned around slowly.

There, next to the rock was the bearded man I had seen at Jensen's farm, his eyes wild, panicked, his arms shaking as he pointed an automatic weapon at my stomach. He seemed to be struggling to remember me.

'Wait a minute,' I stammered, 'I know Jensen.'

He looked at me more closely and lowered the weapon. Then from the woods behind us, we heard the sounds of someone moving. The bearded man ran past me toward the north, holding the rifle in one hand. Instinctively I followed. Both of us were running as fast as we could, dodging rocks and occasionally glancing back.

After several hundred yards, he stumbled and I raced past him. I collapsed between two rocks to rest and to look back, trying to detect movement. I saw a lone soldier, fifty yards away, raise his rifle toward the huge man, who was struggling to his feet. Before I could utter a warning, the soldier fired. The man's chest exploded as bullets tore through from the rear, splattering me with blood. An echo of rifle fire filled the air.

For an instant he stood motionless, his eyes glazed, then his body arched forward and fell. I reacted blindly, running north again away from the soldier, keeping the trees between me and the area from which the bullets had come. The ridge grew constantly more rugged and rocky and began to incline dramatically upwards.

My entire body shook with exhaustion and terror as I struggled up the spaces between the outcroppings. At one point I slipped and dared a glance backward. The soldier was approaching the body. I slithered around a rock just as the soldier looked up, seemingly right at me. I stayed low to the ground and crawled past several other boulders. Then the slope of the ridge leveled off, blocking the soldier's view, so I jumped to my feet again, running as fast as I could between the rocks and trees. My mind was numb. Escape was all I could think of. Though I didn't dare look back, I was sure I heard the soldier running behind me.

The ridge inclined ahead and I fought my way up, my strength beginning to wane. At the top of the rise, the ground leveled out and was thick with tall trees and lush undergrowth. Rising behind them was a sheer rock face that I had to scale delicately, searching for hand and footholds as I proceeded. I struggled to the top and my heart fell at the sight before me. A drop-off of a hundred feet or more blocked my way; I could go no further.

I was doomed, finished. Rocks slid along the outcropping behind me, indicating the soldier was closing fast. I sank to my knees. I was exhausted, spent, and with a final sigh I released the last of my fight, accepting my fate. Soon, I knew, the bullets would come. And interestingly, as an end to the terror, death seemed almost a welcome relief. As I waited, my mind flashed to childhood Sundays and to the innocent contemplation of God. What would it be like, death? I tried to open myself to the experience.

After a long period of waiting during which I had no concept of time, I suddenly became aware that nothing had happened! I looked around and noticed for the first time that I was positioned on the highest peak of the mountain. Other ridges and cliffs fell away from this point, leaving me with a panoramic view in all directions.

A movement caught my eye. There, far down the slope toward the south, walking casually away from me, was the soldier, the gun belonging to Jensen's man slung across one arm.

The sight warmed my body and filled me with ripples of silent laughter. I had somehow survived! I turned and sat cross-legged and savored the euphoria. I wanted to stay here forever. The day was brilliant with sunshine and blue sky.

As I sat there, I was struck by the closeness of the

purple hills in the distance, or rather, the feeling that they were close. The same perception applied to the few puffs of white cloud drifting overhead. I felt as if I could reach out and touch them with my hand.

As I reached up toward the sky, I noticed something different about the way my body felt. My arm had glided upward with incredible ease and I was holding my back, neck and head perfectly straight with absolutely no effort. From my position – sitting cross-legged – I stood up without using my arms, and stretched. The feeling was one of total lightness.

Looking at the distant mountains, I noticed that a day-time moon had been out and was about to set. It looked to be about a quarter full and hung over the horizon like an inverted bowl. Instantly I understood why it had that shape. The sun, millions of miles directly above me, was shining only on the top of the sinking moon. I could perceive the exact line between the sun and the lunar surface, and this recognition somehow extended my consciousness outward even farther.

I could imagine the moon having already dipped below the horizon and the exact reflected shape it would present to those who lived further west and could still see it. Then I imagined how it would look when it moved directly under me on the other side of the planet. To the people there, it would appear full because the sun over my head would shine past the Earth and strike the moon squarely.

This picture sent a rush of sensation up my spine, and my back seemed to straighten even more as I conceived, no, I experienced, the same amount of space commonly felt over my head as also existing under my feet, on the other side of the globe. For the first time in my life, I knew the Earth's roundness not as an intellectual concept but as an actual sensation.

At one level this awareness excited me but at another it seemed perfectly ordinary and natural. All I wanted to do was immerse myself in the feeling of being suspended, floating, amid a space that existed in all directions. Rather than having to push myself away from the Earth with my legs as I stood there, resisting the Earth's gravity, I now felt as though I was held up by some inner buoyancy, as though I was filled like a balloon with just enough helium to hover over the ground and barely touch it with my feet. It was similar to being in perfect athletic condition, as after a year of intense exercise, only far more coordinated and light.

I sat down again on the rock, and, again, everything seemed close: the rugged outcrop on which I was sitting, the tall trees further down the slope and the other mountains on the horizon. And as I watched the limbs of the trees sway gently in the breeze, I experienced not just a visual perception of the event, but a physical sensation as well, as if the limbs moving in the wind were hairs on my body.

I perceived everything to be somehow part of me. As I sat on the peak of the mountain looking out at the landscape falling away from me in all directions, it felt exactly as if what I had always known as my physical body was only the head of a much larger body consisting of everything else I could see. I experienced the entire universe looking out on itself through my eyes.

This perception induced a flash of memory. My mind raced backward in time, past the beginning of my trip to

Peru, past my childhood and my birth. The realization was present that my life did not, in fact, begin with my conception and birth on this planet. It began much earlier with the formation of the rest of me, my real body, the universe itself.

The science of evolution had always bored me, but now, as my mind continued to race backward in time, all the things I had read on the subject began to come back to me, including conversations with the friend who resembled Reneau. I recalled that this was the field he was interested in: evolution.

All knowledge seemed to merge with actual memories. Somehow I was recalling what had happened, and the recollection allowed me to look at evolution in a new way.

I watched as the first matter exploded into the universe, and I realized, as the Third Insight had described, that there was nothing truly solid about it. Matter was only energy vibrating at a certain level, and in the beginning matter existed only in its simplest vibratory form: the element we call hydrogen. That's all there was in the universe, just hydrogen.

I observed the hydrogen atoms begin to gravitate together, as if the ruling principle, the urge, of this energy was to begin a movement into a more complex state. And when pockets of this hydrogen reached a sufficient density, it began to heat up and to burn, to become what we call a star, and in this burning the hydrogen fused together and leaped into the next higher vibration, the element we call helium.

As I continued to watch, these first stars aged and finally blew themselves up and spewed the remaining hydrogen and the newly created helium out into the universe. And the whole process began again. The hydrogen and helium gravitated together until the temperature became hot enough for new stars to form and that in turn fused the helium together, creating the element lithium, which vibrated at the next higher level.

And so on . . . each successive generation of stars creating matter that had not existed before, until the wide spectrum of matter – the basic chemical elements – had been formed and scattered everywhere. Matter had evolved from the element hydrogen, the simplest vibration of energy, to carbon, which vibrated at an extremely high rate. The stage was now set for the next step in evolution.

As our sun formed, pockets of matter fell into orbit around it, and one of them, the Earth, contained all the newly created elements, including carbon. As the Earth cooled, gases once caught in the molten mass migrated to the surface and merged together forming water vapor, and the great rains came, forming oceans on the then barren crust. Then when water covered much of the Earth's surface, the skies cleared and the sun, burning brightly, bathed the new world with light and heat and radiation.

And in the shallow pools and basins, amid the great lightning storms that periodically swept the planet, matter leaped past the vibratory level of carbon to an even more complex state: to the vibration represented by the amino acids. But for the first time, this new level of vibration was not stable in and of itself. Matter had to continually absorb other matter into itself in order to sustain its vibration. It had to eat. Life, the new thrust of evolution, had emerged.

138

Still restricted to living only in water, I saw this life split into two distinct forms. One form – the one we call plants – lived on inorganic matter, and turned these elements into food by utilizing carbon dioxide from the early atmosphere. As a by-product, plants released free oxygen into the world for the first time. Plant life spread quickly through the oceans and finally onto the land as well.

The other form – what we call animals – absorbed only organic life to sustain their vibration. As I watched, the animals filled the oceans in the great age of fishes, and, when the plants had released enough oxygen into the atmosphere, began their own trek toward land.

I saw the amphibians – half fish, half something new – leave the water for the first time and use lungs to breathe the new air. Then matter leaped forward again into reptiles and covered the Earth in the great period of the dinosaurs. Then the warm-blooded mammals came and likewise covered the Earth, and I realized that each emerging species represented life – matter – moving into its next higher vibration. Finally, the progression ended. There at the pinnacle stood humankind.

Humankind. The vision ended. I had seen in one flash the entire story of evolution, the story of matter coming into being and then evolving, as if under some guiding plan, toward ever higher vibrations, creating the exact conditions, finally, for humans to emerge . . . for each of us, as individuals, to emerge.

As I sat there on that mountain, I could almost grasp how this evolution was extended even further in the lives of human beings. Further evolution was related some-how to the experience of life coincidences. Something about these events led us forward in our lives and created a higher vibration that pushed evolution ahead as well. Yet, as hard as I tried, I couldn't quite understand.

For a long time I sat on the rock precipice, consumed by peace and completeness. Then, abruptly, I became aware that the sun was beginning to sink in the west. I also noticed that toward the northwest about a mile was a town of some kind. I could make out the shapes of roof tops. The road on the west ridge seemed to meander right to it.

I got up and began the climb down the rocks. I laughed out loud. I was still connected with the landscape so that I felt I was walking alongside my own body, and more, that I was exploring the regions of my own body. The feeling was exhilarating.

I made my way down the bluffs and into the trees. The afternoon sun cast long shadows along the forest floor. Halfway down I came to a particularly thick area of large trees and as I entered, I experienced a perceptible change in my body; I felt even lighter and more coordinated. I stopped and looked closely at the trees and underlying bushes, focusing on their shape and beauty. I could see flickers of white light and what seemed like a pinkish glow around each plant.

I continued to walk, coming to a stream that radiated a pale blue and filled me with an enhanced tranquility and even a drowsiness. Eventually I made my way across the valley floor and up the next ridge until I came to the road. I pulled myself up to the gravel surface and walked casually along the shoulder toward the north.

Up ahead, I caught sight of a man in a priest's robe rounding the next bend. The sight thrilled me. Totally

140

without fear, I jogged ahead to talk with him. I knew I would know exactly what to say and do. I had a feeling of perfect well-being. But to my surprise he had disappeared. To the right, another road angled back down into the valley, but I could see no one in that direction. I ran farther up the main road, but saw no one there either. I thought about going back and taking the road I had passed, but I knew the town was ahead so I continued to walk that way. Still, I thought several more times of the other road.

A hundred yards farther, as I rounded another curve, I heard the roar of vehicles. Through the trees I could see a line of military trucks approaching at a high rate of speed. For a moment I hesitated, thinking I might stand my ground, but then I remembered the terror of the shooting on the ridge.

I had time only to fling myself off the road to the right and lie still. Ten jeeps sped past me. I had landed in a spot which was completely exposed, and all I could do was hope no one looked my way. Each vehicle passed within twenty feet. I could smell the exhaust fumes and see the expression on every face.

Luckily, no one noticed. After they were well past, I crawled behind a large tree. My hands were shaking and my sensation of peace and connection was totally shattered. A now familiar pang of anxiety knotted in my stomach. Finally, I inched up to the road. The sound of more vehicles sent me scurrying down the slope again as two more jeeps raced past. I felt nauseous.

This time I stayed well off the road and retreated the way I had come, moving very cautiously. I came to the road I had passed earlier. After carefully listening for sound and movement, I decided to walk through the woods beside it, angling back into the valley. My body felt heavy again. What had I been doing, I asked myself. Why had I been walking in the road? I must have been crazy, deluded by the shock of the shooting, entranced in some state of euphoria. Get real, I told myself. You have to be careful. There are people here who will kill you if you make the slightest mistake!

I froze. Ahead of me, perhaps a hundred feet, was the priest. He was sitting under a large tree that was surrounded by numerous rock outcroppings. As I stared at him, he opened his eyes and looked right at me. I flinched but he only smiled and motioned for me to walk up.

Cautiously I approached him. He remained motionless, a thin, tall man of about fifty years of age. His hair was cut short and was dark brown in color, matching his eyes.

'You look as though you need some help,' he said, in perfect English.

'Who are you?' I asked.

'I am Father Sanchez. And you?'

I explained who I was and where I was from, dizzily sinking to one knee and then to my buttocks.

'You were part of what happened in Cula, weren't you?' he asked.

'What do you know of that?' I asked warily, not knowing whether to trust him.

'I know someone in this government is very angry,' he said. 'They don't want the Manuscript publicized.'

'Why?' I asked.

He stood up and looked down at me. 'Why don't you

142

come with me. Our mission is only a half mile away. You'll be safe with us.'

I struggled to my feet, realizing I had no choice, and nodded affirmatively. He led me slowly down the road, his manner respectful and deliberate. He weighed each word.

'Are the soldiers still looking for you?' he asked at one point.

'I don't know,' I replied.

He said nothing for a few minutes, then asked, 'Are you searching for the Manuscript?'

'Not any more,' I said. 'Right now I just want to survive this and go home.'

He nodded reassuringly and I found myself beginning to trust him. Something about his regard and warmth affected me. He reminded me of Wil. Presently we came to the mission, which was a cluster of small houses facing a courtyard and a small church. It was situated in a place of great beauty. As we walked up he told some of the other robed men something in Spanish and they scurried away. I tried to see where they were going but fatigue was engulfing me. The priest led me into one of the houses.

Inside was a small living area and two bedrooms. A fire burned in the fireplace. Soon after we entered, another priest walked in with a tray of bread and soup. Wearily I ate as Sanchez sat politely in a chair beside me. Then, upon his insistence, I stretched out on one of the beds and fell into a deep sleep.

When I walked into the courtyard, I noticed immediately that the grounds were immaculately kept. The gravel walkways were edged with precisely arranged bushes and hedges. Each seemed to be placed so as to accent their full natural shape. None was trimmed.

I stretched and felt the starched shirt I had put on. It was made of coarse cotton and chafed my neck slightly. Still it was clean and freshly ironed. Earlier, I had awakened as two priests poured hot water into a tub and laid out fresh clothes. After I had bathed and dressed I had walked into the other room and found hot muffins and dried fruit on the table. I had eaten ravenously while the priests stood by. After I had finished, the priests had left and I had walked outside to where I now stood.

I walked over and sat on one of the stone benches that faced the courtyard. The sun was just clearing the tops of the trees, warming my face.

'How did you sleep?' a voice asked from behind me. I turned to see Father Sanchez standing very erect, smiling down at me.

'Very well,' I replied. 'May I join you?'

'Sure.'

Neither of us spoke for several minutes, so long in fact that I felt some discomfort. Several times I looked at him, preparing to say something, but he was looking in the direction of the sun, his face tilted slightly back, his eyes squinting.

Finally he spoke: 'This is a nice place you found here.' Apparently he meant the bench at this time of the morning.

'Look, I need to ask your advice,' I said. 'What is the safest way for me to get back to the United States?' He looked at me seriously. 'I don't know. That depends on

144

how dangerous the government thinks you are. Tell me how you happened to be in Cula.'

I told him everything from the time I first heard of the Manuscript. My feeling of euphoria on the ridge now seemed fanciful and pretentious, so I only alluded to it briefly. Sanchez, however, immediately questioned me about it

'What did you do after the soldier failed to notice you and left?' he asked.

'I just sat up there for a few hours,' I replied, 'feeling relieved, I guess.'

'What else did you feel?' he asked.

I squirmed somewhat, then decided to attempt a description. 'It's hard to describe,' I said. 'I felt this euphoric connection with everything, and this total kind of security and confidence. I was no longer tired.'

He smiled. 'You had a mystical experience. Many people report them in that forest near the peak.'

I nodded tentatively.

He turned on the bench to face me more directly. 'This is the experience the mystics of every religion have always described. Have you read anything about such experiences?'

'Some, years ago,' I said.

'But until yesterday it was only an intellectual concept?'

'Yeah, I suppose.'

A young priest walked up and nodded to me, then whispered something to Sanchez. Sanchez nodded and the young priest turned and walked away. The older priest watched every step the young man took. He crossed the courtyard and entered a park-like area about a hundred feet away. I noticed for the first time that this area too was also extremely clean, and full of various plants. The young priest walked to several locations, hesitating at each one as though searching for something, then at one specific location sat down. He appeared to be engaged in an exercise of some kind.

Sanchez smiled and looked pleased, then turned his attention to me.

'I think it is probably unsafe for you to attempt to go back right now,' he said. 'But I will try to find out what the situation is, and if there is any word about your friends.' He stood up and faced me. 'I must attend to some chores. Please understand that we will assist you in any way possible. For now I hope you will be comfortable here. Relax and gain your strength.'

I nodded.

He reached inside his pocket and pulled out some papers and handed them to me. 'This is the Fifth Insight. It speaks about the kind of experience you had. I think you might find it interesting.'

I took it reluctantly as he continued speaking. 'What was your understanding of the last insight you read?' he asked.

I hesitated. I didn't want to think about manuscripts and insights. Finally I said, 'That humans are stuck in a kind of competition for each other's energy. When we can get others to acquiesce to our view, they identify with us and that pulls their energy into us and we feel stronger.'

He smiled. 'So the problem is that everyone is trying to control and manipulate each other for energy, because we feel short of it?'

'That's right.'

'But there is a solution, another source of energy?'

'That's what the last insight implied.'

He nodded and walked very deliberately into the church.

For a few moments, I leaned forward and rested my elbows on my knees, not looking at the translation. I continued to feel reluctant. The events of the last two days had dampened my enthusiasm and I preferred instead to think of how I might return to the United States. Then, in the wooded area across the way, I noticed the young priest stand up and walk slowly to another location about twenty feet from where he was. He turned toward me again and sat down.

I was intrigued over what he might be doing. Then it dawned on me that he might be practicing something that was spelled out in the Manuscript. I looked at the first page and began to read.

It described a new understanding of what has long been called mystical consciousness. During the last decades of the twentieth century, it stated, this consciousness would become publicized as a way of being that is actually attainable, a way that has been demonstrated by the more esoteric practitioners of many religions. For most, this consciousness would remain an intellectual concept, to be only talked of and debated. But for a growing number of humans, this consciousness would become experientially real – because these individuals would experience flashes or glimpses of this state of mind during the course of their lives. The Manuscript said that this experience was the key to ending human conflict in the world, because during this experience we are receiving energy from another source – a source we will eventually learn to tap at will.

I stopped reading and looked at the young priest again. His eyes were open and he appeared to be looking directly at me. I nodded, even though I couldn't make out the details of his face. To my surprise he nodded back to me and smiled faintly. Then he stood up and walked toward my left, heading toward the house in that direction. He avoided my eyes as I watched him cross the courtyard and enter the dwelling.

Behind me I heard footsteps and turned to see Sanchez leaving the church. He smiled as he approached me. 'That didn't take long,' he said. 'Would you like to see more of the grounds?'

'Yes, I would,' I replied. 'Tell me about these sitting areas you have.' I pointed toward the area where the young priest had been.

'Let's walk up there,' he said.

As we strolled across the courtyard, Sanchez told me that the mission was over four hundred years old and was founded by a unique missionary from Spain, who felt the way to convert the local Indians was through their hearts, not through coercion with the sword. The approach had worked, Sanchez went on, and partly because of this success and partly due to the remote location, the priest had been left alone to follow his own course.

'We carry on his tradition of looking inward for the truth,' Sanchez said.

The sitting area was landscaped immaculately. About half an acre of dense forest had been cleared and the bushes and flowering plants beneath were interspersed with walkways made of smooth river stone. Like those in the courtyard, the plants here were also spaced perfectly, accentuating their unique shape.

'Where would you like to sit down?' Sanchez asked. I looked around at my options. In front of us were several arranged areas – nooks which seemed complete unto themselves. All contained open spaces surrounded by beautiful plants and rocks and larger trees of varying shapes. One, to our left, where the young priest had been last sitting, had more outcroppings of stone.

'How about over there?' I said.

He nodded and we walked over and sat down. Sanchez breathed deeply for several minutes, then looked at me.

'Tell me more about your experience on the ridge,' he said.

I felt resistant. 'I don't know what else I can say about it. It didn't last.'

The priest looked at me sternly. 'Just because it ended when you became afraid again doesn't negate its importance, does it? Perhaps it is something to be regained.'

'Maybe,' I said. 'But it's hard for me to concentrate on feeling cosmic when people are trying to kill me.'

He laughed, then looked at me warmly.

'Are you studying the Manuscript here at the mission?' I asked.

'Yes,' he said. 'We teach others how to pursue the kind of experience you had on the ridge. You wouldn't mind getting some of that feeling back, would you?'

A voice from the courtyard interrupted: a priest calling for Sanchez. The older man excused himself and walked down to the courtyard and talked with the priest who had summoned him. I sat back and looked at the plants and rocks nearby, taking my eyes slightly out of focus. Around the bush closest to me I could barely make out an area of light but when I tried it on the rocks, I could see nothing.

Then I noticed Sanchez walking back.

'I must leave for a while,' he said as he reached me. 'I'll be going into town for a meeting so perhaps I can acquire some information concerning your friends, or at least how safe it is for you to travel.'

'Good,' I said. 'Will you be back today?'

'I don't think so,' he replied. 'More like tomorrow morning.'

I must have looked insecure because he walked closer and placed his hand on my shoulder. 'Don't worry. You are safe here. Please make yourself at home. Look around. It is fine to talk with any of the priests, but understand that some of them will be more receptive than others depending on their development.'

I nodded.

He smiled and walked behind the church and entered an old truck I had not noticed. After several attempts it started and he drove around the back side of the church and onto the road leading back up the ridge.

For several hours I remained in the sitting area, content to gather my thoughts, wondering if Marjorie was all right and if Wil had escaped. Several times the image of Jensen's man being killed flashed across my mind, but I fought off the memory and tried to stay calm.

About noon, I noticed several priests were preparing a long table in the center of the courtyard with dishes of food. When they finished, a dozen or more other priests joined them and began serving their own plates and eating on the benches casually. Most of them smiled pleasantly at each other, but I could hear little talking. One of them looked up at me and pointed to the food.

I nodded and walked down to the courtyard and prepared a plate of corn and beans. Each of the priests seemed very conscious of my presence but no one spoke to me. I made several comments about the food, but my words were met only with smiles and polite gestures. If I attempted direct eye contact, they would lower their eyes.

I sat down on one of the benches alone and ate. The vegetables and beans were unsalted but spiced with herbs. When lunch was over and the priests were stacking their plates on the table, another priest walked out of the church and hastily prepared a plate. When he finished, he looked around for a place to sit and our eyes met. He smiled and I recognized him as the priest who had looked at me from the sitting area earlier. I returned his smile and he walked over and spoke to me in broken English.

'May I sit on bench with you?' he asked.

'Yes, please,' I replied.

He sat down and began to eat very slowly, overchewing his food and smiling up at me occasionally. He was short and small with a wiry build and coal black hair. His eyes were a lighter brown.

'You like the food?' he asked.

I was holding my plate in my lap. Several bites of corn remained.

'Oh, yes,' I said, and took a bite. I noticed again how slowly and deliberately he chewed and tried to do the same, and then it struck me that all of the priests had been eating that way.

'Are the vegetables grown here at the mission?' I asked.

He hesitated before answering, swallowing slowly.

'Yes, food is very important.'

'Do you meditate with the plants?' I asked.

He looked at me with obvious surprise. 'You have read Manuscript?' he asked.

'Yes, the first four insights.'

'Have you grown food?' he asked.

'Oh no. I'm just learning about all this.'

'Do you see energy fields?'

'Yes, sometimes.'

We sat in silence for a few minutes while he carefully ate several more bites.

'Food is the first way of gaining energy,' he said.

I nodded.

'But in order to totally absorb energy in food, the food must be appreciated, eh . . .'

He seemed to be struggling for the right English word. 'Savored,' he finally said. 'Taste is the doorway. You must appreciate taste. This is the reason for prayer before eating. It is not just about being thankful, it is to make eating a holy experience, so the energy from the food can enter your body.'

He looked closely at me, as though to see whether I understood.

I nodded without comment. He looked thoughtful.

What he was telling me, I reasoned, was that this kind of deliberate appreciation of food was the real purpose behind the normal religious custom of being thankful, with the result being a higher energy absorption of the food.

152

'But taking in food is only first step,' he said. 'After personal energy is increased in this way, you become more sensitive to energy in all things ... and then you learn to take this energy into yourself without eating.'

I nodded affirmatively.

'Everything around us,' he continued, 'has energy. But each has its own special kind. That is why some places increase energy more than others. It depends on how your shape fits with the energy there.'

'Is that what you were doing up there earlier?' I asked. 'Increasing your energy?'

He looked pleased. 'Yes.'

'How do you do that?' I asked.

'You have to be open, to connect, to use your sense of appreciation, as in seeing fields. But you take this one step further so that you get the sensation of being filled up.'

'I'm not sure I follow you.'

He frowned at my denseness. 'Would you like to walk back to the sitting place? I can show you.'

'Okay,' I said. 'Why not?'

I followed as he led the way across the courtyard and back to the sitting area. As we arrived, he stopped and looked around, as if surveying the area for something.

'Over there,' he said, pointing to a spot that bordered the dense forest.

We followed the path as it wound through the trees and bushes. He picked a spot in front of a large tree that grew out of a mound of boulders so that its huge trunk seemed to be perched on the rocks. Its roots wrapped around and through the boulders before finally reaching the soil. Flowering shrubs of some type grew in semi-circles in front of the tree and I could detect a strange sweet fragrance from the shrub's yellow blossoms. The dense forest provided a solid sheet of green in the background.

The priest directed me to sit down in a clear spot amid the bushes, facing the gnarled tree. He sat beside me.

'Do you think the tree is beautiful?' he asked.

'Yes.'

'Then, uh . . . feel it . . . uh . . .'

He seemed to be struggling again to find the word. He thought for a moment and then asked, 'Father Sanchez told me that you had an experience on the ridge; can you remember how you felt?'

'I felt light and secure and connected.'

'How connected?'

'That's hard to describe,' I said. 'Like the whole land-scape was part of me.'

'But what was the feeling?'

I thought for a minute. What was the feeling? Then it came to me.

'Love,' I said. 'I guess I felt a love for everything.'

'Yes,' he said. 'That is it. Feel that for the tree.'

'But wait a minute,' I protested. 'Love is something that just happens. I can't make myself love anything.'

'You do not make yourself love,' he said. 'You allow love to enter you. But to do this you must position your mind by remembering what it felt like and try to feel it again.'

I looked at the tree and tried to remember the emotion on the ridge. Gradually, I began to admire its shape and presence. My appreciation grew until I actually felt an emotion of love. The feeling was exactly the one I remember as a child for my mother and as a youth for the special little girl that was the object of my 'puppy love.' Yet even though I had been looking at the tree, this particular love existed as a general background feeling. I was in love with everything.

The priest slid away several feet and looked back at me intensely. 'Good,' he said.'You are accepting the energy.'

I noticed his eyes were slightly out of focus.

'How do you know?' I asked.

'Because I can see your energy field getting larger.'

I closed my eyes and tried to reach the intense feelings I had acquired on the ridge top but I couldn't duplicate the experience. What I was feeling was on the same continuum but to a lesser degree than before. The failure made me frustrated.

'What happened?' he asked. 'Your energy fell.'

'I don't know,' I said. 'I just couldn't do it as strongly as before.'

He just looked at me, amused at first, then with impatience.

'What you experienced on the ridge was a gift, a breakthrough, a look at a new way. Now you must learn to get that experience by yourself, a little at a time.'

He slid back a foot farther and looked at me again. 'Now try more.'

I closed my eyes and tried to feel deeply. Eventually the emotion swept over me again. I stayed with it, attempting to increase the feeling by small increments. I focused my regard on the tree.

'That is very good,' he suddenly said. 'You are receiving energy and giving it to the tree.'

I looked at him squarely. 'I'm giving it back to the tree?'

'When you appreciate the beauty and uniqueness of things,' he explained, 'you receive energy. When you get to a level where you feel love, then you can send the energy back just by willing it so.' For a long time I sat there with the tree. The more I focused attention on the tree and admired its shape and color, the more love I seemed to acquire generally, an unusual experience. I imagined my energy flowing over and filling up the tree, but I couldn't see it. Without changing my focus, I noticed the priest get up and begin to walk away.

'What does it look like when I'm giving energy to the tree?' I asked.

He described the perception in detail and I recognized it as the same phenomenon I had witnessed when Sarah projected energy onto the philodendron at Viciente. Though Sarah was successful, she apparently wasn't aware that a state of love was necessary for the projection to take place. She must have been acquiring a love state naturally, without realizing it.

The priest walked down toward the courtyard and out of my range of vision. I remained in the sitting area until dusk.

The two priests nodded politely as I entered the house. A roaring fire fended off the evening chill and several oil lamps illuminated the front room. The air was filled with the smell of vegetable, or perhaps potato, soup. On the table was a ceramic bowl, several spoons, and a plate holding four slices of bread.

One of the priests turned and left without looking at me and the other kept his eyes lowered and nodded at a large cast iron pot sitting on the hearth by the fire. A handle protruded from under its lid. As soon as I saw the pot, the second priest asked, 'Is there anything else you need?'

'I think not,' I said. 'Thank you.'

He nodded and left the house as well, leaving me alone. I lifted the lid from the pot – potato soup. It smelled rich and delicious. I poured several ladles full into a bowl and sat down at the table, then pulled the part of the Manuscript Sanchez had given me from my pocket and placed it beside my plate, intending to read. But the soup tasted so good that I focused entirely on eating. After I finished, I placed the dishes in a large pan and stared at the fire, hypnotized, until the flames burned low. Then I turned down the lamps and went to bed.

The next morning, I awakened at dawn feeling totally refreshed. Outside a morning mist rolled through the courtyard. I stoked up the fire and put several pieces of kindling on the coals and fanned it until it caught up. I was about to look through the kitchen for food when I heard Sanchez's truck approaching.

I walked outside as he emerged from behind the church, a backpack in one arm and several packages in the other.

'I have some news,' he said, motioning me to follow him back inside the house.

Several other priests appeared with hot corn cakes and grits and more dried fruit. Sanchez greeted the men, then sat with me at the table as the priests scurried away.

'I attended a meeting of some of the priests of the Southern Council,' he said. 'We were there to talk about the Manuscript. At issue was the government's aggressive actions. This was the first time any group of priests has met publicly in support of this document, and we were just beginning our discussion when a government representative knocked on the door and asked to be admitted.'

He paused as he served his plate and took several bites, chewing them thoroughly. 'The representative,' he continued, 'assured us that the government's sole purpose was to protect the Manuscript from outside exploitation. He informed us that all copies being held by Peruvian citizens must be licensed. He said he understood our concern but asked us to comply with this law and turn in our copies. He promised that government duplicates would be issued back to us at once.'

'Did you turn them in?' I asked.

'Of course not.'

We both ate for a few minutes. I tried to overchew, to appreciate the taste.

'We asked about the violence in Cula,' he went on, and he told us that this was a necessary reaction against a man called Jensen, that several of his men were armed agents from another country. He said they planned to find and steal the undiscovered part of the Manuscript and remove it from Peru, so the government had no choice but to arrest them. There was no mention of you or your friends.'

'Did you believe the government man?'

'No, we didn't. After he left we continued the meeting. We agreed that our policy would be one of quiet resistance. We will continue to make copies and distribute them carefully.'

'Will your church leaders allow you to do that?' I asked.

158

'We don't know,' Sanchez said. 'The church elders have disapproved of the Manuscript but so far have not seriously investigated who is involved with it. Our main concern is a cardinal who resides farther north, Cardinal Sebastian. He is the most vocal in opposition to the Manuscript and is very influential. If he convinces the leadership to issue strong proclamations, then we will have a very interesting decision to make.'

'Why is he so opposed to the Manuscript?'

'He is afraid.'

'Why?'

'I haven't spoken with him in a long time, and we always avoid the subject of the Manuscript. But I believe he thinks man's role is to participate in the cosmos ignorant of spiritual knowledge – by faith alone. He thinks the Manuscript will undermine the status quo, the lines of authority in the world.'

'How would it do that?'

He smiled and tilted his head back slightly. 'The truth shall set you free.'

I was looking at him, trying to understand what he meant, eating the last of the bread and fruit on my plate. He ate several more tiny bites and pushed his chair back.

'You seem much stronger,' he said. 'Did you talk with anyone here?'

'Yes,' I replied. 'I learned a method of connecting with the energy from one of the priests. I . . . didn't catch his name. He was in the sitting area while we were talking in the courtyard yesterday morning, remember? When I spoke with him later, he showed me how to absorb energy and then to project it back.'

'His name is John,' Sanchez said, then nodded for me to go on.

'It was an amazing experience,' I said. 'By remembering the love I felt I was able to open up. I sat up there all day simmering in it. I didn't reach the state I experienced on the ridge but I got close.'

Sanchez looked more serious. 'The role of love has been misunderstood for a long time. Love is not something we should do to be good or to make the world a better place out of some abstract moral responsibility, or because we should give up our hedonism. Connecting with energy feels like excitement, then euphoria, and then love. Finding enough energy to maintain that state of love certainly helps the world, but it most directly helps us. It is the most hedonistic thing we can do.'

I agreed, then noticed he had moved his chair back several more feet and was looking at me intensely, his eyes unfocused.

'So what does my field look like,' I asked.

'It is much larger,' he said. 'I think you feel very good.'

'I do.'

'Good. That is what we do here.'

'Tell me about that,' I said.

'We train priests to go farther into the mountains and work with the Indians. It is a lonely job and the priests must have great strength. All of the men here have been screened thoroughly, and all have one thing in common: each has had one experience he calls mystical.

'I have been studying this kind of experience for many years,' he continued, 'even before the Manuscript was found, and I believe that when one has already encountered a mystical experience, getting back into this state and raising one's personal energy level comes much easier. Others can also connect but it takes longer. A strong memory of the experience, as I think you learned, facilitates its re-creation. After that, one slowly builds back.'

'What does a person's energy field look like when this is happening?'

'It grows outward and changes color slightly.'

'What color?'

'Normally from a dull white toward green and blue. But the most important thing is that it expands. For instance, during your mystical encounter on the ridge top, your energy flashed outward into the whole universe. Essentially you connected and drew energy from the entire cosmos and in turn your energy swelled to encompass everything, everywhere. Can you remember how that felt?'

'Yeah,' I said. 'I felt as though the entire universe was my body and I was just the head, or perhaps more accurately, the eyes.'

'Yes,' he said, 'and at that moment, your energy field and that of the universe were the same. The universe was your body.'

'I had a strange memory during that time,' I said. 'I seemed to remember how this larger body, this universe of mine, evolved. I was there. I saw the first stars formed from simple hydrogen and then saw more complex matter evolve in successive generations of these suns. Only I didn't see matter. I saw matter as simple vibrations of energy that were evolving systematically into ever more complex higher states. Then . . . life began and evolved to a point where humans appeared . . .'

I stopped suddenly and he noticed my changed mood.

'What's wrong?' he said.

'That's where the memory of evolution stopped,' I explained, 'with humans. I felt as if the story continued, but I couldn't quite grasp it.'

'The story does go on,' he said. 'Humans are carrying forth the universe's evolution toward higher and higher vibrational complexity.'

'How?' I asked.

He smiled but didn't answer. 'Let's talk about this later. I really must check on a few things. I'll see you in an hour or so.'

I nodded. He picked up an apple and walked out. I wandered outside behind him, then remembered the copy of the Fifth Insight in the bedroom and retrieved it. Earlier I had been thinking of the forest where Sanchez had been sitting when I had first met him. Even in my fatigue and panic I had noticed that the place was extraordinarily beautiful, so I walked down the road toward the west until I came to the exact spot, then sat down there myself.

Leaning back against a tree, I cleared my mind and spent several minutes looking around The morning was bright and breezy and I watched the wind as it whipped the branches above my head. The air felt refreshing as I took in several deep breaths. During a lull in the wind, I took out the Manuscript and looked for the page where I had stopped reading. Before I could locate it, however, I heard the sound of a truck engine.

I lay flat beside the tree and attempted to determine its direction. The sound was coming from the mission. As it grew closer, I could see it was Sanchez's old truck, with him driving.

'I thought you might be here,' he said, as he pulled up to where I was standing. 'Get in. We need to leave.'

'What's going on?' I asked, sliding into the passenger seat.

He drove on toward the main road. 'One of my priests told me of a conversation he overheard in the village. Some government officials are in town and they were asking questions about me and the mission.'

'What do you think they want?'

He looked at me reassuringly. 'I don't know. Let's just say I'm not as certain as before that they will leave us alone. I thought, as a precaution, that we should drive up into the mountains. One of my priests lives near Machu Picchu. His name is Father Carl. We'll be safe at his house until we can better read the situation.' He smiled. 'I want you to see Machu Picchu anyway.'

I suddenly had a flash of suspicion that he had made a deal and was taking me somewhere to turn me in. I decided to proceed cautiously and to stay alert until I found out for sure.

'Did you finish the translation?' he asked.

'Most of it,' I said.

'You had asked about human evolution. Did you finish that part?'

'No.'

He turned his eyes from the road and looked at me intensely. I pretended not to notice.

'Is something wrong?' he asked.

'Nothing,' I said. 'How long will it take to get to Machu Picchu?'

'About four hours.'

I wanted to remain silent and let Sanchez talk, hoping he might give himself away, but I couldn't control my curiosity about evolution.

'So how do humans further evolution?' I asked.

He glanced at me. 'What do you think?'

'I don't know,' I said. 'But when I was up on the ridge I thought it might have something to do with the meaningful coincidences that the First Insight talks about.'

'That's right,' he said. 'That would fit with the other insights, wouldn't it?'

I was confused. I almost understood but I couldn't quite grasp it. I remained silent.

'Think of how the Insights fall into sequence,' he said. 'The First Insight occurs when we take the coincidences seriously. These coincidences make us feel there is something more, something spiritual, operating underneath everything we do.

'The Second Insight institutes our awareness as something real. We can see that we have been preoccupied with material survival, with focusing on controlling our situation in the universe for security, and we know our openness now represents a kind of waking up to what is really going on.

'The Third Insight begins a new view of life. It defines the physical universe as one of pure energy, an energy that somehow responds to how we think.

'And the Fourth exposes the human tendency to steal energy from other humans by controlling them, taking over their minds, a crime in which we engage because we so often feel depleted of energy, and cut off. This shortage of energy can be remedied, of course, when we connect with the higher source. The universe can provide all we need if we can only open up to it. That is the revelation of the Fifth Insight.

'In your case,' he continued, 'you had a mystical experience that allowed you to briefly see the magnitude of energy one can acquire, But this state is like leaping ahead of everyone else and glimpsing the future. We can't maintain it for very long. Once we try to talk to someone who is operating in normal consciousness, or try to live in a world where conflict is still happening, we get knocked out of this advanced state and fall back to the level of our old selves.

'And then,' he continued, 'it is a matter of slowly regaining what we glimpsed, a little at a time, and to begin a progression back toward that ultimate consciousness. But to do this, we must learn to consciously fill up with energy because this energy brings on the coincidences, and the coincidences help us actualize the new level on a permanent basis.'

I must have looked puzzled because he said, 'Think about it: when something occurs beyond chance to lead us forward in our lives, then we become more actualized people. We feel as though we are attaining what destiny is leading us to become. When this occurs, the level of energy that brought on the coincidences in the first place is instituted in us. We can be knocked out of it and lose energy when we are afraid, but this level serves as a new outer limit which can be regained quite easily. We have become a new person. We exist at a level of higher energy, at a level – get this – of higher vibration.

'Can you see the process now? We fill up, grow, fill up

and grow again. That is how we as humans continue the evolution of the universe to a higher and higher vibration.'

He paused for a moment then seemed to think of something he wanted to add. 'This evolution has been going on unconsciously throughout human history. That explains why civilization has progressed and why humans have grown larger, lived longer, and so forth. Now however, we are making the whole process conscious. That is what the Manuscript is telling us. That is what this movement toward a world-wide spiritual consciousness is all about.'

I was listening intensely, totally fascinated with what Sanchez was telling me. 'So all we have to do is fill up with energy, as I learned to do with John, and the co-incidences begin to happen more consistently?'

'Well yes, but that's not as easy as you think. Before we can connect with the energy on a permanent basis there is one more hurdle we must pass. The next insight, the Sixth, deals with this issue.'

'What is it?'

He looked squarely at me. 'We must face up to our particular way of controlling others. Remember, the Fourth Insight reveals that humans have always felt short of energy and have sought to control each other to acquire the energy that flows between people. The Fifth then shows us that an alternative source exists, but we can't really stay connected with this source until we come to grips with the particular method that, we, as individuals, use in our controlling, and stop doing it because whenever we fall back into this habit, we get disconnected from the source.

'Getting rid of this habit isn't easy because it's always unconscious at first. The key to letting it go is to bring it fully into consciousness, and we do that by seeing that our particular style of controlling others is one we learned in childhood to get attention, to get the energy moving our way, and we're stuck there. This style is something we repeat over and over again. I call it our unconscious *control drama*.

'I call it a drama because it is one familiar scene, like a scene in a movie, for which we write the script as youths. Then we repeat this scene over and over in our daily lives without being aware of it. All we know is that the same kind of events happen to us repeatedly. The problem is if we are repeating one particular scene over and over, then the other scenes of our real life movie, the high adventure marked by coincidences, can't go forward. We stop the movie when we repeat this one drama in order to manipulate for energy.'

Sanchez slowed the truck and moved carefully forward through a series of deep ruts in the road. I realized I was frustrated. I couldn't quite grasp how a control drama worked. I almost expressed my feelings to Sanchez but I couldn't. I realized I still felt distant from him and I didn't care to reveal myself.

'Did you understand?' he asked.

'I don't know,' I said curtly. 'I don't know if I have a control drama.'

He looked at me with the warmest regard and chuckled out loud. 'Is that so?' he asked. 'Then why do you always act so aloof?'

Clearing the Past

Ahead the road narrowed and bent sharply around the sheer rock face of the mountain. The truck bounced over several large rocks and slowly proceeded through the curve. Below, the Andes rose in massive gray ridges above banks of snow-white clouds.

I looked at Sanchez. He was leaning over the steering wheel, tense. For most of the day we had been scaling steep inclines and edging through passages made more narrow by fallen rock. I had wanted to broach the subject of control dramas again but the time seemed inappropriate. Sanchez appeared to need every ounce of energy for driving, and besides, I wasn't clear on what I wanted to ask. I had read the rest of the Fifth Insight and it had echoed exactly the points Sanchez had related to me. The idea of getting rid of my style of controlling seemed desirable, especially if it would make my evolution accelerate, but I still couldn't grasp how a control drama operated.

'What are you thinking about?' Sanchez asked.

'I finished reading the Fifth Insight,' I said. 'And I was thinking about these dramas. Considering what you said about me, I assume you think my drama has something to do with being aloof?'

He didn't reply. He was staring up the road. A hundred feet ahead, a large four-wheel drive vehicle blocked the way. A man and a woman stood on a rock precipice fifty feet from the vehicle. They returned our gaze.

Sanchez stopped the truck and looked them over for an instant, then smiled. 'I know the woman,' he said. 'That's Julia. It's all right. Let's talk with them.'

Both the man and woman were of dark complexion and appeared Peruvian. The woman was older, appearing to be about fifty, while the man looked approximately thirty. As we got out of the truck, the woman walked toward us.

'Father Sanchez!' she said as she approached.

'How are you, Julia?' Sanchez replied. The two embraced, then Sanchez introduced me to Julia. Julia, in turn, introduced her companion, Rolando.

Saying nothing else, Julia and Sanchez turned their backs on us and walked toward the overhang where Julia and Rolando had previously been standing. Rolando looked at me intensely and I instinctively turned and walked in the direction of the other two people. Rolando followed, still looking at me as though he wanted something. Although his hair and features were young, his complexion was ruddy and red. For some reason I felt anxious.

Several times as we walked to the edge of the mountain, he looked as though he was going to speak, but each time I turned my eyes away and increased my pace. He remained silent. When we reached the precipice, I sat on a ledge to prevent him from sitting next to me. Julia and

Sanchez were above me about twenty-five feet, sitting together on a large boulder.

Rolando sat as close to me as possible. Although his constant stare bothered me, I was slightly curious about him at the same time.

He caught me looking at him and asked, 'Are you here for the Manuscript?'

I took a long time to answer. 'I've heard of it.'

He looked perplexed. 'Have you seen it?'

'Some,' I said. 'Do you have something to do with it?'

'I am interested,' he said, 'but I have not seen any copies yet.' A period of silence followed.

'Are you from the United States?' he asked.

The question disturbed me, so I decided not to answer. Instead I asked, 'Does the Manuscript have anything to do with the ruins at Machu Picchu?'

'I don't think so,' he replied. 'Except that it was written about the same time they were built.'

I remained silent, looking out at the incredible view of the Andes. Sooner or later, if I remained quiet, he would divulge what he and Julia were doing here and how it concerned the Manuscript. We sat for twenty minutes with no conversation. Finally, Rolando stood and walked up to where the others were talking.

I was perplexed as to what to do. I had avoided sitting with Sanchez and Julia because I had the distinct impression they wanted to talk alone. For perhaps another thirty minutes, I remained there, gazing out at the rocky peaks and straining to overhear the conversation above me. None of them paid me the slightest bit of attention. Finally I decided to join them, but before I could move, the three of them stood and began walking toward

Julia's vehicle. I cut across the rocks toward them.

'They have to go,' Sanchez remarked as I approached.

'I'm sorry we did not have time to talk,' Julia said. 'I hope we see you again.' She was looking at me with the same warmth Sanchez often displayed. As I nodded, she cocked her head slightly and added, 'In fact, I have a feeling we will see you soon.'

As we strolled down the rocky path, I felt the need to say something in response but I couldn't think. When we reached her vehicle Julia only nodded slightly and said a quick good-bye. Both she and Rolando got in and Julia drove away toward the north, the way Sanchez and I had come. I felt puzzled by the entire experience.

Once we were in our vehicle, Sanchez asked, 'Did Rolando fill you in on Wil?'

'No!' I said. 'Had they seen him?'

Sanchez looked confused, 'Yes, they saw him at a village forty miles east of here.'

'Did Wil say anything about me?'

'Julia said Wil mentioned being separated from you. She said Wil talked mainly with Rolando. Didn't you tell Rolando who you were?'

'No, I didn't know if I could trust him.'

Sanchez looked at me in total bewilderment. 'I told you it was fine to talk with them. I have known Julia for years. She owns a business in Lima, but since the discovery of the Manuscript she has been looking for the Ninth Insight. Julia would not be traveling with anyone untrustworthy. There was no danger. Now you missed what could have been important information.'

Sanchez looked at me with a serious expression. 'This is a perfect example of how a control drama interferes,' he said. 'You were so aloof you didn't allow an important coincidence to take place.'

I must have appeared defensive. 'It's all right,' he said, 'everyone plays a drama of one kind or another. At least now you understand how yours works.'

'I don't understand!' I said. 'What exactly am I doing?'

'Your way of controlling people and situations,' he explained, 'in order to get energy coming your way, is to create this drama in your mind during which you withdraw and look mysterious and secretive. You tell yourself that you're being cautious but what you're really doing is hoping someone will be pulled into this drama and will try to figure out what's going on with you. When someone does, you remain vague, forcing them to struggle and dig and try to discern your true feelings.

'As they do so, they give you their full attention and that sends their energy to you. The longer you can keep them interested and mystified, the more energy you receive. Unfortunately, when you play aloof, your life tends to evolve very slowly because you're repeating this same scene over and over again. If you had opened up to Rolando, your life movie would have taken off in a new and meaningful direction.'

I felt myself becoming depressed. All this was just another example of what Wil had pointed out when he saw me resisting giving information to Reneau. It was true. I did tend to hide what I really thought. I looked out the window as we followed the road higher into the peaks. Sanchez concentrated again on avoiding the fatal drop-offs. When the road straightened, he looked over at me and said, 'The first step in the process of getting clear, for each of us, is to bring our particular control drama

172

into full consciousness. Nothing can proceed until we really look at ourselves and discover what we are doing to manipulate for energy. This is what has just happened to you.'

'What is the next step?' I asked.

'Each of us must go back into our past, back into our early family life, and see how this habit was formed. Seeing its inception keeps our way of controlling in consciousness. Remember, most of our family members were operating in a drama themselves, trying to pull energy out of us as children. This is why we had to form a control drama in the first place. We had to have a strategy to win energy back. It is always in relation to our family members that we develop our particular dramas. However, once we recognize the energy dynamics in our families, we can go past these control strategies and see what was really happening.'

'What do you mean, really happening?'

'Each person must reinterpret his family experience from an evolutionary point of view, from a spiritual point of view, and discover who he really is. Once we do that, our control drama falls away and our real lives take off.'

'So how do I begin?'

'By first understanding how your drama was formed. Tell me about your father. '

'He is a good man who is fun-loving and capable but . . .' I hesitated, not wanting to sound ungrateful toward my father.

'But what?' Sanchez asked.

'Well,' I said, 'he was always critical. I could never do anything right.'

'How did he criticize you?' Sanchez asked.

173

A picture of my father, young and strong, appeared in my mind. 'He asked questions, then found something wrong with the answers.'

'And what happened to your energy?'

'I guess I felt drained so I tried to keep from telling him anything.'

'You mean you got vague and distant, trying to say things in a way that would get his attention but not reveal enough to give him something to criticize. He was the interrogator and you dodged around him with your aloofness?'

'Yeah, I guess. But what is an interrogator?'

'An interrogator is another kind of drama. People who use this means of gaining energy, set up a drama of asking questions and probing into another person's world with the specific purpose of finding something wrong. Once they do, then they criticize this aspect of the other's life. If this strategy succeeds then the person being criticized is pulled into the drama. They suddenly find themselves becoming self-conscious around the interrogator and paying attention to what the interrogator is doing and thinking about, so as not to do something wrong that the interrogator would notice. This psychic deference gives the interrogator the energy he desires.

'Think about the times you have been around someone like this. When you get caught up in this drama, don't you tend to act a certain way so that the person won't criticize you? He pulls you off your own path and drains your energy because you judge yourself by what he might be thinking.'

I remembered the feeling exactly, and the person that came to mind was Jensen.

'So my father was an interrogator?' I asked.

'That's what it sounds like.'

For a moment I was lost in thought about my mother's drama. If my father was an interrogator, what was my mother?

Sanchez asked me what I was thinking.

'I was wondering about my mother's control drama,' I said 'How many different kinds are there?'

'Let me explain the classifications spoken of in the Manuscript,' Sanchez said. 'Everyone manipulates for energy either aggressively, directly forcing people to pay attention to them, or passively, playing on people's sympathy or curiosity to gain attention. For instance, if someone threatens you, either verbally or physically, then you are forced, for fear of something bad happening to you, to pay attention to him and so to give him energy. The person threatening you would be pulling you into the most aggressive kind of drama, what the Sixth Insight calls the intimidator.

'If, on the other hand, someone tells you all the horrible things that are already happening to them, implying perhaps that you are responsible, and that, if you refuse to help, these horrible things are going to continue, then this person is seeking to control at the most passive level, with what the Manuscript calls a poor me drama. Think about this one for a moment. Haven't you ever been around someone who makes you feel guilty when you're in their presence, even though you know there is no reason to feel this way?'

'Yes.'

'Well, it's because you have entered the drama world of a poor me. Everything they say and do puts you in a place where you have to defend against the idea that you're not doing enough for this person. That's why you feel guilty just being around them.'

I nodded.

'Anyone's drama can be examined,' he continued, 'according to where it falls on this spectrum from aggressive to passive. If a person is subtle in their aggression, finding fault and slowly undermining your world in order to get your energy, then, as we saw in your father, this person would be an interrogator. Less passive than the poor me would be your aloofness drama. So the order of dramas goes this way: intimidator, interrogator, aloof, and poor me. Does that make sense?'

'I guess. You think everyone falls somewhere among these styles?'

'That's correct. Some people use more than one in different circumstances, but most of us have one dominant control drama that we tend to repeat, depending on which one worked well on the members of our early family.'

It suddenly dawned on me. My mother did exactly the same thing to me as my father. I looked at Sanchez. 'My mother. I know what she was. She was also an interrogator.'

'So you had a double dose,' Sanchez said. 'No wonder you're so aloof. But at least they weren't intimidating you. At least you never feared for your safety.'

'What would have happened in that case?'

'You would have become stuck in a poor me drama. Do you see how this works? If you are a child and someone is draining your energy by threatening you with bodily harm then being aloof doesn't work. You can't get them

176

to give you energy by playing coy. They don't give a damn what's going on inside you. They're coming on too strong. So you're forced to become more passive and to try the poor me approach, appealing to the mercy of the person, guilt tripping them about the harm they are doing.

'If this doesn't work, then, as a child you endure until you are big enough to explode against the violence and fight aggression with aggression.' He paused. 'Like the child you told me about, the one in the Peruvian family that served you dinner.

'A person goes to whatever extreme necessary to get attention energy in their family. And after that, this strategy becomes their dominant way of controlling to get energy from everyone, the drama they constantly repeat.'

'I understand the intimidator,' I said, 'but how does the interrogator develop?'

'What would you do if you were a child and your family members were either not there or ignored you because they were preoccupied with their careers or something?'

'I don't know.'

'Playing aloof would not get their attention; they wouldn't notice. Wouldn't you have to resort to probing and prying and finally finding something wrong in these aloof people in order to force attention and energy? This is what an interrogator does.'

I began to get the insight. 'Aloof people create interrogators!'

'That's right.'

'And interrogators make people aloof! And intimidators

create the poor me approach, or if this fails, another intimidator!'

'Exactly. That's how control dramas perpetuate themselves. But remember, there is a tendency to see these dramas in others but to think that we ourselves are free from such devices. Each of us must transcend this illusion before we can go on. Almost all of us tend to be stuck, at least some of the time, in a drama and we have to step back and look at ourselves long enough to discover what it is.'

I was silent for a moment. Finally I looked at Sanchez again and asked, 'Once we see our drama, what happens next?'

Sanchez slowed the truck in order to look me in the eyes. 'We are truly free to become more than the unconscious act we play. As I said before, we can find a higher meaning for our lives, a spiritual reason we were born to our particular families. We can begin to get clear about who we really are.'

'We're almost there,' Sanchez said. The road was cresting between two peaks. As we passed the huge formation on our right, I saw a small house ahead. It backed up to another majestic pinnacle of rock.

'His truck isn't here,' Sanchez said.

We parked and walked to the house. Sanchez opened the door and walked inside while I waited. I took in several breaths. The air was cool and very thin. Overhead, the sky was dark gray and thick with clouds. It looked as though it might rain.

Sanchez walked back to the door, 'No one is inside. He must be at the ruins.'

'How do we get there?'

He suddenly looked exhausted. 'They're up ahead about a half mile,' he said, handing me the keys to the truck. 'Follow the road past the next ridge and you'll see them down below. Take the truck. I want to stay here and meditate.'

'Okay, I will,' I said, walking around to get in the vehicle.

I drove forward into a little valley and then up the next ridge, anticipating the view. The sight did not disappoint me. As I crested the ridge I saw the full splendor of the ruins at Machu Picchu: a temple complex of massive, carefully shaped rocks weighing tons sitting atop each other on the mountain. Even in the dull cloudy light, the beauty of the place was overwhelming.

I stopped the truck and soaked up the energy for ten or fifteen minutes. Several groups of people were walking through the ruins. I saw a man wearing a priest's collar leave the remains of a building and walk toward a vehicle parked nearby. Because of the distance, and because the man wore a leather jacket rather than a priest's robe, I couldn't be sure it was Father Carl.

I started the truck and drove closer. As soon as he heard the sound he looked up and smiled, apparently recognizing the vehicle as belonging to Sanchez. When he saw me inside he looked interested and walked over. His build was short and squat, with dull brown hair and pudgy features, with deep blue eyes. He looked to be about thirty. 'I'm with Father Sanchez,' I said, stepping from the vehicle and introducing myself. 'He's up at your house.'

He offered his hand. 'I'm Father Carl.'

I glanced past him to the ruins. The cut stone was even more impressive when in close proximity.

'Is this the first time you've been here?' he asked.

'Yes, it is,' I replied. 'I've heard about this place for years but I never anticipated this.'

'It is one of the highest energy centers in the world,' he said.

I looked closely at him. Clearly he spoke about energy in the same sense it was used in the Manuscript. I nodded affirmatively, then said, 'I'm at a point where I'm consciously trying to build energy and deal with my control drama.' I felt somewhat pretentious at saying that but comfortable enough to be honest.

'You don't seem too aloof,' he said.

I was startled. 'How did you know that was my drama?' I asked.

'I've developed an instinct for it. That's why I'm here.'

'You help people see their way of controlling?'

'Yes, and their true self.' His eyes shone with sincerity. He was totally direct, with no hint of embarrassment at revealing himself to a stranger.

I remained silent so he said, 'You understand the first five insights?'

'I've read most of them,' I said, 'and I've talked with several people.'

As soon as I made this statement, I realized I was being too vague. 'I think I understand the first five,' I added. 'It's number six that I'm not clear about.'

He nodded, then said, 'Most of the people I talk with haven't even heard of the Manuscript. They come up here and are entranced by the energy. That alone makes them rethink their lives.'

'How do you meet these people?'

He looked at me with a knowing expression. 'They seem to find me.'

'You said you help them find their true self; how?'

He took a long breath, then said, 'There's only one way. Each of us has to go back to our family experience, that childhood time and place, and review what happened. Once we become conscious of our control drama, then we can focus on the higher truth of our family, the silver lining so to speak, that lies beyond the energy conflict. Once we find this truth, it can energize our lives, for this truth tells us who we are, the path we are on, what we are doing.'

'That's what Sanchez has told me,' I said. 'I want to know more about how to find this truth.'

He zipped up his coat against the late afternoon chill. 'I hope we can talk more about it later,' he said. 'Right now I would like to greet Father Sanchez.'

I looked out at the ruins, and he added, 'Feel free to look around as long as you would like. I'll see you back at my house later.'

For the next hour and a half, I walked through the ancient site. At certain spots I would linger, feeling more buoyant than at others. I wondered with fascination about the civilization that had built these temples. How did they move these stones up here and place them atop one another in this fashion? It seemed impossible.

As my intense interest in the ruins began to wane, my thoughts turned to my personal situation. Although my circumstances had not changed, I felt less fearful now. Sanchez's confidence had reassured me. I had been stupid to doubt him. And I already liked Father Carl.

As darkness descended I walked back to the truck and returned to Father Carl's house. As I drove up I could see the two men standing close to each other inside. When I entered I heard laughter. Both were busy in the kitchen, preparing dinner. Father Carl greeted me and escorted me to a chair. I sat down lazily in front of a large fire in the fireplace and looked around.

The room was large, and paneled with wide boards which were lightly stained. I could see two other rooms, bedrooms apparently, linked by a narrow hallway. 'The house was lit with low wattage bulbs and I thought I could detect the faint hum of a generator.

When the preparations were completed, I was summoned to a rough plank table. Sanchez offered a brief prayer, and then we ate, the two men continuing to talk. Afterward we sat together by the fire.

'Father Carl has spoken with Wil,' Sanchez said.

'When?' I asked, immediately excited.

'Wil came through here several days ago,' Father Carl said. 'I had met him a year ago and he came by to bring me some information. He said he thought he knew who was behind the governmental action against the Manuscript.'

'Who?' I asked.

'Cardinal Sebastian,' Sanchez interjected.

'What is he doing?' I asked.

'Apparently,' Sanchez said, 'he is using his influence with the government to increase the military pressure against the Manuscript. He has always preferred to work quietly through the government rather than force a division within the church. Now he is intensifying his efforts. Unfortunately, it may be working.'

'What do you mean?' I asked.

'Except for the few priests of the Northern Council and a few others like Julia and Wil, no one else seems to have copies any longer.'

'What about the scientists at Viciente?' I asked.

Both men were silent for a moment, then Father Carl said, 'Wil told me the government has closed it down. All the scientists were arrested and their research data was confiscated.'

'Will the scientific community stand for that?' I asked.

'What choice do they have?' Sanchez said. 'Besides, that research wasn't accepted by most scientists anyway. The government is apparently selling the idea that these people were breaking the law.'

'I can't believe the government could get away with doing that.'

'Apparently they have,' Father Carl said. 'I made some calls to check and I received the same story. Though they're keeping it very quiet, the government is intensifying its crackdown.'

'What do you think will happen?' I asked them both.

Father Carl shrugged his shoulders and Father Sanchez said, 'I don't know. It may depend on what Wil finds.'

'Why?' I asked.

'He appears to be close to finding the missing part of the Manuscript, the Ninth Insight. Perhaps when he does there will be enough interest to create world-wide intervention here.'

'Where did he say he was going?' I asked Father Carl.

'He didn't know, exactly, but he said his intuitions were leading him further north, near Guatemala.'

'His intuitions were leading him?'

'Yes, you'll understand that after you get clear about who you are and go on to the Seventh Insight.'

I looked at both of them, at how incredibly serene they appeared. 'How can you remain so calm?' I asked. 'What if they come crashing in here and arrest all of us?'

They gazed at me patiently, then Father Sanchez spoke. 'Don't confuse calmness with carelessness. Our peaceful countenance is a measure of how well we are connected with the energy. We stay connected because it is the best thing for us to do, regardless of the circumstances. You understand that, don't you?'

'Yes,' I said, 'of course. I guess I'm having trouble staying connected myself.'

Both men smiled.

'Staying connected,' Father Carl said, 'will be easier once you get clear on who you are.'

Father Sanchez stood up then and walked away, announcing that he would be doing the dishes.

I looked at Father Carl. 'Okay,' I said. 'How do I start getting clear about myself?'

'Father Sanchez tells me,' he replied, 'that you already understand the control dramas of your parents.'

'That's right. They were both interrogators and that made me aloof.'

'Okay, now you must look past the energy competition that existed in your family and search for the real reason you were there.'

I looked at him blankly.

'The process of finding your true spiritual identity involves looking at your whole life as one long story, trying to find a higher meaning. Begin by asking yourself this question: why was I born to this particular

184

family? What might have been the purpose for that?'

'I don't know,' I said.

'Your father was an interrogator; what else was he?'

'You mean, what did he stand for?'

'Yes.'

I thought for a moment, then said, 'My father genuinely believes in enjoying life, in living with integrity but making the most of what life has to offer. You know, living life to the fullest.'

'Has he been able to do this?'

'To some extent, but somehow he always seems to have a run of bad luck just when he thinks he's about to enjoy life the most.'

Father Carl squinted his eyes in contemplation. 'He believes life is for fun and enjoyment but he hasn't quite pulled it off?'

'Yes.'

'Have you thought about why?'

'Not really. I always figured he was unlucky.'

'Maybe he hasn't found the way to do it yet?'

'Maybe not.'

'What about your mother?'

'She's no longer living.'

'Can you see what her life represented?'

'Yes, her life was her church. She stood for Christian principles.'

'In what way?'

'She believed in community service and in following God's laws.'

'Did she follow God's laws?'

'To the letter, at least so far as her church taught.'

185

'Was she able to convince your father to do the same thing?'

I laughed. 'Not really. My mother wanted him to go to church every week, and to be involved in community programs. But as I told you, he was more of a free spirit than that.'

'So where did that leave you?'

I looked at him. 'I've never thought about it.'

'Didn't they both want your allegiance? Wasn't that why they were interrogating you, to make sure you weren't siding with the values of the other? Didn't they both want you to think their way was the best?'

'Yes, you're right.'

'How did you respond?'

'I just tried to avoid taking a stand, I guess.'

'They both monitored you to see if you were measuring up to their particular views, and unable to please both, you became aloof.'

'That's about it,' I said.

'What happened to your mother?' he asked.

'She developed Parkinson's disease and died after being sick for a long time.'

'Did she remain true to her faith?'

'Absolutely,' I said. 'Throughout it all.'

'So what meaning did she leave you with?'

'What?'

'You're looking for the meaning her life has for you, the reason you were born to her, what you were there to learn. Every human being, whether they are conscious of it or not, illustrates with their lives how he or she thinks a human being is supposed to live. You must try to discover what she taught you and at the same time what

186

about her life could have been done better. What you would have changed about your mother is part of what you yourself are working on.'

'Why only part?'

'Because how you would improve on your father's life is the other part.'

I was still confused.

He placed his hand on my shoulder. 'We are not merely the physical creation of our parents; we are also the spiritual creation. You were born to these two people and their lives had an irrevocable effect on who you are. To discover your real self, you must admit that the real you began in a position between their truths. That's why you were born there: to take a higher perspective on what they stood for. Your path is about discovering a truth that is a higher synthesis of what these two people believed.'

I nodded.

'So how would you express what your parents taught you?'

'I'm not sure,' I replied.

'What do you think?'

'My father thought life was about maximizing his aliveness, his enjoyment of who he was, and he tried to pursue that end. My mother believed more in sacrifice and in spending her time in service to others, denying herself. She felt this is what the scriptures command.'

'And you, how do you feel about this?'

'I don't know really.'

'Which viewpoint would you choose for yourself, that of your mother, or that of your father?'

'Neither. I mean, life is not that simple.'

He laughed. 'You're being vague.'

'I guess I don't know.'

'But if you had to choose one or the other?'

I hesitated, trying to think honestly, then the answer came to me.

'They're both correct,' I said, 'and incorrect.'

His eyes beamed. 'How?'

'I'm not sure exactly. But I think a correct life must include both views.'

'The question for you,' Father Carl said, 'is how. How does one live a life that is both? From your mother you received the knowledge that life is about spirituality. From your father you learned that life is about self-enhancement, fun, adventure.'

'So my life,' I interrupted, 'is about somehow combining the two approaches?'

'Yes, for you, spirituality is the question. Your whole life will be about finding one that is self-enhancing. This is the problem your parents were unable to reconcile, the one they left for you. This is your evolutionary question, your quest this lifetime.'

The idea propelled me into deep thought. Father Carl said something else but I couldn't concentrate on what he was saying. The waning fire was having a calming effect on me. I realized I was tired.

Father Carl sat up straight and said, 'I think you're out of energy for tonight. But let me leave you with one thought. You can go to sleep and never think again of what we have discussed. You can go right back into your old drama, or you can wake up tomorrow and hold on to this new idea of who you are. If you do then you can take the next step in the process, which is to look closely at all the other things that have happened to you since birth.

If you view your life as one story, from birth to right now, you'll be able to see how you have been working on this question all along. You'll be able to see how you came to be here in Peru and what you should do next.'

I nodded and looked at him closely. His eyes were warm and caring and held the same expression I had seen so often on Wil's face, and Sanchez's.

'Good night,' Father Carl said, and walked into the bedroom and closed the door. I unrolled my sleeping bag on the floor and fell quickly to sleep.

I woke up with Wil on my mind. I wanted to ask Father Carl what else he knew of Wil's plans. As I lay there thinking, still zipped in the sleeping bag, Father Carl walked into the room quietly and began rebuilding the fire.

I unzipped the bag and he looked over at me, alerted by the sound.

'Good morning,' he said. 'How did you sleep?'

'Okay,' I replied, standing.

He put fresh kindling on the coals and then larger pieces of firewood.

'What did Wil say he was going to do?' I asked.

Father Carl stood and faced me. 'He said he was going to a friend's house to wait for some information he expected, apparently information about the Ninth Insight.'

'What else did he say?' I asked.

'Wil told me that he thought Father Sebastian intends to find the last insight himself and seems to be close. Wil thinks that the person who controls the last insight will determine whether the Manuscript ever becomes widely distributed and understood.'

'Why?'

'I'm not sure really. Wil was one of the first to ever collect and read the insights. He may understand them better than any man alive. He feels, I think, that the last insight will make all the others become more clear and accepted.'

'Do you think he is right?' I asked.

'I don't know,' he replied. 'I don't understand as much as he does. All I understand is what I am supposed to do.'

'What is that?'

He paused momentarily, then replied, 'As I said before, my truth is to help people discover who they really are. When I read the Manuscript, this mission became clear to me. The Sixth Insight is my special insight. My truth is helping others grasp this insight. And I'm effective because I've gone through the process myself.'

'What was your control drama?' I asked.

He looked at me with amusement. 'I was an interrogator.'

'You controlled people by finding something wrong with the way they lived their lives?'

'That's right. My father was a poor me and my mother was aloof. They completely ignored me. The only way I could get any attention energy was to pry into what they were doing and then point out something wrong with it.'

'And when did you work through this drama?'

'About eighteen months ago, when I met Father Sanchez and began to study the Manuscript. After I really looked at my parents, I realized what my experience with them was preparing me to do. You see, my father stood for accomplishment. He was very goal oriented. He planned his time to the minute and judged himself according to how much he got done. My mother was very intuitive and mystical. She believed that each of us received spiritual guidance and that life was about following this direction.'

'What did your father think about that?'

'He thought it was crazy.'

I smiled but said nothing.

'Can you see where that left me?' Father Carl asked.

I shook my head. I couldn't quite grasp it.

'Because of my father,' he said, 'I was sensitized to the idea that life was about accomplishment: having something important to do and getting it done. But at the same time my mother was there to tell me life was about inner direction, an intuitive guidance of some sort. I realized that my life was a synthesis of both viewpoints. I was trying to discover how we are guided inwardly toward the mission only we can do, knowing it is of supreme importance to pursue this mission if we are to feel happy and fulfilled.'

I nodded.

'And,' he continued, 'you can see why I was excited about the Sixth Insight. As soon as I read it, I knew that my work was to help people get clear so that they could develop this sense of purpose.'

'Do you know how Wil got on the path he is on?'

'Yes, he shared some of this information with me. Wil's drama was to be aloof, like yours. Also, as in your case, each of his parents was an interrogator and each had a strong philosophy they wanted Wil to adopt. Wil's father was a German novelist who argued that the ultimate destiny of the human race was to perfect itself. His father never advocated anything but the purest of humanitarian principles, but the Nazis used his basic idea of perfection to help legitimize their murderous liquidation of inferior races.

'The corruption of his theme destroyed the old man and led him to move to South America with his wife and Wil. His wife was a Peruvian who grew up in America and was educated there. She was a writer too, but she was basically Eastern in her philosophical beliefs. She held that life was about reaching an inner enlightenment, a higher consciousness marked by peace of mind and detachment from the things of the world. According to her, life was not about perfection; it was about letting go of the need to perfect anything, to go anywhere . . . Can you see where this left Wil?'

I shook my head.

'He was left,' Father Carl continued, 'in a difficult position. His father championed the Western idea of working for progress and perfection and his mother held the Eastern belief that life was only about reaching inner peace, nothing else.

'These two people had prepared Wil to work on integrating the main philosophical differences between Eastern and Western culture, although he didn't know it at first. He first became an engineer dedicated to progress and then a simple guide who sought peace by bringing people to the beautiful, inwardly moving places in this country.

'But searching out the Manuscript awakened all this in him. The insights speak directly to his main question. They reveal that the thought of both East and West can indeed be integrated into a higher truth. They show us that the West is correct in maintaining that life is about progress, about evolving toward something higher. Yet the East is also correct in emphasizing that we must let go of control with the ego. We can't progress by using logic alone. We have to attain a fuller consciousness, an inner connection with God, because only then can our evolution toward something better be guided by a higher part of ourselves.

'When Wil began to discover the insights, his whole life began to flow. He met Jose, the priest who first found the Manuscript and had it translated. Soon after that, he met the owner of Viciente and helped start the research there. And at about the same time, he met Julia, who was in business, but was also guiding people to the virgin forests.

'It was with Julia that Wil had the most affinity. They hit it off immediately because of the similarity in the questions they pursued. Julia grew up with a father who talked of spiritual ideas but in a capricious and flaky way. Her mother on the other hand was a college speech teacher, a debater, who demanded clear thinking. Naturally, Julia found herself wanting information about spirituality but insisting that it be intelligible and precise.

'Wil wanted a synthesis between East and West that explained human spirituality, and Julia wanted this explanation to be perfectly clear. Something the Manuscript was providing for both.'

'Breakfast is ready,' Sanchez called from the kitchen.

I turned around, surprised. I didn't realize Sanchez was up. Without pursuing the conveisation any further, Father Carl and I got up and joined Sanchez in a meal of fruit and cereal. Afterwards Father Carl asked me to take a walk to the ruins with him. I agreed, wanting very much to go there again. Both of us looked at Father Sanchez and he gracefully declined, explaining that he needed to drive down the mountain and make some phone calls.

Outside, the sky was crystal clear and the sun shone brightly over the peaks. We walked briskly.

'Do you think there is a way to contact Wil?' I asked.

'No,' he replied. 'He did not tell me who his friends were. The only way would be to drive to Iquitos, a town near the northern border, and I think that might be unsafe right now.'

'Why there?' I asked.

'He said he thought his search would take him to this town. There are many ruins near there. Also Cardinal Sebastian has a mission nearby.'

'Do you think Wil will find the last insight?'

'I don't know.'

We walked in silence for several minutes, then Father Carl asked, 'Have you made a decision about what course to take personally?'

'What do you mean?'

'Father Sanchez said you were talking at first about going back immediately to the United States but that lately you seemed to be more interested in exploring the insights. How are you feeling now?'

'Precarious,' I said. 'But for some reason I also want to continue.'

'I understand a man was killed right beside you.'

'That's right.'

'And still you want to stay?'

'No,' I said. 'I want to get away, save my life . . . yet here I am.'

'Why do you think that is?' he asked.

I scrutinized his expression. 'I don't know. Do you?'

'Do you remember where we left our conversation last night?'

I remembered exactly. 'We had discovered the question my parents left me with: to find a spirituality that is self-enhancing, that gives one a sense of adventure, and fulfillment. And you said if I looked closely at how my life has evolved, this question would put my life in perspective and clear up what's happening to me now.'

He smiled mysteriously. 'Yes, according to the Manuscript, it will.'

'How does that occur?'

'Each of us must look at the significant turns in our lives and reinterpret them in light of our evolutionary question.'

I shook my head, not comprehending.

'Try to perceive the sequence of interests, important friends, coincidences that have occurred in your life. Weren't they leading you somewhere?'

I thought about my life since childhood but could find no pattern.

'How did you spend your time as you grew up?' he asked.

'I don't know. I was a typical child, I guess. I read a lot.'

'What did you read?'

'Mystery stuff mostly, science fiction, ghost stories, that kind of thing.'

'What happened in your life after that?'

I thought about the effect my grandfather had on me, and told Father Carl about the lake and the mountains.

He nodded his head knowingly. 'And after you grew up, what happened?'

'I went away to college. My grandfather died while I was away.'

'What did you study at college?'

'Sociology.'

'Why?'

'I met a professor I liked. His knowledge of human nature interested me. I decided to study with him.'

'What happened then?'

'I graduated and went to work.'

'Did you enjoy it?'

'Yes, for a long time.'

'Then things changed?'

'I felt that what I was doing wasn't complete. I was working with emotionally disturbed adolescents and I thought I knew how they could transcend their pasts and stop the acting out that was so self-defeating. I thought I could help them go on with their lives. I finally realized something was missing in my approach.'

'Then what?'

'I quit.'

'And?'

'And then an old friend called and told me of the Manuscript.'

'Is that when you decided to come to Peru?'

'Yes.'

'What do you think of your experience here?'

'I think I'm crazy,' I said. 'I think I'm going to get myself killed.'

'But what do you think of the way your experience has progressed?'

'I don't understand.'

'When Father Sanchez told me what had happened to

196

you since coming to Peru,' he said, 'I was amazed at the series of coincidences that brought you face to face with the different insights of the Manuscript just when you needed them.'

'What do you think that means?' I asked.

He stopped walking and faced me. 'It means you were ready. You are like the rest of us here. You came to the point where you needed the Manuscript in order to continue your life evolution.

'Think about how the events of your life fit together. From the beginning you were interested in mysterious topics, and that interest finally led you to study human nature. Why do you think you happened to meet that particular teacher? He crystallized your interests and led you into looking at the greatest mystery: the human situation on this planet, the question of what life is about. Then at some level, you knew that life's meaning was connected to the problem of transcending our past conditioning and moving our lives forward. That's why you were working with those kids.

'But, as you can understand now, it has taken the insights to clear up what was missing in your technique with those youths. In order for emotionally disturbed children to evolve, they have to do what we all have to do: get connected with enough energy to see through their intense control drama, what you call "acting out," and go forward in what turns out to be a spiritual process, a process you have been trying to understand all along.

'See the higher perspective on these events. All the interests that led you forward in your past, all these stages of growth, were just preparing you to be here, now, exploring the insights. You've been working on your evolutionary search for a self-enhancing spirituality throughout your entire life, and the energy you acquired from that natural spot where you grew up, an energy your grandfather was trying to show you, finally gave you the courage to come to Peru. You are here because this is where you need to be to continue the evolution. Your whole life has been a long road leading directly to this moment.'

He smiled. 'When you fully integrate this view of your life, you will have achieved what the Manuscript calls a clear awareness of your spiritual path. According to the Manuscript we all must spend as much time as necessary going through this process of clearing our past. Most of us have a control drama we have to transcend but once we do, we can comprehend the higher meaning for why we were born to our particular parents, and what all the twists and turns of our lives were preparing us to do. We all have a spiritual purpose, a mission, that we have been pursuing without being fully aware of it, and once we bring it completely into consciousness, our lives can take off.

'In your case, you've discovered this purpose. Now, you must go forward, allowing the coincidences to lead you into a clearer and clearer idea of how to pursue this mission from this point on, what else you must do here. Since you've been in Peru, you've been riding along on Wil's energy and Father Sanchez's. But now it's time to learn to evolve by yourself . . . consciously.'

He was about to tell me something more, but we were both distracted by the sight of Sanchez's truck racing up behind us. He pulled alongside and rolled down his window.

'What's wrong?' Father Carl asked.

'I must return to the mission as soon as I can get packed,' Sanchez said. 'Government troops are there . . . and Cardinal Sebastian.'

We both jumped into the truck and Sanchez drove back toward Father Carl's house, telling us along the way that the troops were at his mission to confiscate all copies of the Manuscript and possibly to close it down.

We drove up to Father Carl's house and hurriedly walked inside. Father Sanchez immediately began to pack his belongings. I stood there, deliberating on what to do. As I watched, Father Carl approached the other priest and said, 'I think I should go with you.'

Sanchez turned. 'Are you sure?'

'Yes, I believe I should.'

'For what purpose?'

'I don't know yet.'

Sanchez stared at him for a moment, then returned to packing. 'If you think that is best.'

I was leaning against the door frame. 'What should I do?' I asked.

Both men looked at me.

'That's up to you,' Father Carl said.

I just stared.

'You'll have to make the decision,' Sanchez interjected.

I couldn't believe they were so detached about my choice. To go with them meant certain capture by the Peruvian troops. Yet how could I stay here, alone?

'Look,' I said, 'I don't know what to do. You two must help me. Is there anyone else who can hide me?'

Both men looked at one another.

'I don't think so,' Father Carl said.

I looked at them, a knot of anxiety growing in my stomach.

Father Carl smiled at me and said, 'Stay centered. Remember who you are.'

Sanchez walked over to a bag and pulled out a folder. 'This is a copy of the Sixth Insight,' he said. 'Perhaps it will help you decide what to do.'

As I took the copy, Sanchez looked at Father Carl and asked, 'How long before you can leave?'

'I'll need to contact some people,' Father Carl said. 'Probably an hour.'

Sanchez looked at me. 'Read and think for a while, then we will talk.'

Both men returned to their preparations, and I walked outside and sat down on a large rock, then opened the Manuscript. It echoed exactly the words of Father Sanchez and Father Carl. Clearing the past was a precise process of becoming aware of our individual ways of controlling learned in childhood. And once we could transcend this habit, it said, we would find our higher selves, our evolutionary identities.

I read the entire text in less than thirty minutes and when I finished I finally understood the basic insight: before we could fully enter the special state of mind that so many people were glimpsing – the experience of ourselves moving onward in life guided by mysterious coincidences – we had to wake up to who we really were.

At that moment Father Carl walked around the house, spotted me, and came to where I was sitting.

'Have you finished?' he asked. His manner was warm and friendly as usual.

'Yes.'

'Do you mind if I sit here with you for a moment?'

'I wish you would.'

He positioned himself to my right and after a period of silence asked, 'Do you understand that you are on your path of discovery here?'

'I guess, but now what?'

'Now you must really believe it.'

'How, when I feel this afraid?'

'You must understand what is at stake. The truth you are pursuing is as important as the evolution of the universe itself, for it enables evolution to continue.

'Don't you see? Father Sanchez told me of your vision of evolution on the ridge top. You saw how matter evolved from the simple vibration of hydrogen all the way to humankind. You wondered how humans carried on this evolution. You have now discovered the answer: humans are born into their historical situations and find something to stand for. They form a union with another human being who also has found some purpose.

'The children born to this union then reconcile these two positions by pursuing a higher synthesis, guided by the coincidences. As I'm sure you learned in the Fifth Insight, each time we fill up with energy and a co-incidence occurs to lead us forward in our lives, we institute this level of energy in ourselves, and so we can exist at a higher vibration. Our children take our level of vibration and raise it even higher. This is how we, as humans, continue evolution.

'The difference now, with this generation, is that we are ready to do it consciously and to accelerate the process. No matter how afraid you become, you now have no choice. Once you learn what life is about, there is no way to erase the knowledge. If you try to do something else with your life you will always sense that you are missing something.'

'But what do I do now?'

'I don't know. Only you know that. But I suggest you first try to gain some energy.'

Father Sanchez rounded the corner of the house and joined us, carefully avoiding eye contact or noise as if he desired not to interrupt. I tried to center myself and to focus on the rock peaks that encircled the house. I took a deep breath and realized that I had been totally self-absorbed since coming outside, as if I had had tunnel vision. I had cut myself off from the beauty and majesty of the mountains.

As I gazed out at the surroundings, consciously trying to appreciate what I was seeing, I began to experience that now familiar feeling of closeness. Suddenly everything seemed to exhibit more presence and to glow slightly. I began to feel lighter, my body more buoyant.

I looked at Father Sanchez and then at Father Carl.

They were gazing intensely at me and I could tell they were observing my energy field.

'How do I look?' I asked.

'You look as if you feel better,' Sanchez said. 'Stay here and increase your energy as much as possible. We have about twenty more minutes of packing.'

He smiled wryly. 'After that,' he continued, 'you will be ready to begin.'

Engaging the Flow

The two priests walked back to the house and I spent several more minutes observing the beauty of the mountains in an attempt to gain more energy. Then, I lost my focus and drifted absently into a reverie about Wil. Where was he? Was he close to finding the Ninth Insight?

I imagined him running through the jungle, the Ninth Insight in his hand, troops everywhere, pursuing. I thought of Sebastian orchestrating the chase. Yet in my daydream, it was clear that Sebastian, even with all his authority, was wrong, that he misunderstood something about the impact the insights would have on people. I felt that someone could persuade him to take a different view, if only we could discover what part of the Manuscript threatened him so.

As I mused over this thought, Marjorie popped into my mind. Where was she? I pictured seeing her again. How might that happen?

The sound of the front door closing brought me back to reality. I felt weak and nervous again. Sanchez walked around the house toward where I was sitting. His pace was quick, purposeful.

He sat down beside me, then asked, 'Have you decided what to do?'

I shook my head.

'You don't look very strong,' he said.

'I don't feel very strong.'

'Perhaps you're not being very systematic in the way you build your energy.'

'What do you mean?'

'Let me offer you the way that I personally gain energy. Perhaps my method will help you as you create your own procedure.'

I nodded for him to go on.

'The first thing I do,' he said, 'is to focus on the environment around me, as I think you do also. Then I try to remember how everything looks when I'm being filled with energy. I do this by recalling the presence everything displays, the unique beauty and shape of everything, especially plants, and the way colors seem to glow and appear brighter. Do you follow me?'

'Yes, I try to do the same thing.'

'Then,' he continued. 'I try to experience that feeling of closeness, the feeling that no matter how far away something is, that I can touch it, connect with it And then I breathe it in.'

'Breathe it in?'

'Did Father John not explain this to you?'

'No, he didn't.'

Sanchez appeared confused. 'Perhaps he intended to come back and tell you about it later. Often he's very dramatic. He walks away and leaves his pupil alone to ponder what he has taught, then he shows up later at just the right time to add something else to the instruction. I suppose he intended to talk with you again but we left too quickly.'

'I'd like to hear about it,' I said.

'Do you remember the feeling of buoyancy that you experienced on the ridge top?' he asked.

'Yes,' I said.

'To regain this buoyancy, I try to breathe in the energy with which I have just connected.'

I had been following along as Sanchez spoke. Just hearing his procedure was increasing my connection. Everything around me had increased in presence and beauty. Even the rocks seemed to have a whitish glow and Sanchez's energy field was wide and blue. He was now taking deep, conscious breaths, holding each about five seconds before exhaling. I followed his example.

'When we visualize,' he said, 'that each breath pulls energy into us and fills us like a balloon, we actually become more energized and feel much lighter and more buoyant.'

After several breaths, I began to feel exactly that way.

'After I breathe in the energy,' Sanchez continued, 'I check to see if I have the right emotion. As I've told you before, I consider this the true measure of whether I am really connected.'

'You are speaking of love?'

'That's correct. As we discussed at the mission, love is not an intellectual concept or a moral imperative or anything else. It is a background emotion that exists when one is connected to the energy available in the universe, which, of course, is the energy of God.'

Father Sanchez was gazing at me, his eyes slightly out of focus. 'There,' he said, 'you've reached it. That's the level of energy you need to have. I'm helping you some, but you are ready to maintain it on your own.'

'What do you mean, you're helping me some?'

Father Sanchez shook his head. 'Don't worry about that now. You'll learn about it later, in the Eighth Insight.'

Father Carl walked around the house then and looked at both of us, as though pleased. As he approached he glanced at me. 'Have you decided yet?'

The question irritated me; I fought against the resulting loss of energy.

'Don't fall back into your aloof drama,' Father Carl said. 'You can't avoid taking a stand here. What are you thinking you need to do?'

'I'm not thinking anything,' I said. 'That's the problem.'

'Are you sure? Thoughts feel different once you get connected with the energy.'

I gave him a puzzled look.

'The words you have habitually willed through your head in an attempt to logically control events,' he explained, 'stop when you give up your control drama. As you fill up with inner energy, other kinds of thoughts enter your mind from a higher part of yourself. These are your intuitions. They feel different. They just appear in the back of your mind, sometimes in a kind of daydream or mini-vision, and they come to direct you, to guide you.'

I still didn't understand.

'Tell us what you were thinking about when we left you alone earlier,' Father Carl said.

'I'm not sure I remember it all,' I said.

'Try.'

I tried to concentrate. 'I was thinking about Wil, I guess, about whether he was close to finding the Ninth

Insight, and about Sebastian's crusade against the Manuscript.'

'What else?'

'I was wondering about Marjorie, about what happened to her. But I don't understand how this helps me know what to do.'

'Let me explain,' Father Sanchez said. 'When you have acquired enough energy, you are ready to consciously engage evolution, to start it flowing, to produce the coincidences that will lead you forward. You engage your evolution in a very specific way. First, as I said, you build sufficient energy, then you remember your basic life question – the one your parents gave you because this question provides the overall context for your evolution. Next you center yourself on your path by discovering the immediate, smaller questions that currently confront you in life. These questions always pertain to your larger question and define where you currently are in your life-long quest.

'Once you become conscious of the questions active in the moment, you always get some kind of intuitive direction of what to do, of where to go. You get a hunch about the next step. Always. The only time this will not occur is when you have the wrong question in mind. You see, the problem in life isn't in receiving answers. The problem is in identifying your current questions. Once you get the questions right, the answers always come.

'After you get an intuition of what might happen next,' he continued, 'then the next step is to become very alert and watchful. Sooner or later coincidences will occur to move you in the direction indicated by the intuition. Do you follow me?'

'I think I do.'

'So,' he continued, 'don't you think those thoughts of Wil and Sebastian and Marjorie are important? Think about why these thoughts are coming now, considering the story of your life. You know that you came out of your family wanting to find out how to make the spiritual life an inwardly self-enhancing adventure, right?'

'Yes.'

'Then, as you grew up, you became interested in mysterious topics, you studied sociology and worked with people, although you didn't yet know why you were doing these things. Then as you began to wake up, you heard about the Manuscript and came to Peru and found the insights one by one, and each has taught you something about the kind of spirituality you seek. Now that you've become clear, you can become super conscious of this evolution by defining your current questions and then watching the answers come.'

I just looked at him.

'What are your current questions?' he asked.

'I guess I want to know about the other insights,' I said. 'Especially, I want to know if Wil is going to find the Ninth Insight. I want to know what happened to Marjorie. And I want to know about Sebastian.'

'And what were your intuitions suggesting about these questions?'

'I don't know. I was thinking of seeing Marjorie again, and of Wil running with troops chasing him. What does it mean?'

'Where was Wil running?'

'In the jungle.'

'Perhaps that indicates where you should go. Iquitos is in the jungle. What about Marjorie?'

'I saw myself seeing her again.'

'And Sebastian?'

'I fantasized that he was against the Manuscript because he misunderstood, that his mind could be changed if one could find out what he was thinking, what exactly he feared about the Manuscript.'

Both men looked at each other in total amazement.

'What does it mean?' I asked.

Father Carl replied with another question, 'What do you think?'

For the first time since the ridge top I was beginning to feel fully energized again and confident. I looked at them and said, 'I guess it means I should go toward the jungle and try to discover which aspects of the Manuscript the church dislikes.'

Father Carl smiled. 'Exactly! You can take my truck.'

I nodded and we walked around to the front of the house where the vehicles were parked. My things, along with a supply of food and water, were already packed in Father Carl's truck. Father Sanchez's vehicle was also packed.

'I want to tell you this,' Sanchez said. 'Remember to stop as often as necessary to re-connect your energy. Stay full, stay in a state of love. Remember that once you achieve this state of love, nothing nor anyone can pull more energy from you than you can replace. In fact, the energy flowing out of you creates a current that pulls energy into you at the same rate. You can never run out. But you must stay conscious of this process in order for it to work. This is especially important when you interact with people.'

He paused. Simultaneously, as if on cue, Father Carl walked closer and said, 'You have read all but two insights: the Seventh and Eighth. Seven deals with the process of consciously evolving yourself, of staying alert to every coincidence, every answer the universe provides for you.'

He handed me a small folder. 'This is the Seventh. It is very short and general,' he continued, 'but it talks about the way objects jump out at us, the way certain thoughts come as guidance. As for the Eighth, you will find it yourself when the time is right. It explains how we can aid others as they bring us the answers we seek. And further, it describes a whole new ethic governing the way humans should treat each other in order to facilitate everyone's evolution.'

'Why can't you give me the Eighth Insight now?' I asked.

Father Carl smiled and put his hand on my shoulder. 'Because we don't feel we should. We must follow our intuitions also. You will get the Eighth Insight as soon as you ask the right question.'

I told him I understood. Then both priests hugged me and wished me well. Father Carl stressed that we would soon meet again and that I would indeed find the answers I was here to receive.

We were all about to board our respective vehicles when Sanchez turned suddenly and faced me. 'I have an intuition to tell you something. You will learn more about it later. Let your perception of beauty and iridescence lead your way. Places and people who have answers for you will appear more luminous and attractive.'

I nodded and climbed into Father Carl's truck, then

followed them down the rocky road for several miles until we came to a fork. Sanchez waved out the back window as he and Father Carl headed east. I watched them for a moment then turned the old truck north toward the Amazon basin.

A surge of impatience rose up within me. After making good time for over three hours, I now sat at a crossroads, unable to decide between two particular routes.

To my left was one possibility. Judging from the map, this road bore north along the edge of the mountains for a hundred miles, then turned sharply east toward Iquitos. The other route led to the right and maintained an eastern angle through the jungle to the same destination.

I took a deep breath and tried to relax, then quickly checked the rear view mirror. No one was in sight. In fact, I hadn't seen anyone – no traffic, no locals walking – in over an hour. I tried to shake off a rush of anxiety. I knew I had to relax and stay connected if I expected to make the right decision.

I focused on the scene. The jungle route to my right progressed between a group of large trees. Several huge outcroppings of rock punctuated the ground around them. Most were encircled by large tropical bushes. The other route through the mountains seemed comparatively bare. One tree grew in that direction, but the remainder of the landscape was rocky, with very little plant life.

I looked to the right again and tried to induce a love state. The trees and bushes were a rich green. I looked to the left and tried the same procedure. Immediately I noticed a patch of flowering grass that bordered the road. The blades of grass were pale and spotty, but the white flowers, viewed together, created a unique pattern into the distance. I wondered why I hadn't noticed the flowers earlier. They now seemed to almost glow. I broadened my focus to include everything in that direction. The small rocks and brown patches of gravel seemed extraordinarily colorful and distinct. Hues of amber and violet and even dark red ran through the entire scene.

I glanced back to the right to the trees and bushes. Although beautiful, they now paled in comparison to the other route. But how could that be, I thought. Initially, the road to the right seemed more attractive. Glancing back to the left, my intuition strengthened. The richness of shape and color amazed me.

I was convinced. I started the truck and headed to the left, sure of the correctness of my decision. The road was bumpy with rocks and ruts. As I bounced along, my body felt lighter. My weight was centered on my buttocks, and my back and neck were straight. My arms were holding the steering wheel but were not resting on it

For two hours I drove without incident, nibbling from the food basket Father Carl had packed and again seeing no one. The road meandered up and down one small foothill after another. At the top of one hill, I observed two older cars parked to my right. They were pulled far off to the side of the road in a stand of small trees. I could see no occupants and assumed the vehicles were abandoned. Ahead the road turned sharply to the left and circled downward into a wide valley. From the peak I could see for several miles.

I stopped the truck abruptly. Halfway across the valley

three or four military vehicles sat along both sides of the road. A small group of soldiers stood among the trucks. A chill ran through me. That was a roadblock. I backed off the crest and pulled my vehicle behind two large rocks, then got out and walked back to the overlook to again observe the activity in the valley. One vehicle was driving away in the opposite direction.

Suddenly I heard something behind me. I turned around quickly. It was Phil, the ecologist I had met at Viciente.

He was equally shocked. 'What are you doing here?' he asked, as he rushed up to me.

'I'm trying to get to Iquitos,' I said.

His face was filled with anxiety. 'So are we, but the government's getting crazy over this Manuscript. We're trying to decide whether to risk passing through that roadblock. There are four of us.' He nodded to his left. I could see several men through the trees.

'Why are you going to Iquitos?' he asked.

'I'm trying to find Wil. We got separated in Cula. But I heard he might be headed to Iquitos, looking for the rest of the Manuscript.'

He looked horrified. 'He shouldn't be doing that! The military has prohibited anyone having copies. Didn't you hear what occurred at Viciente?'

'Yeah, some, but what did you hear?'

'I wasn't there but I understand the authorities rushed in and arrested everyone who had copies. All the guests were detained for questioning. Dale and the other scientists were taken away. No one knows what happened to them.'

'Do you know why the government is so disturbed about this Manuscript?' I asked.

'No, but when I heard how unsafe it was getting, I decided to return to Iquitos for my research data and then to leave the country myself.'

I told him the details of what had happened to Wil and myself after leaving Viciente, especially the shooting on the ridge top.

'Damn,' he said. 'And you're still fooling around with this thing?'

His statement jarred my confidence, but I said, 'Look, if we do nothing, the government is going to suppress the Manuscript completely. The world will be denied its knowledge, and I think the insights are important!'

'Important enough to die for?' he asked.

The sound of vehicles attracted our attention. The trucks were driving across the valley toward us.

'Oh shit!' he said. 'Here they come.'

Before we could move, we heard the sound of vehicles approaching from the other direction as well.

'They've surrounded us!' Phil shouted. He looked panicked.

I ran to the truck and dumped the basket of food into a small pack. I took the folders containing the Manuscript and placed them in the pack as well, then thought better of it and pushed them under the seat instead.

The sounds were growing louder so I ran across the road to my right in the direction Phil had headed. Down the slope I could see him and the other men huddled behind a group of rocks. I hid with them. My hope was that the military trucks would pass and keep going. My truck was out of sight. Hopefully they would think, as I had, that the other cars were abandoned.

The trucks approaching from the south arrived

first and to our horror stopped even with the vehicles.

'Don't move. Police!' a voice shouted. We froze as several soldiers walked up from behind us. All were heavily armed and very cautious. The soldiers searched us thoroughly and took everything, then forced us to walk back to the road. There, dozens of soldiers were searching the vehicles. Phil and his companions were taken and placed in one of the military trucks, which quickly drove away. As he rode past me, I caught sight of him. He looked pale and ghostly.

I was led on foot in the opposite direction and asked to sit near the crest of the hill. Several soldiers stood near me, each carrying an automatic weapon on his shoulder. Finally an officer walked over and tossed the folders containing my copies of the insights on the ground at my feet. On top of them he threw the keys to Father Carl's truck.

'Are these copies yours?' he asked.

I looked at him without answering.

'These keys were found on you,' he said. 'Inside the vehicle we found these copies. I ask you again, are they yours?'

'I don't think I'll answer until I see a lawyer,' I stammered. The remark brought a sarcastic smile to the officer's face. He said something to the other soldiers and walked away. The soldiers directed me to one of the jeeps and into the front seat by the driver. Two other soldiers sat in the back seat, their weapons ready. Behind us, more soldiers climbed aboard a second truck. After a short wait, both vehicles headed north into the valley.

Anxious thoughts filled my mind. Where were they taking me? Why had I put myself into this position? So much for the preparation the priests had given me; I hadn't lasted a day. Back at the crossroads, I had been so certain I had chosen the correct road. This route was the one most attractive; I was sure of it. Where did I make my mistake?

I took a deep breath and attempted to relax, wondering what would happen now. I would plead ignorance, I thought, and present myself as a misguided tourist meaning no harm. I just got mixed up with the wrong people, I would say. Let me go home.

My hands were resting in my lap; they were shaking slightly. One of the soldiers sitting behind me offered a canteen of water and I took it, though I could not drink. The soldier was young and when I handed the canteen back to him, he smiled without a trace of malice on his face. The image of Phil's panicked look flashed across my mind. What would they do with him?

The thought occurred to me that meeting Phil on that hilltop had been a coincidence. What was its meaning? What would we have talked about had we not been interrupted? As it was, all I did was stress the Manuscript's importance, and all he did was warn me about the danger here and counsel me to get out before being captured. Unfortunately, his advice had come too late.

For several hours we rode without anyone speaking. The terrain outside grew progressively more flat. The air warmed. At one point, the young soldier handed me an open can of C rations, something like beef hash, but again I couldn't force anything down. After sunset the light faded quickly.

I rode along without thought, staring straight ahead

with the truck's headlights, then I slipped into a restless sleep during which I dreamed of being in flight. I was running desperately from an unknown foe amid hundreds of huge bonfires, certain that somewhere was a secret key that would open the way to knowledge and safety. In the middle of one of the giant fires I saw the key. I darted in to retrieve it!

I jerked awake, sweating profusely. The soldiers glanced at me nervously. I shook my head and leaned against the truck's door. For a long time, I looked out the side window at the dark shapes of the landscape, fighting the urge to panic. I was alone and under guard, heading into blackness, and no one cared about my nightmares.

About midnight we pulled up to a large, dimly lit building constructed of cut stone and two stories high. We walked along a walkway past the front entrance and entered a side door. Steps led down to a narrow hall. The inner walls were also of stone and the ceiling was constructed of large timbers and rough cut planks. Bare bulbs hanging from the ceiling lit our way. We walked through another door and then into an area of cells. One of the soldiers who had disappeared caught up with us and opened one of the cell doors and motioned for me to enter.

Inside were three cots, a wooden table and a vase of flowers. To my surprise, the cell was very clean. As I walked in, a young Peruvian, no more than eighteen or nineteen years old, looked at me meekly from behind the door. The soldier locked the door behind me and walked away. I sat down on one of the cots as the young man reached over and turned up an oil lamp. When the light hit his face I noticed that he was an Indian.

'Do you speak English?' I asked.

'Yes, some,' he said.

'Where are we?'

'Near Pullcupa.'

'Is this a prison?'

'No, everyone is here for questioning about the Manuscript.'

'How long have you been here?' I asked.

He looked up at me with shy, brown eyes. 'Two months.'

'What have they done to you?'

'They try to make me disbelieve the Manuscript and tell about others who have copies.'

'How?'

'By talking to me.'

'Just talking, no threats?'

'Just talking,' he repeated.

'Have they said when they will let you go?'

'No.'

I paused for a moment and he looked at me questioningly. 'Were you caught with copies of the Manuscript?' he asked.

'Yes. Were you?'

'Yes. I live near here, in an orphanage. My headmaster was teaching from the Manuscript. He allowed me to teach the children. He was able to escape but I was captured.'

'How many insights have you seen?' I asked.

'All that have been found,' he said. 'You?'

'Eh, I've seen all but the Seventh and Eighth Insights. I had the Seventh but I didn't get a chance to read it before the soldiers showed up.'

The young man yawned and asked, 'Can we sleep now?'

'Yeah,' I said absently. 'Sure.'

I laid on my cot and shut my eyes, my mind racing. What should I do now? How had I let myself be caught? Could I escape? I concocted several strategies and scenarios before I finally drifted off to sleep.

Again I dreamed vividly. I was searching for the same key but this time I was lost in a deep forest. For a long time I had been walking aimlessly, wishing for some sort of guidance. After a while, a huge thunderstorm came and flooded the landscape. During the deluge, I was washed down a deep ravine and into the river, which was flowing in the wrong direction and threatening to drown me. With all my might I fought against the current, struggling for what seemed like days. Finally, I was able to pull myself from the torrent by clinging to the rocky shoreline. I climbed up the rocks and along the sheer cliffs that bordered the river, ascending higher and higher and into ever more treacherous areas. Although I had summoned all my willpower and expertise to negotiate the cliffs, at one point I found myself clinging perilously to the rock face, unable to proceed any further. I looked down at the terrain below me. In shock, I realized that the river I had been fighting flowed out of the forest and gently up to a beautiful beach and meadow. In the meadow, surrounded by flowers, was the key. Then I slipped and fell screaming down and down until I hit the river and sank.

I sat up quickly in my cot, gasping for air. The young Indian, apparently already awake, walked over to me.

'What is wrong?' he asked.

I caught my breath and looked around, realizing where I was. I also noticed that the room had a window and that it was already light outside.

'Just a bad dream,' I said.

He smiled at me as though he was pleased at what I said. 'Bad dreams have the most important messages,' he commented.

'Messages?' I asked, getting up and putting on my shirt.

He looked embarrassed at having to explain. 'The Seventh Insight talks of dreams,' he said.

'What does it say about dreams?'

'It tells how to, eh . . .'

'Interpret dreams?'

'Yes.'

'What does it say about that?'

'It says to compare the story of the dream to the story of your life.'

I thought for a moment, unsure of what that instruction meant. 'What do you mean, compare stories?'

The young Indian could barely look me in the eye. 'Do you want to interpret your dream?'

I nodded and told him what I had experienced.

He listened intently, then said, 'Compare parts of the story with your life.'

I looked at him. 'Where do I start?'

'At the beginning. What are you doing at the beginning of the dream?'

'I was searching for a key in a forest.'

'How did you feel?'

'Lost.'

'Compare this situation to your real situation.'

'Maybe it does relate,' I said 'I'm looking for some answers about this Manuscript and I'm damn sure feeling lost.'

'And what else is happening to you in real life?' he asked.

'I've been caught,' I said. 'In spite of everything I tried to do, I've been locked up. All I can hope for now is to talk someone into letting me go home.'

'You are struggling against being caught?'

'Of course.'

'What happened next in the dream?'

'I fought against the current.'

'Why?' he asked.

I began to pick up on where he was headed. 'Because at the time I thought it would drown me.'

'And if you hadn't fought the water?'

'It would have carried me to the key. What are you saying? That if I don't fight against this situation that I might still get the answers I want?'

He looked embarrassed again. 'I'm not saying anything. The dream is saying.'

I thought for a moment. Was this interpretation correct?

The young Indian looked up at me, then asked, 'If you had to experience the dream again, what would you do different?'

'I wouldn't resist the water, even though it looked as though it might kill me. I would know better.'

'What is threatening you now?'

'I guess the soldiers. Being detained.'

'So what is the message to you?'

'You think the message of the dream is to look at this capture positively?'

221

He didn't answer; he only smiled.

I was sitting on my cot leaning back against the wall. The interpretation excited me. If it was accurate, it would mean that I hadn't made a mistake at the crossroads after all, that this was all part of what should be happening.

'What is your name?' I asked.

'Pablo,' he said.

I smiled and introduced myself, then briefly told him the story of why I was in Peru and what had happened. Pablo was sitting on his cot, his elbows resting on his knees. He had short, black hair and was very thin.

'Why are you here?' he asked.

'To find out about this Manuscript,' I replied.

'Why specifically?' he asked again.

'To find out about the Seventh Insight and to find out about some friends, Wil and Marjorie . . . and I guess to find out why the church is so against the Manuscript.'

'There are many priests here to talk to,' he said.

I thought about his statement for a moment then asked, 'What else does the Seventh Insight say about dreams?'

Pablo told me that dreams come to tell us something about our lives that we are missing. Then he said something else but instead of listening, I started to think about Marjorie. I could see her face clearly in my mind and I wondered where she might be, then I saw her running up to me smiling.

Suddenly I became aware that Pablo was no longer talking. I looked over at him. 'Sorry, my mind was wandering,' I said. 'What were you saying?'

'That is all right,' he replied. 'What were you thinking about?'

'Just a friend of mine. It was nothing.'

He looked as though he wanted to press the question, but someone was approaching the cell door. Through the bars we could see a soldier sliding back the bolt lock.

'Time for breakfast,' Pablo said.

The soldier opened the door and motioned with his head for us to walk into the hall. Pablo led the way down the stone corridor. We proceeded to a stairway and up one flight of stairs to a small dining area. Four or five soldiers stood at the corner of the room while several civilians, two men and a woman, waited in line to be served.

I stopped, not believing my eyes. The woman was Marjorie. Simultaneously, she saw me and covered her mouth with her hand, her eyes opening wide with surprise. I glanced at the soldier behind me. He was walking toward the other military men in the corner, smiling nonchalantly and saying something in Spanish. I followed Pablo as he led us across the room and to the end of the line.

Marjorie was being served. The two other men took their trays to a table, talking. Several times Marjorie gazed over and met my eyes, struggling not to say anything. After the second glance, Pablo guessed that we knew each other and looked at me questioningly. Marjorie carried her food to a table, and after being served, we walked over and sat with her. The soldiers were still talking among themselves, seemingly oblivious to our movements.

'God, I'm glad to see you,' she said. 'How did you get here?'

'I hid for a while with some priests,' I replied. 'Then I left to find Wil and was captured yesterday. How long have you been here?'

'Since they found me on the ridge,' she said.

I noticed Pablo was looking at us intensely and I introduced him to Marjorie.

'I guessed that this must be Marjorie,' he said.

They talked briefly, then I asked Marjorie, 'What else has happened?'

'Not much,' she said. 'I don't even know why I'm being detained. Every day I've been taken to one of the priests or to one of the officers for questioning. They want to know who my contacts were at Viciente, and if I know where any other copies are. Over and over again!'

Marjorie smiled and looked vulnerable and when she did, I felt another strong attraction to her. She looked at me sharply, out of the corner of her eyes. We both laughed quietly. A period of silence followed as we ate our food, and then the door opened and in walked a priest, dressed formally. He was accompanied by a man appearing to be a high ranking military officer.

'That's the head priest,' Pablo said.

The officer said something to the soldiers, who had snapped to attention, and then he and the priest walked across the room toward the kitchen. The priest looked directly at me, our eyes meeting for a long second. I looked away and took a bite of food, not wanting to attract attention. Both men continued through the kitchen and out a door there.

'Was that one of the priests you've talked to?' I asked Marjorie.

'No,' Marjorie said. 'I've never seen him.'

'I know that priest,' Pablo said. 'He arrived yesterday. His name is Cardinal Sebastian.'

I sat up straight. 'That was Sebastian?'

'It sounds like you've heard of him,' Marjorie said.

'I have,' I replied. 'He's the main person behind the church's opposition to the Manuscript. I thought he was at Father Sanchez's mission.'

'Who is Father Sanchez?' Marjorie asked.

I was about to tell her when the soldier who had escorted us walked over to the table and motioned for Pablo and me to follow.

'Time for exercise,' Pablo said.

Marjorie and I looked at each other. Her eyes revealed an inner anxiety.

'Don't worry,' I said, 'I'll talk to you at the next meal. Everything will be fine.'

As I walked away, I wondered if my optimism was realistic. These people could make any of us disappear without a trace at any time. The soldier guided us into a short hall and through a door that led to an outside stairway. We walked down to a side yard which was surrounded by a tall rock wall. The soldier stood by the entrance. Pablo nodded for me to walk with him around the borders of the yard. As we walked, Pablo bent down several times to pick some of the flowers growing in beds by the wall.

'What else does the Seventh Insight say?' I asked.

He bent down and picked another flower. 'It says that not only dreams guide us. Also thoughts or daydreams guide us.'

'Yes, Father Carl said that. Tell me how daydreams guide us.'

'They show us a scene, a happening, and this is an indication that this event might happen. If we pay attention then we can be ready for this turn in our lives.'

225

I looked at him. 'You know, Pablo, an image came to me that I would run into Marjorie. Then I did.'

He smiled.

A chill went up my spine. I must indeed be in the right place. I had intuited something that had come true. I had thought several times of finding Marjorie again and now it had happened. The coincidences were taking place. I felt lighter.

'I don't have thoughts like that happen very often,' I said.

Pablo looked away, then said, 'The Seventh Insight says that we all have many more such thoughts than we realize. To recognize them we must take an observer position. When a thought comes, we must ask why? Why did this particular thought come now? How does it relate to my life questions? Taking this observer position helps us release our need to control everything. It places us in the flow of evolution.'

'But what about negative thoughts?' I asked. 'Those fear images of something bad happening, such as someone we love getting hurt, or of not achieving something we very much want?'

'Very simple,' Pablo said. 'The Seventh Insight says that fear images should be halted as soon as they come. Then another image, one with a good outcome, should be willed through the mind. Soon, negative images will almost never happen. Your intuitions will be about positive things. When negative images come after that, the Manuscript says they should be taken very seriously, and not followed. For instance, if the idea comes to you that you're going to have a wreck in a truck and someone comes along and

226

offers you a ride in a truck, then do not accept it.'

We had come full circle in our walk around the court-yard and were approaching the guard. Neither of us talked as we passed him. Pablo picked a flower and I took a deep breath. The air was warm and humid, and the plant life outside the wall was dense and tropical. I had noticed several mosquitoes.

'Come!' the soldier suddenly called out.

He prodded us inside and down to our cell. Pablo entered ahead of me, but the soldier put his arm up blocking my way.

'Not you,' he said, then nodded for me to walk down the hallway and up the other steps and outside through the same door we had entered the night before. In the parking lot, Father Sebastian was entering the back seat of a large car. A driver shut the door behind him. For an instant Sebastian looked at me again, then he turned and said something to the driver. The car sped away.

The soldier nudged me toward the front of the build-ing. We walked inside and into an office. I was directed to sit in a wooden chair across from a white metal desk. Within minutes a small, sandy-haired priest of about thirty entered and sat at the desk without acknowledging my presence. He looked through a file for a full minute, then looked up at me. His round, gold-rimmed glasses produced an intellectual appearance.

'You've been arrested with illegal state documents,' he said matter-of-factly. 'I'm here to help determine whether prosecution is in order. I would appreciate your cooperation.'

I nodded.

'Where did you get the translations?'

'I don't understand,' I said. 'Why would copies of an old manuscript be illegal?'

'The government of Peru has its reasons,' he said. 'Please answer the question.'

'Why is the church involved?' I asked.

'Because this Manuscript contradicts the traditions of our religion,' he said. 'It misrepresents the truth of our spiritual nature. Where . . .'

'Look,' I said, interrupting. 'I'm just trying to understand this. I'm just a tourist who got interested in this Manuscript. I'm a threat to no one. I only want to know why it is so alarming.'

He looked puzzled, as if trying to decide the best strategy for dealing with me. I was consciously pressing for details.

'The church feels the Manuscript is confusing to our people,' he said carefully. 'It gives the impression that people can decide on their own how to live, without regard to the scriptures.'

'Which scriptures?'

'The commandment to honor thy father and mother, for one.'

'What do you mean?'

'The Manuscript blames problems on parents, undermining the family.'

'I thought it spoke of ending old resentments,' I said. 'And finding a positive view of our early life.'

'No,' he said. 'It is misleading. There should never have been a negative feeling to begin with.'

'Can't parents be wrong?'

'Parents do the best they can. Children must forgive them.'

228

'But isn't that what the Manuscript is clarifying? Doesn't forgiveness take place when we see the positive about our childhoods?'

His voice rose with anger. 'But from what authority does this Manuscript speak? How can it be trusted?'

He walked around the desk and stared down at me, still angry. 'You don't know what you're talking about,' he said. 'Are you a religious scholar? I think not. You're direct evidence of the kind of confusion this Manuscript evokes. Don't you understand that there is order in the world only because of law and authority? How can you question the authorities in this matter?'

I said nothing, which seemed to infuriate him even more. 'Let me tell you something,' he said, 'the crime you have committed is punishable by years in prison. Have you ever been in a Peruvian prison? Does your Yankee curiosity yearn to find out what our prisons are like? I can arrange that! Do you understand? I can arrange that!'

He put his hand over his eyes and paused, taking a deep breath, obviously trying to calm down. 'I am here to find out who has copies, where they are coming from. I will ask you one more time. Where did you get your translations?'

His outburst had filled me with anxiety. I was making my situation worse with all my questions. What might he do if I failed to cooperate? Still, how could I implicate Father Sanchez and Father Carl?

'I need some time to think before I answer you,' I said.

Momentarily he looked as if he might fly into another rage. Then he relaxed and looked very tired.

'I will give you until tomorrow morning,' he said, motioning for the soldier standing in the doorway to take me away. I followed the soldier back down the hall and directly to the cell.

Without saying anything I walked over and lay down on my cot, feeling exhausted myself. Pablo was looking out the barred window.

'Did you talk to Father Sebastian?' he asked.

'No, it was another priest. He wanted to know who gave me the copies I had.'

'What did you say?'

'Nothing. I asked for time to think and he gave me until tomorrow.'

'Did he say anything about the Manuscript?' Pablo asked.

I looked into Pablo's eyes and this time he did not lower his head. 'He talked a little about how the Manuscript undermines traditional authority,' I said. 'Then he started raving and threatening me.'

Pablo looked genuinely surprised. 'Did he have brown hair and round glasses?'

'Yes.'

'His name is Father Costous,' Pablo said. 'What else did you say?'

'I disagreed with him on whether the Manuscript undermines tradition,' I replied. 'He threatened me with prison. Do you think he meant that?'

'I don't know,' Pablo said. He walked over and sat on his cot across from me. I could tell he had something else on his mind but I was so tired and scared that I closed my eyes. When I awoke Pablo was shaking me.

'Time for lunch,' he said.

We followed a guard upstairs and were served a plate of gristly beef and potatoes. The two men who we saw earlier came in after us. Marjorie wasn't with them.

'Where is Marjorie?' I asked them, trying to whisper. The two men looked horrified that I would speak to them and the soldiers stared at me intensely.

'I don't think they speak English,' Pablo said.

'I wonder where she is,' I said.

Pablo said something in response but again I wasn't listening. I suddenly felt like running away and was picturing myself fleeing down a street of some kind, then ducking through a doorway, to freedom.

'What are you thinking about?' Pablo asked.

'I was fantasizing about an escape,' I said. 'What were you saying?'

'Wait,' Pablo said. 'Don't dismiss your thought. It may be important. What kind of escape?'

'I was running down an alley, or a street, then through a doorway. I got the impression I was successfully escaping.'

'What do you think of this image?' Pablo asked.

'I don't know,' I said. 'It didn't seem to be logically connected to what we were talking about.'

'Do you remember what we were talking about?'

'Yes. I was asking about Marjorie.'

'You don't think there is a connection between Marjorie and your thought?'

'Not an obvious link I can think of.'

'What about a hidden link?'

'I can't see a connection. How could escaping be related to Marjorie? Do you think she escaped?'

He looked thoughtful. 'Your thought was of you escaping.'

'Oh yeah, that's right,' I said. 'Maybe I'm going to

escape without her.' I looked at him. 'Maybe I'm going to escape *with* her.

'That would be my guess,' he said.

'But where is she?'

'I don't know!'

We finished eating without talking. I was hungry but the food seemed too heavy. For some reason, I felt tired and sluggish. My hunger left me quickly.

I noticed Pablo wasn't eating either.

'I think we should go back to the cell,' Pablo said.

I nodded, and he motioned for the soldier to take us back. When we arrived, I stretched out on my cot and Pablo sat looking at me.

'Your energy seems down,' he said.

'It is,' I replied. 'I'm not sure what is wrong.'

'Are you trying to take in energy?' he asked.

'I guess I haven't,' I replied. 'And that food doesn't help.'

'But you don't need much food if you are taking everything in.' He swept his arm in front of him to emphasize everything.

'I know. It's hard for me to get the love flowing in a situation like this.'

He looked at me quizzically. 'But not to do so is to harm yourself.'

'What do you mean?'

'Your body is vibrating at a certain level. If you let your energy get too low your body suffers. That is the relationship between stress and disease. Love is the way we keep our vibration up. It keeps us healthy. It is that important.'

'Give me a few minutes,' I said.

I practiced the method Father Sanchez had taught me.

Immediately I felt better. The objects around me stood out with presence. I closed my eyes and concentrated on the feeling.

'That's good,' he said.

I opened my eyes and saw him smiling broadly at me. His face and body were still boyish and immature, but his eyes now seemed full of wisdom.

'I can see the energy coming into you,' he said.

I could detect a slight field of green around Pablo's body. The new flowers he had placed in the vase on the table seemed radiant.

'To grasp the Seventh Insight and truly enter the movement of evolution,' he said, 'one must pull all the insights into one way of being.'

I didn't say anything.

'Can you sum up how the world has changed for you as a result of the insights?'

I thought for a moment. 'I guess I've woken up and seen the world as a mysterious place that provides everything we need, if we get clear and get on the path.'

'Then what happens?' he asked.

'Then, we're ready to begin the evolutionary flow.'

'And how do we engage this process?'

I thought for a moment. 'By keeping our current life questions firmly in mind,' I said. 'And then watching for direction, either in a dream or in an intuitive thought or in the way the environment illuminates and jumps out at us.'

I paused again, trying to pull the whole insight together, then added, 'We build our energy and center ourselves in our situations, in the questions we have, then we receive some form of intuitive guidance, an idea

233

of where to go or what to do, and then coincidences occur to allow us to move in that direction.'

'Yes! Yes!' Pablo said. 'That is the way. And each time that these coincidences lead us into something new, we grow, we become fuller persons, existing at a higher vibration.'

He was leaning toward me, and I noticed the incredible energy around him. He was beaming, no longer appearing shy or even young. He seemed full of power.

'Pablo, what has happened to you?' I asked. 'Compared to when I first met you, you seem more confident and knowledgeable and full somehow.'

He laughed. 'When you first came, I had allowed my energy to dissipate. At first, I thought that you might be able to help me with my energy flow, but I realized that you haven't learned to do this yet. That ability is learned in the Eighth Insight.'

I was puzzled. 'What was it that I didn't do?'

'You must learn that all the answers that mysteriously come to us really come from other people. Think about all that you have learned since you have been in Peru. Haven't all the answers come to you through the actions of other people you mysteriously met?'

I thought about it. He was right. I had met just the right people at just the right time: Charlene, Dobson, Wil, Dale, Marjorie, Phil, Reneau, Father Sanchez and Father Carl, now Pablo.

'Even the Manuscript was written by a person,' Pablo added. 'But not all the people you meet will have the energy or the clarity to reveal the message they have for you. You must help them by sending them energy.' He paused. 'You told me of learning to project your energy toward a plant by focusing on its beauty, remember?'

'Yes.'

'Well, you do exactly the same thing toward a person. When the energy goes into them, it helps them see their truth. Then they can give this truth to you.

'Father Costous is an example,' he continued. 'He had an important message for you which you did not help him reveal. You tried to demand answers from him and that created a competition between you and him for energy. When he felt that, his childhood drama, his intimidator, took over the conversation.'

'What was I supposed to have said?' I asked.

Pablo didn't answer. Again we heard someone at the cell door.

Father Costous entered.

He nodded at Pablo, a slight smile on his face. Pablo smiled broadly, as if he actually liked the priest. Father Costous shifted his gaze to me, his face becoming stern. Anxiety gripped my stomach.

'Cardinal Sebastian has asked to see you,' he said. 'You will be transported to Iquitos this afternoon. I would advise you to answer all his questions.'

'Why does he want me?' I asked.

'Because the truck you were caught with belongs to one of our priests. We are assuming you received your copies of the Manuscript from him. For one of our own priests to disregard the law is very serious.' He looked at me with determination.

I glanced at Pablo, who nodded for me to continue.

'You think that the Manuscript is undermining your religion?' I asked Costous gently.

He looked at me with condescension. 'Not just our

religion; everyone's religion. Do you think there is no plan for this world? God is in control. He assigns our destiny. Our job is to obey the laws set forth by God. Evolution is a myth. God creates the future the way he wants it. To say humans can make themselves evolve takes the will of God out of the picture. It allows people to be selfish and separate. They think that their evolution is the important thing, not God's plan. They will treat each other even worse than they do now.'

I couldn't think of another question. The priest looked at me for a moment, then said, almost kindly, 'I hope you will cooperate with Cardinal Sebastian.'

He turned and looked at Pablo, obviously proud of the way he had handled my questions. Pablo only smiled at him and nodded again. The priest walked out and a soldier locked the door behind him. Pablo leaned forward on his cot and beamed at me, his demeanor still completely transformed, confidence on his face.

I looked at him for a moment, then smiled.

'What do you think happened just now?' he asked.

I struggled for humor. 'I found out I'm in more trouble than I thought?'

He laughed. 'What else occurred?'

'I'm not sure what you're getting at.'

'What were your questions when you arrived here?'

'I wanted to find Marjorie and Wil?'

'Well, you found one of them. What was your other question?'

'I had a sense that these priests were against the Manuscript not out of malice but because they misunderstood. I wanted to know what they were thinking. For some reason I had the idea they could be talked out of their opposition.' After saying this I suddenly understood what Pablo was leading to. I had met Costous, here, now, so that I could find out what bothered him about the Manuscript.

'And what was the message you received?' he asked.

'The message?'

'Yes, the message.'

I looked at him. 'It's the idea of participating in evolution that bothers them, isn't it?'

'Yes,' he said.

'That would figure,' I added. 'The idea of physical evolution is bad enough. But to extend the idea to everyday life, to the individual decisions we make, to history itself. That's unacceptable. They think humans will run amuck with this evolution, that relations between people will degenerate. No wonder they want to see the Manuscript suppressed.'

'Could you convince them otherwise?' Pablo asked.

'No . . . I mean, I don't know enough myself.'

'What would it take for someone to be able to convince them?'

'One would have to know the truth. One would have to know how humans would be treating each other if everyone was following the insights and evolving.'

Pablo appeared pleased.

'What?' I asked, smiling along with him.

'How humans will act toward each other is in the very next insight, the Eighth. Your question of why the priests were against the Manuscript has been answered, and the answer, in turn, has evolved into another question.'

'Yes,' I said, deep in thought. 'I've got to find the Eighth. I've got to get out of here.'

'Don't go too fast,' Pablo cautioned. 'You must make sure you fully grasp the Seventh before you go further.'

'Do you think I grasp it?' I asked. 'Am I staying in the flow of evolution?'

'You will,' he said, 'if you remember to keep your questions always in mind. Even people who are still unaware can stumble into answers and see coincidences in retrospect. The Seventh Insight occurs when we can see these answers as they arrive. It heightens everyday experience.

'We must assume every event has significance and contains a message that somehow pertains to our questions. This especially applies to what we used to call bad things. The Seventh Insight says that the challenge is to find the silver lining in every event, no matter how negative. You first thought that being captured had ruined everything. But now you can see that you were supposed to be here. This is where your answers were.'

He was right, but if I was receiving answers here and evolving to a higher level, then Pablo must certainly be doing the same thing.

Suddenly we heard someone coming down the hall. Pablo looked directly at me, a serious look on his face.

'Listen,' he said. 'Remember what I told you. The Eighth Insight is next for you. It is about an Interpersonal Ethic, a way of treating other people so more messages are shared. But remember not to go too fast. Stay centered in your situation. What are your questions?'

'I want to find out where Wil is,' I said. ' And I want to find the Eighth Insight. And I want to find Marjorie.'

'And what was your guiding intuition concerning Marjorie?'

I thought for a moment 'That I would escape . . . that we would escape.'

We could hear someone right outside the door.

'Did I bring you a message?' I asked Pablo hurriedly.

'Of course,' he said. 'When you arrived I didn't know why I was here. I knew it had something to do with communicating the Seventh Insight, but I doubted my ability. I didn't think that I knew enough. Because of you,' he continued, 'I now know that I can. That was one of the messages that you brought to me.'

'Was there another?'

'Yes, your intuition that the priests can be convinced to accept the Manuscript is a message for me also. It makes me think I'm here to convince Father Costous.'

As he finished speaking, a soldier opened the door and motioned for me.

I looked at Pablo.

'I want to tell you one of the concepts the next insight talks about,' he said.

The soldier glared at him and took my arm, ushering me out the door and closing it. As I was led away, Pablo stared through the bars.

'The Eighth Insight warns against something,' he called out. 'It warns against your growth being stopped . . . It happens when you become addicted to another person.'

The Interpersonal Ethic

I followed the soldier up the steps and out into the bright sunshine. Pablo's warning was echoing in my head. Addiction to another person? What did he mean by that? What kind of addiction?

The soldier led me down the path toward the parking area where two other soldiers stood beside a military jeep. They watched us intensely as we walked their way. When I was close enough to see inside the jeep, I noticed that a passenger was already sitting in the back. Marjorie! She looked pale and anxious. Before I could catch her eye, the soldier behind me grabbed my arm and directed me into the seat beside her. Two other soldiers climbed into the front seats. The one sitting on the driver's side glanced back at us briefly, then he started the vehicle and headed north.

'Do you speak English?' I asked the soldiers.

The soldier in the passenger seat, a beefy man, looked at me blankly and said something in Spanish that I couldn't understand, then turned curtly away.

I turned my attention to Marjorie. 'Are you all right?' I asked, in a whisper.

'I . . . uh . . .' Her voice faded, and I noticed tears were flowing down her face.

'It's going to be okay,' I said, putting my arm around her. She looked up at me, forcing a smile, then rested her head on my shoulder. A ripple of passion filled my body.

For an hour we bounced along the unpaved road. Outside, the landscape grew continuously more lush and jungle-like. Then, around one bend, the dense vegetation opened up into what appeared to be a small town. Wood frame buildings lined both sides of the road.

A hundred yards ahead, a large truck blocked the way. Several soldiers motioned for us to stop. Beyond them were other vehicles, some with flashing yellow lights. I became more alert. As we pulled to a stop, one of the soldiers outside walked up and said something I couldn't understand. The only word I recognized was 'gasoline.' Our escorts left the jeep and stood outside talking with the other soldiers. They glanced at us occasionally, weapons at their side.

I noticed a small street which angled to the left. As I looked at the shops and doorways, something changed in my perception. The shapes and colors of the buildings suddenly stood out and became more distinct.

I whispered Marjorie's name and felt her look up, but before she could say anything, an enormous explosion rocked the jeep. A blast of fire and light shot up from the area in front of us, and the soldiers were blown to the ground. Immediately, our vision was obscured by smoke and falling ash.

'Come on!' I yelled, pulling Marjorie from the vehicle.

Amid the confusion we ran down the street in the direction I had been looking. Behind us I could hear distant shouts and moans. Still engulfed with smoke, we ran perhaps fifty yards. Suddenly, I noticed a doorway to the left.

'In here!' I shouted. The door was open and we both ran inside. I fell against the door, closing it securely. When I turned around, I saw a middle-aged woman staring at us. We had dashed into someone's home.

As I looked at her, attempting a smile, I noticed that the woman's expression was not one of horror, nor anger, at having had two strangers rush into her house after an explosion. Instead, what she displayed was an amused half smile that looked more like resignation, as though she half expected us and now had to *do* something. On a chair nearby was a small child about four years old.

'Hurry!' she said in English. 'They will be looking for you!' She ushered us to the back of the sparsely furnished living room, through a hall, and down some wooden steps to a long cellar. The child walked at her side. We moved quickly through the cellar and up some other steps to an outside door leading to an alley.

The woman unlocked a small compact car which was parked there and hurried us inside. She directed us to lie down in the back seat, threw a blanket over us, and pulled away in what seemed to be a northerly direction. Through it all, I remained speechless, carried along by the woman's initiative. A rush of energy filled my body as I fully realized what had happened. My intuition of escape had occurred.

Marjorie lay beside me, her eyes tightly closed. 'Are you all right?' I whispered.

She looked up at me with tearful eyes and nodded.

After about fifteen minutes, the woman said, 'I think you can sit up now.'

I pushed away the blanket and looked around. We seemed to be on the same road as before the explosion, only farther north.

'Who are you?' I asked.

She turned and looked at me with her half smile. She was a shapely woman of about forty with shoulder length dark hair.

'I'm Karla Deez,' she said. 'This is my daughter, Mareta.'

The child was smiling and looking over the passenger seat at us with large, inquisitive eyes. Her hair was jet black and also long.

I told them who we were, then asked, 'How did you know to help us?'

Karla's smile grew wider. 'You are running from the soldiers because of the Manuscript, aren't you?'

'Yes, but how did you know?'

'I know the Manuscript, too.'

'Where are you taking us?' I asked.

'I don't know that,' she said. 'You will have to help me.'

I glanced at Marjorie. She was watching me closely as I spoke. 'Right now I don't know where to go,' I said. 'Before I was captured, I was trying to get to Iquitos.'

'Why did you want to go there?' she asked.

'I'm trying to find a friend. He's looking for the Ninth Insight.'

'That is a dangerous thing.'

'I know.'

'We will take you there, won't we, Mareta?'

The little girl giggled and said with a sophistication beyond her years, 'Of course.'

'What kind of explosion was that back there?' I asked.

'I think it was a gas truck,' she answered. 'Earlier, an accident had occurred, a leak.'

I was still amazed at how quickly Karla had decided to help us so I decided to press the question.'How did you know we were running from the soldiers?'

She took a deep breath. 'Yesterday, many military trucks were passing through the village going north. This is unusual and it made me think of the time two months ago when my friends were taken away. My friends and I studied the Manuscript together. We were the only ones in this village who had all eight insights. Then the soldiers came and took my friends. I have not heard from them.

'As I watched the trucks yesterday,' she continued, 'I knew the soldiers were continuing to hunt copies of the Manuscript and that others, like my friends, would need help. I envisioned myself helping those people if I could. Of course, I suspected that it was meaningful that I was having that particular thought at that particular time. So, when you came into my house, I was not surprised.'

She paused, then asked, 'Have you ever experienced this?'

'Yes,' I said.

Karla slowed the car. Ahead was a crossroads.

'I think we should turn to the right here,' she said. 'It will take longer but it will be safer.'

As Karla turned the car to the right, Mareta slid to the left and had to hold onto the seat to keep from falling over. She giggled. Marjorie was staring appreciatively at the little girl

'How old is Mareta?' Marjorie asked Karla.

Karla looked disturbed, then said gently, 'Please don't talk about her as if she wasn't here. If she was an adult you would have addressed the question to her.'

'Oh, I'm sorry,' Marjorie said.

'I'm five,' Mareta said proudly.

'Have you studied the Eighth Insight?' Karla asked.

'No,' Marjorie said, 'I have only seen the Third Insight.'

'I'm at the Eighth,' I said. 'Do you have any copies?'

'No,' Karla said. 'All the copies were taken away by the soldiers.'

'Does the Eighth talk about how to relate to children?'

'Yes, it is about how humans will eventually learn to relate to each other, and talks of many things, such as how to project energy to others and how to avoid addictions to people.'

There was that warning again. I was about to ask Karla what it meant when Marjorie spoke.

'Tell us about the Eighth Insight,' she said.

'The Eighth Insight,' Karla explained, 'is about using energy in a new way when relating to people in general, but it begins at the beginning, with children.'

'How should we view children?' I asked.

'We should view them as they really are, as end points in evolution that lead us forward. But in order to learn to evolve they need our energy on a constant basis, unconditionally. The worst thing that can be done to children is to drain their energy while correcting them. This is what creates control dramas in them, as you already know. But these learned manipulations on the child's part can be avoided if the adults give them all the energy they need no matter what the situation. That is why they should always be included in conversations,

245

especially conversations about them. And you should never take responsibility for more children than you can give attention to.'

'The Manuscript says all this?' I asked.

'Yes,' she said, 'and the point about the number of children is highly stressed.'

I felt confused. 'Why is the number of children one has important?'

She glanced at me for an instant as she drove. 'Because any one adult can only focus on and give attention to one child at a time. If there are too many children for the number of adults, then the adults become overwhelmed and unable to give enough energy. The children begin to compete with each other for the adult's time.'

'Sibling rivalry,' I said.

'Yes, but the Manuscript says that this problem is more important than people think. Adults often glamorize the idea of large families and children growing up together. But children should learn the world from adults, not from other children. In too many cultures, children are running in gangs. The Manuscript says humans will slowly understand that they should not bring children into the world unless there is at least one adult committed to focus full attention, all of the time, on each child.'

'But wait a minute,' I said. 'In many situations both parents must work to survive. This denies them the right to have children.'

'Not necessarily,' she replied. 'The Manuscript says humans will learn to extend their families beyond blood ties. So that someone else is able to provide one on one attention. All the energy does not have to come from the parents alone. In fact, it is better if it does not. But whoever cares for the children must provide this one on one attention.'

'Well,' I said, 'you've done something right. Mareta certainly seems mature.'

Karla frowned and said, 'Don't tell me, tell her.'

'Oh, right.' I looked at the child. 'You act very grown-up, Mareta.'

She looked away shyly for a moment, then said, 'Thank you.' Karla hugged her warmly.

Karla looked at me proudly. 'For the last two years I have been trying to relate to Mareta according to the Manuscript's guidelines, haven't I, Mareta?'

The child smiled and nodded.

'I have tried to give her energy and to always tell her the truth of every situation in language she can understand. When she asked the questions a young child asks, I treated them very seriously, avoiding the temptation of giving her a fanciful answer which is plainly for the entertainment of adults.'

I smiled. 'Do you mean untruths like, "storks bring babies," that sort of thing?'

'Yes, but these cultural expressions aren't so bad. Children figure these out quickly because they stay the same. Worse are the distortions created on the spot by adults just because they want to have a little fun, and because they believe the truth is too complicated for a child to comprehend. But this is not right; the truth can always be expressed at a child's level of understanding. It just takes some thought.'

'What does the Manuscript say about this issue?'

'It says we should always find a way to tell a child the truth.'

Part of me resisted this idea. I was one who enjoyed kidding around with children.

'Don't kids usually understand that adults are just playing?' I said. 'All this seems to make them grow up too fast and take some of the fun out of childhood.'

She looked at me sternly. 'Mareta is full of fun. We chase and tumble and play all the childhood fantasy games. The difference is that when we are fantasizing, she knows it.'

I nodded. She was right, of course.

'Mareta seems confident,' Karla continued, 'because I was there for her. I gave her one on one attention when she needed it. And if I wasn't there, my sister, who lives next door, was there. She always had an adult to answer her questions, and because she has had this sincere attention, she has never felt she had to act out or show off. She has always had enough energy and that makes her assume she will continue to have enough, which makes the transition from receiving energy from adults to getting it from the universe – which we already talk about – much easier for her to grasp.'

I noticed the terrain outside. We were traveling through deep jungle now and though I couldn't see it, I knew the sun was low in the afternoon sky.

'Can we get to Iquitos tonight?' I asked.

'No,' Karla said. 'But we can stay at a house I know.'

'Near here?' I asked.

'Yes, it is the house of a friend. He works for the wild-life service.'

'He works for the government?'

'Some of the Amazon is a protected area. He is the local agent, but influential. His name is Juan Hinton. Do not

248

worry. He believes in the Manuscript and they have never bothered him.'

By the time we arrived, the sky was completely dark. Around us the jungle was alive with night sounds, the air muggy. A large well-lit, wood frame house stood at the end of a clearing in the dense foliage. Nearby were two large buildings and several jeeps. Another vehicle was up on blocks and two men worked around lights underneath.

A thin Peruvian, dressed in expensive clothing, answered Karla's knock and smiled at her until he noticed Marjorie, Mareta and myself waiting on the steps. His face turned nervous and displeased as he talked to her in Spanish. She said something pleadingly in return, but his mannerism and inflection indicated that he did not want us to stay.

Then, through the crack in the door, I noticed a lone female figure standing in the foyer. I moved a little to bring her face into view. It was Julia. As I looked, she turned her head and saw me, then quickly walked forward with a surprised look on her face. She touched the shoulder of the man at the door and said something quietly into his ear. The man nodded, then opened the door with a look of resignation. We all introduced ourselves as Hinton led the way into the den area. Julia looked at me and said, 'We meet again.' She wore khaki pants with pockets on the legs and a bright red T-shirt.

'Yes we do,' I said.

A Peruvian servant stopped Hinton, and after talking for a minute, the two walked into another part of the house. Julia sat in a chair by a coffee table and motioned for the rest of us to sit on a couch across from her.

Marjorie appeared panicked. She looked at me intensely. Karla also seemed to be aware of Marjorie's distress. She walked over and took her by the hand. 'Let's get some hot tea,' she suggested.

As they walked away, Marjorie glanced back at me. I smiled and watched them until they turned the corner into the kitchen, then I turned to face Julia.

'So what do you think it means? she asked.

'What does what mean?' I replied, still distracted.

'That we have run into each other again.'

'Oh . . . I don't know.'

'How did you wind up with Karla and where are you going?'

'She saved us. Marjorie and I had been detained by Peruvian troops. When we escaped, she happened to be there to help us.'

Julia looked intense. 'Tell me what occurred.'

I leaned back and told her the whole story, beginning at the point in which I had taken Father Carl's truck and then all about the capture and our eventual escape.

'And Karla agreed to take you to Iquitos?' Julia asked.

'Yes.'

'Why do you want to go there?'

'That's where Wil told Father Carl he was going. Wil apparently has a lead about the Ninth Insight Also, Sebastian is there for some reason.'

Julia nodded. 'Yes, Sebastian has a mission near there. It's where he made his reputation, converting the Indians.'

'What about you?' I asked. 'What are you doing here?'

Julia told me that she too wanted to find the Ninth Insight, but that she had no leads. She had come to this house after thinking repeatedly of her old friend, Hinton.

I was hardly listening. Marjorie and Karla had walked out of the kitchen and were standing in the hall, talking, cups of tea in their hands. Marjorie caught my eye but said nothing.

'Has she read much of the Manuscript?' Julia asked, nodding toward Marjorie.

'Just the Third Insight,' I said.

'We can probably get her out of Peru if that's what she wants.'

I turned and looked at her. 'How?'

'Rolando is leaving tomorrow for Brazil. We have some friends at the American Embassy there. They can get her back to the United States. We have helped other Americans this way.'

I looked at her and nodded tentatively. I realized I was having mixed feelings about what she had said. Part of me knew that leaving would be best for Marjorie. But another part wanted her to stay, to remain with me. I felt changed, energized, when she was around.

'I think I need to talk with her,' I finally said.

'Of course,' Julia replied. 'We can talk later.'

I got up and walked toward her. Karla was heading back toward the kitchen. Marjorie stepped around the corner of the hall out of sight. When I walked up, she was leaning back against the wall.

I pulled Marjorie into my arms. My body pulsated.

'Feel that energy?' I asked, whispering into her ear.

'It's incredible,' she said. 'What does it mean?'

'I don't know. We have some kind of connection.'

I glanced around. No one could see us. We kissed passionately.

When I pulled back to look at her face, she looked different, stronger somehow, and I thought back to the day we had met at Viciente and to the conversation in the restaurant at Cula. I couldn't believe the amount of energy I felt in her presence and when she touched me.

She held me tightly. 'Since that day at Viciente,' she said, 'I've wanted to be with you. I didn't know what to think about it then, but the energy is wonderful. I've never experienced anything like this.'

Out of the corner of my eye I noticed Karla walking up, smiling. She told us that dinner was ready so we made our way into the dining room and found a huge buffet of fresh fruits and vegetables and breads. Everyone served their plates and sat around a large table. After Mareta sang a blessing song we spent an hour and a half eating and talking casually. Hinton had lost his nervousness and he set a light-hearted mood which helped to ease the tension of our escape. Marjorie was talking freely and laughing. Sitting beside her filled me with warm love.

After dinner, Hinton took us back into the den where a custard dessert was served with a sweet liqueur. Marjorie and I sat on the couch and fell into a long conversation about our pasts and significant life experiences. We seemed to grow closer and closer. The only difficulty we discovered was that she lived on the west coast and I resided in the south. Later Marjorie dismissed the problem and laughed heartily.

'I can't wait until we get back to the United States,' she said. 'We'll have so much fun traveling back and forth.'

I sat back and gave her a serious look. 'Julia said she could arrange a way for you to go home now.'

'You mean both of us, don't you?' she replied.

'No, I . . . I can't go.'

'Why?' she asked, 'I can't leave without you. But I can't stand to stay here any longer either. I'll go crazy.'

'You'll have to go on ahead. I'll be able to leave soon.'

'No!' she said loudly. 'I can't stand that!'

Karla, who was walking back into the den from putting Mareta in bed, glanced toward us, then looked quickly away. Hinton and Julia were still talking, seemingly oblivious to Marjorie's outburst.

'Please,' Marjorie said. 'Let's just go home.'

I looked away.

'Okay, fine!' she said. 'Stay!' She stood and walked briskly toward the bedroom area.

My gut wrenched as I watched Marjorie walk away. The energy I had gained with her collapsed, and I suddenly felt weak and confused. I tried to shake it off. After all, I told myself, I hadn't known her that long. On the other hand, I thought, maybe she was correct. Maybe I should just go home. What difference could I make here anyway? Back at home I could perhaps marshal some support for the Manuscript, and stay alive, as well. I stood up and started to follow her down the hall, but for some reason I sat back down. I couldn't decide what to do.

'May I join you for a minute?' Karla was suddenly asking. I hadn't noticed that she was standing beside the sofa.

'Sure,' I said.

She sat down and looked at me with regard. 'I couldn't help overhearing what is going on,' she said. 'And I thought that before you made your decision, you might want to hear what the Eighth Insight says about addictions to people.'

'Yes, please, I want to know what that means.'

'When one first learns to be clear and to engage one's evolution, any of us can be stopped, suddenly, by an addiction to another person.'

'You're speaking of Marjorie and me, aren't you?'

'Let me explain the process,' she said. 'And you judge for yourself.'

'Okay.'

'First, let me say that I had a very hard time with this part of the insight. I don't think I would have ever understood if I had not met Professor Reneau.'

'Reneau?!' I exclaimed. 'I know him. We met when I was learning the Fourth Insight.'

'Well,' she said,' we met when we both had reached the Eighth Insight. He stayed at my house for several days.'

I nodded in amazement.

'He said that the idea of an addiction, as used in the Manuscript, explains why power struggles arise in romantic relationships. We've always wondered what causes the bliss and euphoria of love to end, to suddenly turn into conflict, and now we know. It is a result of the flow of energy between the individuals involved.

'When love first happens, the two individuals are giving each other energy unconsciously and both people feel buoyant and elated. That's the incredible high we all call being "in love." Unfortunately, once they expect this feeling to come from the other person, they cut themselves off from the energy in the universe and begin to rely even more on the energy from each other – only now there doesn't seem to be enough and so they stop giving each other energy and fall back into their dramas in an attempt to control each other and force the other's energy their way. At this point the relationship degenerates into the usual power struggle.'

She hesitated for a moment, as if checking whether I understood, then added, 'Reneau told me that our susceptibility to this kind of addiction can be described psychologically, if that will help you understand?'

I nodded again for her to continue. 'Reneau said the problem starts in our early family. Because of the energy competition there, none of us were able to complete an important psychological process. We weren't able to integrate our opposite sexual side.'

'Our what?'

'In my case,' she continued. 'I wasn't able to integrate my male side. In your case you weren't able to integrate your female side. The reason we can become addicted to someone of the opposite sex is that we've yet to access this opposite sex energy ourselves. You see, the mystical energy that we can tap as an inner source is both male and female. We can eventually open up to it, but when we first begin to evolve, we have to be careful. The integration process takes some time. If we connect prematurely with a human source for our female or male energy, we block the universal supply.'

I told her I didn't understand.

'Think of how this integration is supposed to work in an ideal family,' she explained, 'and then perhaps you can see what I mean. In any family, the child must first receive energy from the adults in his life. Usually, identifying with and integrating the energy of the same-sexed parent is accomplished easily, but receiving energy from the other parent can be more difficult because of the differences in the sexes.

'Let's use a female child as an example. All the little girl knows as she first attempts to integrate her male side is that she is extremely attracted to her father. She wants him around and close to her all the time. The Manuscript explains that what she really wants is male energy because this male energy complements her female side. From this male energy she receives a sense of completion and euphoria. But she mistakenly thinks that the only way to have this energy is by sexually possessing her father and keeping him close physically.

'Interestingly, because she intuits that this energy is really supposed to be her own and that she should be able to command this energy at will, she wants to direct the father as if he were that part of herself. She thinks he is magical and perfect and able to supply her every whim. In a less than ideal family, this sets up a power conflict between the little girl and her dad. Dramas are formed as she learns to posture herself in order to manipulate him into giving her the energy she desires.

'But in an ideal family, the father would remain un-competitive. He would continue to relate honestly and have enough energy so as to supply her unconditionally even though he can't do everything she asks. The important thing to know here, in our ideal example, is that the father would remain open and communicative. She thinks he is ideal and magical but if he honestly explains who he is and what he is doing and why, then the little girl can integrate his particular style and abilities and proceed past an unrealistic view of her father. In the end she will see him as just a particular human being, a human being with his own talents and faults. Once this true emulation takes place, then the child makes an easy transition from receiving her opposite-sex energy from her father to receiving it as part of the overall energy existing in the universe at large.

'The problem,' she went on, 'is that most parents, up to now, have been competing with their own children for energy, and that has affected all of us. Because this competition was taking place, none of us have quite resolved this opposite-sex issue. We're all stuck at the stage where we are still looking for our opposite-sex energy outside of ourselves, in the person of a male or female we can think of as ideal and magical and can possess sexually. See the problem?'

'Yes,' I said. 'I think I do.'

'In terms of our ability to evolve consciously,' she continued, 'we are faced with a critical situation. As I said before, according to the Eighth Insight, when we first begin to evolve, we automatically begin to receive our opposite-sex energy. It comes in naturally from the energy in the universe. But we must be careful, because if another person comes along who offers this energy directly we can cut ourselves off from the true source . . . and regress.' She chuckled to herself.

'What are you laughing at?' I asked.

'Reneau once made this analogy,' she said. 'He said that until we learn how to avoid this situation, we are walking around like a circle half complete. You know, we look like the letter C. We are very susceptible to a person of the opposite sex, some other circle half complete, coming up and joining with us – completing the circle that way – and giving us a burst of euphoria and energy that feels like the wholeness that a full connection with the universe produces. In reality, we have only joined up with another person who is looking for their other half on the outside too.

'Reneau said that this is a classical co-dependent relationship and that it has built-in problems that begin to arise immediately.'

She hesitated, as though she expected me to say something. But I only nodded.

'You see, the problem with this completed person, this O, that both people think they have reached, is that it has taken two people to make this one whole person, one supplying the female energy and one supplying the male. This one whole person consequently has two heads, or egos. Both people want to run this whole person they have created and so, just as in childhood, both people want to command the other, as if the other were themselves. This kind of illusion of completeness always breaks down into a power struggle. In the end, each person must take the other for granted and even invalidate them so that they can lead this whole self in the direction they want to go. But of course that doesn't work, at least not any more. Perhaps in the past, one of the partners was willing to submit themselves to the other – usually the woman, sometimes the man. But we are waking up now. No one wants to be subservient to anyone else any longer.'

I thought of what the First Insight had conveyed about power struggles within intimate relationships, and of the woman's outburst at the restaurant with Charlene. 'So much for romance,' I said.

'Oh, we can still have romance,' Karla replied. 'But first

we have to complete the circle on our own. We have to stabilize our channel with the universe. That takes time, but afterward we are never susceptible to this problem again and we can have what the Manuscript calls a higher relationship. When we connect romantically with another whole person after that, we create a super-person ... but it never pulls us from the path of our individual evolution.'

'Which is what you think Marjorie and I are doing to each other now, isn't it? Pulling ourselves off our paths?'

'Yes.'

'So how do we avoid these encounters?' I asked.

'By resisting the "love at first sight" feeling for a while, by learning to have platonic relationships with members of the opposite sex. But remember the process. You must have these relationships only with people who will reveal themselves totally, telling you how and why they are doing what they doing – just as this would have happened with the opposite-sexed parent during an ideal childhood. By understanding who these opposite-sexed friends really are on the inside, one breaks past one's own fantasy projection about that gender, and that releases us to connect again with the universe.

'Remember, also,' she continued, 'that this is not easy, especially if one has to break away from a current co-dependent relationship. It is a real pulling apart of energy. It hurts. But it must be done. Co-dependence is not some new malady some of us have. We're all co-dependent, and we're all growing out of it now.

'The idea is to begin to experience that sense of well-being and euphoria experienced in the first moment of a co-dependent relationship when you are alone. You get to have him or her on the inside. After that, you evolve forward and can find that special romantic relationship that really fits you.'

She paused. 'And who knows, if both you and Marjorie evolve further, perhaps you will find that you truly belong with each other. But understand: your relationship with her has no way of working now.'

Our conversation was interrupted as Hinton walked over and explained that he was retiring for the night, and that our rooms had been prepared. We both expressed our appreciation for his hospitality, and as he walked away, Karla said, 'I think I'm going to bed also. We'll talk later.'

I nodded and watched her as she left. Then I felt a hand on my shoulder. It was Julia.

'I'm going to my room,' she said. 'Do you know where yours is? I can show you.'

'Please,' I said, then asked, 'Where is Marjorie's room?'

She smiled as we walked down the hall and stopped in front of a particular door. 'Nowhere near yours,' she said. 'Mr Hinton is a very conservative man.'

I smiled back and bid her good night, then entered my room and held my stomach until I went to sleep.

I awoke to the smell of rich coffee. The aroma permeated the entire house. After I dressed, I walked into the den. An older male houseworker offered me a glass of fresh grape juice which I accepted.

'Good moming,' Julia said from behind me. I turned around. 'Good morning.'

She looked at me intensely, then asked, 'Have you discovered yet why we've run into each other again?'

'No,' I said. 'I haven't been able to think about it. I've been trying to understand addictions.'

'Yes,' she replied. 'I saw.'

'What do you mean?'

'I could tell what was happening by the way your energy field looked.'

'How did it look?' I asked.

'Your energy was connected to Marjorie's. When you were sitting here and she was in the other room, your field stretched all the way in there and attached to hers.'

I shook my head.

She smiled and put her hand on my shoulder. 'You had lost your connection with the universe. You had become addicted to Marjorie's energy as a substitute. It is the same way with all addictions – one goes through someone or something else to connect with the universe. The way to deal with this is to get your energy up and then center yourself again in what you are really doing here.'

I nodded and walked outside. She waited in the den. For about ten minutes I practiced the method of building energy that Sanchez had taught me. Gradually the beauty returned and I felt much lighter. I returned to the house. 'You look better,' Julia said.

'I feel better,' I replied.

'So what are your questions at this point?'

I thought for a minute. I had found Marjorie. That question had been answered. But I still wanted to find out where Wil was. And I still wanted to understand how people would be acting toward each other if they follow this Manuscript. If the Manuscript's effect was positive, why would Sebastian and the other priests be worried?

I looked at Julia. 'I need to grasp the rest of the Eighth

Insight and I still want to find Wil. Maybe he has the Ninth.'

'I'm going to Iquitos tomorrow,' she said. 'Would you like to go?'

I hesitated.

'I think Wil is there,' she added.

'How do you know?'

'Because of the thoughts I had about him last night.'

I said nothing.

'I had thoughts of you, too,' Julia continued. 'Of both of us going to Iquitos. You're involved in this somehow.'

'Involved in what?' I asked.

She grinned. 'In finding this last insight before Sebastian does.'

As she spoke, the image came to my mind of Julia and me arriving at Iquitos, but then deciding to go in separate directions for some reason. I felt I had a purpose but it was unclear.

I focused again on Julia. She was smiling.

'Where were you?' she asked.

'Sorry,' I said. 'I was thinking about something.'

'Was it important?'

'I don't know. I was thinking that once we get to Iquitos . . . that we would go in two different directions.'

Rolando came into the room.

'I brought the supplies you wanted,' he said to Julia. He recognized me and nodded politely.

'Good, thank you,' Julia replied. 'Did you see many soldiers?'

'No, I did not see any,' he said.

Marjorie walked into the room then and distracted me but I could hear Julia explaining to Rolando that she

262

thought Marjorie wanted to go with him to Brazil, where she would arrange passage back to the States.

I went over to Marjorie. 'How did you sleep?' I asked.

She looked at me as though deciding whether to remain angry. 'Not very well,' she said.

I nodded toward Rolando. 'He is Julia's friend. He is leaving this morning for Brazil. From there he will help you get back to the States.'

She appeared frightened.

'Look, you're going to be okay,' I said. 'They've helped other Americans. They know people at the American Embassy in Brazil. In no time you will be home.'

She nodded. 'I'm worried about you.'

'I'll be fine. Don't worry. As soon as I get back to the U.S., I'll call you.'

From behind me, Hinton announced that breakfast was being served. We walked into the dining room and ate. Afterward, Julia and Rolando seemed to be in a hurry. Julia explained that it was important for Rolando and Marjorie to get across the border before dark and the journey would take all day.

Marjorie packed some clothes that Hinton had given her, and later, while Julia and Rolando were talking by the door, I pulled Marjorie to the side.

'Don't worry about anything,' I said. 'Just keep your eyes open and perhaps you'll see the other insights.'

She smiled but said nothing. I watched with Julia as Rolando helped her load her things into his small car. Her eyes met mine briefly as they drove away.

'Do you think they will get through all right?' I asked Julia.

She looked at me and winked. 'Of course. And now, we

had better go, as well. I have some clothes for you.' She handed me a satchel of clothes and we loaded these and several boxes of foodstuff into the pick-up truck. We then said good-bye to Hinton and Karla and Mareta, and drove northeast toward Iquitos.

As we traveled, the landscape grew even more jungle-like and we saw very few signs of people. I began thinking of the Eighth Insight. Clearly it was a new understanding of how to treat others, but I didn't understand it completely. Karla had told me of the way one should treat children and the dangers of an addiction to a person. But both Pablo and Karla had alluded to a way to consciously project energy onto others. What was this about?

I caught Julia's eye and said, 'I haven't quite grasped the Eighth Insight.'

'How we approach other people determines how quickly we evolve, how quickly our life questions are answered,' she said.

'How does that work?' I asked.

'Think about your own situation,' she said. 'How have your questions been answered?'

'By people who came along, I guess.'

'Were you completely open to their messages?'

'Not really. I was mainly aloof.'

'Were the people who brought messages to you pulled back also?'

'No, they were very open and helpful. They . . .' I hesitated, unable to think of the correct way to express my idea.

'Did they help you by opening you up?' she asked. 'Did they fill you with warmth and energy somehow?'

Her remark uncapped an eruption of memories. I

recalled Wil's soothing attitude when I was on the verge of panic in Lima, and Sanchez's fatherly hospitality, and Father Carl's and Pablo's and Karla's concerned counsel. And now Julia's. They all had the same look in their eyes.

'Yes,' I said. 'All of you have done that.'

'That's right,' she said. 'We have, and we were doing it consciously, following the Eighth Insight. By lifting you up and helping you to get clear, we could search for the truth, the message, that you had for us. Do you understand that? Energizing you was the best thing we could do for ourselves.'

'What does the Manuscript say about all this, exactly?' 'It says that whenever people cross our paths, there is always a message for us. Chance encounters do not exist. But how we respond to these encounters determines whether we're able to receive the message. If we have a conversation with someone who crosses our path and we do not see a message pertaining to our current questions, it does not mean there was no message. It only means we missed it for some reason.'

She thought for a moment, then continued. 'Have you ever run into an old friend or acquaintance, talked for a minute and left, then run into him or her again the same day or the same week?'

'Yes, I have,' I replied.

'And what do you usually say? Something like "Well, fancy seeing you again," and laugh and, go on your way.'

'Something like that.'

'The Manuscript says that what we should do instead in that situation is to stop what we are doing, no matter what, and find out the message we have for that person, and that the person has for us. The Manuscript predicts that once humans grasp this reality, our interaction will slow down and become more purposeful and deliberate.'

'But isn't that hard to do, especially with someone who wouldn't know what you were talking about?'

'Yes, but the Manuscript outlines the procedures.'

'You mean, the exact way we're supposed to treat each other?'

'That's right.'

'What does it say?'

'Do you remember the Third Insight, that humans are unique in a world of energy in that they can project their energy consciously?'

'Yes.'

'Do you remember how this is done?'

I recalled John's lessons. 'Yes, it is done by appreciating the beauty of an object until enough energy comes into us to feel love. At that point we can send energy back.'

'That's right. And the same principle holds true with people. When we appreciate the shape and demeanor of a person, really focus on them until their shape and features begin to stand out and to have more presence, we can then send them energy, lifting them up.

'Of course, the first step is to keep our own energy high, then we can start the flow of energy coming into us, through us, and into the other person. The more we appreciate their wholeness, their inner beauty, the more the energy flows into them, and naturally, the more that flows into us.'

She laughed. 'It's really a rather hedonistic thing to do,' she said. 'The more we can love and appreciate others, the more energy flows into us. That's why loving and energizing others is the best possible thing we can do for ourselves.'

'I've heard that before,' I said. 'Father Sanchez says it often.'

I looked at Julia closely. I had the feeling I was seeing her deeper personality for the first time. She returned my gaze for an instant, then focused again on the road. 'The effect on the individual of this projection of energy is immense,' she said. 'Right now, for instance, you're filling me with energy. I can feel it. What I feel is a greater sense of lightness and clarity as I'm formulating my thoughts to speak.

'Because you are giving me more energy than I would have otherwise, I can see what my truth is and more readily give it to you. When I do that, you have a sense of revelation about what I'm saying. This leads you to see my higher self even more fully and so appreciate and focus on it at an even deeper level, which gives me even more energy and greater insight into my truth and the cycle begins over again. Two or more people doing this together can reach incredible highs as they build one another up and have it immediately returned. You must understand, though, that this connection is completely different from a co-dependent relationship. A co-dependent relationship begins this way but soon becomes controlling because the addiction cuts them off from their source and the energy runs out. Real projection of energy has no attachment or intention. Both people are just waiting for the messages.'

As she spoke I thought of a question. Pablo had said that I didn't get Father Costous's message at first because I set off his childhood drama.

'What do we do,' I asked Julia, 'if the person we are speaking with is already operating in a control drama and trying to pull us into it? How do we cut through that?'

Julia answered quickly. 'The Manuscript says if we do not assume the matching drama, then the person's own drama will fall apart.'

'I'm not sure I understand,' I said.

Julia was looking at the road ahead. I could tell she was in thought. 'Somewhere right through here is a house where we can buy some gasoline.'

I looked down at the gas gauge. It indicated the truck's tank was half full.

'We still have plenty of gas,' I said.

'Yes, I know,' she replied. 'But I had a thought about stopping and filling it up, so I think we should.'

'Oh, okay.'

'There's the road,' she said, pointing to the right.

We made the turn and drove almost a mile into the jungle before arriving at what looked like a supply house for fishermen and hunters. The dwelling was built at the edge of a river and several fishing boats were tied to the dock. We pulled up to a rusty pump and Julia went inside to find the owner.

I climbed out and stretched then walked around the building to the water's edge. The air was extremely humid. Although the thick canopy of trees blocked the sun, I could tell it was almost directly overhead. Soon the temperature would be scorching.

Suddenly a man behind me was speaking angrily in Spanish. I turned to see a short stocky Peruvian. He looked at me menacingly and repeated the statement.

'I don't understand what you're saying.'

He switched to English. 'Who are you? What are you doing here?'

I tried to ignore him. 'We're just here for gas. We'll be gone in a few minutes.' I turned around and faced the water again, hoping he would go away.

He walked to the side of me. 'I think you better tell me who you are, Yankee.'

I looked at him again. He appeared to be serious.

'I'm an American,' I said. 'I'm not sure where I'm going. I'm riding with a friend.'

'A lost American,' he said hostilely.

'That's right,' I said.

'What are you after here, American?'

'I'm not after anything,' I said, trying to walk back to the car, 'and I've done nothing to you. Leave me alone.'

I noticed suddenly that Julia was standing at the vehicle. When I looked, the Peruvian turned and looked too.

'It's time to leave,' Julia said. 'They're not in business any longer.'

'Who are you?' the Peruvian asked her in his hostile tone.

'Why are you so angry?' Julia asked in response.

The man's demeanor changed. 'Because it is my job to look after this place.'

'I'm sure you do a good job. But it's hard for people to talk if you're frightening them.'

The man stared, trying to figure Julia out.

'We're on our way to Iquitos,' Julia said. 'We're working with Father Sanchez and Father Carl. Do you know them?'

He shook his head, but the mention of the two priests settled him down even more. He finally nodded and walked away.

'Let's go,' Julia said.

We got in the truck and drove away. I realized how anxious and nervous I had been. I tried to shake it off.

'Did anything happen inside?' I asked.

Julia looked at me. 'What do you mean?'

'I mean did anything happen inside to explain why you had the thought to stop?'

She laughed, then said, 'No, all the action was outside.'

I looked at her.

'Have you figured it out?' she asked.

'No,' I replied.

'What were you thinking about just before we arrived?'

'That I wanted to stretch my legs.'

'No, before that. What were you asking about when we were talking?'

I tried to think. We were talking about childhood dramas. Then I remembered. 'You had said something that had confused me,' I said. 'You had said that a person cannot play a control drama with us unless we play the matching drama. I didn't understand that.'

'Do you understand now?'

'Not really. What are you getting at?'

'The scene outside clearly demonstrated what happens if you *do* play the matching drama.'

'How?'

She glanced at me briefly. 'What drama was the man playing with you?'

'He was obviously the intimidator.'

'Right, and what drama did you play?'

270

'I was just trying to get him off my back.'

'I know, but what drama were you playing?'

'Well, I started off in my aloofness drama, but he kept coming after me. '

'Then?'

The conversation was irritating me but I tried to get centered and stay with it. I looked at Julia and said, 'I guess I was playing a poor me.'

She smiled. 'That's right.'

'I noticed you handled him with no problem,' I said.

'Only because I didn't play the drama he expected. Remember that each person's control drama was formed in childhood in relation to another drama. Therefore each drama needs a matching drama to be fully played out. What the intimidator needs in order to get energy is either a poor me, or another intimidator.

'How did you handle it?' I asked, still confused.

'My drama response would have been to play the intimidator myself, trying to out-intimidate him. Of course, this would probably have resulted in violence. But instead I did what the Manuscript instructs. I named the drama he was playing. All dramas are covert strategies to get energy. He was trying to intimidate you out of your energy. When he tried that on me, I named what he was doing.'

'That's why you asked why he was so angry?'

'Yes. The Manuscript says that covert manipulations for energy can't exist if you bring them into conscious-ness by pointing them out. They cease to be covert. It is a very simple method. The best truth about what's going on in a conversation always prevails. After that the person has to be more real and honest.'

271

'That makes sense,' I said. 'I guess I've even named dramas myself before, though I didn't know what I was doing.'

'I'm sure. That's something all of us have done. We're just learning more about what is at stake. And the key to making it work is to simultaneously look beyond the drama at the real person in front of you, and send as much energy their way as possible. If they can feel energy coming in anyway, then it's easier for them to give up their way of manipulating for it.'

'What could you appreciate in that guy?' I said.

'I could appreciate him as a little insecure boy needing energy desperately. Besides, he brought you a very timely message, right?'

I looked at her. She appeared to be on the verge of laughter.

'You think we stopped there just so I could grasp how to deal with someone playing a drama?'

'That was the question you asked, wasn't it?'

I smiled, my good feeling beginning to return. 'Yes, I guess it was.'

A mosquito buzzing around my face forced me awake. I looked over at Julia. She was smiling as though recalling something humorous. For several hours after leaving the river camp we had ridden in silence, munching on the food Julia had prepared for the trip.

'You're awake,' Julia said.

'Yes,' I replied. 'How far is Iquitos?'

'The town is about thirty miles, but the Stewart Inn is only a few minutes ahead. It's a small inn and hunting camp. The owner is English and supports the

Manuscript.' She smiled again. 'We have had many good times together. Unless something has happened, he should be there. I hope we can get a lead on where Wil is.'

She pulled the truck to the side of the road and looked at me. 'We'd better get centered in where we are,' she said. 'Before I ran into you again, I had been floundering around wanting to help find the Ninth Insight but not knowing where to go. At one point I realized I had been thinking repeatedly of Hinton. I get to his house and who should show up but you. And you tell me that you're looking for Wil and that he's rumored to be in Iquitos. I have the intuition that we'll both be involved in finding the Ninth Insight, and then you have the intuition that at some point we separate and go in different directions. Is that pretty much it?'

'Yes,' I said.

'Well, I want you to know that after that, I got to thinking about Willie Stewart and the inn. Something is going to happen there.'

I nodded.

She drove the vehicle back on the road and around a curve. 'There's the inn,' Julia said.

Ahead about two hundred yards, where the road took another sharp bend to the right, was a two-story, Victorian style home.

We pulled into a gravel parking area and stopped. Several men were talking on the porch. I opened the door of the vehicle and was about to get out when Julia touched my shoulder.

'Remember,' she said, 'no one is here by accident. Stay alert for the messages.'

I followed her as we walked up on the porch. The men,

well-dressed Peruvians, nodded distractedly as we walked by them and into the house.

Once in the large foyer, Julia pointed to a dining room and asked me to pick a table and wait there while she looked for the owner.

I surveyed the room. It contained a dozen or so tables lined in two rows. I picked a table about halfway down and sat with my back against the wall. Three more men, all Peruvians, came in behind me and sat down across from my table. Another man came in soon after and took a table about twenty feet to my right. He sat at an angle where his back was slightly toward me. I noticed he was a foreigner, perhaps European.

Julia entered the room, spotted me, and then walked over and sat down facing me.

'The owner isn't here,' she said, 'and his clerk knew nothing of Wil.'

'Now what?' I asked.

She looked at me and shrugged. 'I don't know. We'll have to assume that someone here has a message for us.'

'Who do you think it is?'

'I don't know.'

'How do you know it will happen?' I asked, suddenly feeling skeptical. Even after all the mysterious co-incidences that had happened to me since I had been in Peru, I still had trouble believing one would occur now just because we wanted it to.

'Don't forget the Third Insight,' Julia replied. 'The universe is energy, energy that responds to our expectations. People are part of that energy universe too, so when we have a question, the people show up who have the answer.'

She cut her eyes to the other people in the room. 'I don't know who these people are, but if we could talk with them long enough, we would find a truth each had for us, some part of the answer to our questions.'

I looked at her askance. She leaned toward me across the table. 'Get it into your head. Everyone who crosses our path has a message for us. Otherwise they would have taken another path, or left earlier or later. The fact that these people are here means that they are here for some reason.'

I looked at her, still not sure whether I believed it was that simple.

'The hard part,' she said, 'is figuring out who to take time to talk with when talking with everyone is impossible.'

'How do you decide?' I asked.

'The Manuscript says there are signs.'

I was listening intently to Julia but for some reason I glanced around and looked at the man to my right He turned around at exactly the same time and looked back at me. As I caught his eye, he shifted his gaze back to his food. I also looked away.

'What signs?' I asked.

'Signs like that,' she said.

'Like what?'

'Like what you just did.' She nodded toward the man to my right.

'What do you mean?'

Julia leaned toward me again. 'The Manuscript says we will learn that sudden, spontaneous eye contact is a sign that two people should talk.'

'But doesn't that happen all the time?' I asked.

'Yes, it does,' she said. 'And after it happens, most people just forget about it and go on with what they are doing.'

I nodded. 'What other signs does the Manuscript mention?' I asked.

'A sense of recognition,' she replied. 'Seeing someone who looks familiar, even though you know you've never seen the person before.'

When she said that, I thought of Dobson and Reneau, of how familiar they looked when I had first seen them.

'Does the Manuscript say anything about why some people look familiar?' I asked.

'Not much. It just says we are members of the same thought group with certain other people. Thought groups are usually evolving along the same lines of interest. They think the same and that creates the same expression and outward experience. We intuitively recognize members of our thought group and very often they provide messages for us.'

I looked at the man to my right one more time. He did look vaguely familiar. Incredibly, as I gazed at him, he turned and glanced at me again. I quickly looked back at Julia.

'You *must* talk with this man,' Julia said.

I didn't respond. I felt uncomfortable with the idea of just walking up to him. I wanted to leave, to go on to Iquitos. I was about to make that suggestion when Julia spoke again, 'This is where we need to be,' she said, 'not Iquitos. We have to play this out. The trouble with you is that you're resisting the idea of walking up to him and starting a conversation.'

'How did you do that?' I asked.

'Do what?' she replied.

'Know what I was thinking.'

'There is nothing mysterious about it. It is a matter of looking closely at your expressions.'

'What do you mean?'

'When you are appreciating someone at a deeper level, you can see their most honest self beyond any facades they may put up. When you really focus at this level, you can perceive what someone is thinking as a subtle expression on their face. This is perfectly natural.'

'It sounds telepathic to me,' I said.

She grinned. 'Telepathy is perfectly natural.'

I glanced over at the man again. He did not look.

'You had better get your energy together and talk with him,' Julia said, 'before you lose the opportunity.'

I focused on increasing my energy until I felt stronger, then asked, 'What am I going to say to this guy?'

'The truth,' she said. 'Put the truth in a form you think he would recognize.'

'Okay, I will.'

I slid back my chair and walked over to where the man was sitting. He looked shy and nervous, the way I remembered Pablo looking the night I met him. I tried to look beyond the man's nervousness to a deeper level. When I did I seemed to perceive a new look on his face, one with more energy.

'Hello,' I said. 'You appear not to be a native Peruvian. I'm hoping you can help me. I'm looking for a friend of mine, Wil James.'

'Please sit down,' he said in a Scandinavian accent. 'I'm Professor Edmond Connor.'

He offered me his hand and said, 'I'm sorry. I do not know your friend, Wil.'

I introduced myself and then explained – just on a hunch that it would mean something to him – that Wil was searching for the Ninth Insight.

'I'm familiar with the Manuscript,' he said. 'I'm here to study its authenticity.'

'Alone?'

'I was to meet a Professor Dobson here. But so far he has not come. I don't understand the delay. He assured me that he would be here when I arrived.'

'You know Dobson?!'

'Yes. He is the one who is organizing an inspection of the Manuscript.'

'And he's all right? He's coming here?'

The Professor looked at me questioningly. 'Those were the plans we made. Has something been wrong?'

My energy fell. I realized that Dobson's meeting with Connor had been set up before Dobson's arrest. 'I met him on the airplane,' I explained, 'when I came to Peru. He was arrested in Lima. I have no idea what happened to him.'

'Arrested! My God!'

'When did you last speak with him?' I asked

'Several weeks ago, but our meeting time here was firm. He said he would call me if anything changed.'

'Do you remember why he wanted you to meet him here instead of in Lima?' I asked.

'He said there were some ruins around here and that he would be up in this area speaking with another scientist.'

'Did he mention where he would be talking to this scientist?'

'Yes, he said he had to go to, uh, San Luis, I believe. Why?'

'I don't know . . . I was just wondering.'

As I said this, two things happened simultaneously. First, I began thinking of Dobson, of seeing him again. We were meeting along a road with large trees. And then, at the same time, I looked out the window and saw, to my amazement, Father Sanchez walking up the porch steps. He looked tired and his clothes were dirty. In the parking lot another priest waited in an old car.

'Who is that?' Professor Connor asked.

'It's Father Sanchez!' I replied, barely able to contain my excitement.

I turned around and looked for Julia but she was no longer sitting at our table. I got up just as Sanchez walked into the room. When he saw me, he stopped abruptly, a look of total surprise on his face, then he walked over and embraced me.

'Are you all right?' he asked.

'Yes, fine,' I said. 'What are you doing here?'

Through his fatigue, he chuckled lightly. 'I didn't know where else to go. And I almost didn't make it here. Hundreds of troops are headed this way.'

'Why are the troops coming?' Connor asked from behind me, walking up to where Sanchez and I were standing.

'I'm sorry,' Sanchez replied. 'I do not know what the troops have in mind. I just know there are many.'

I introduced the two men and told Father Sanchez of Connor's situation. Connor appeared panicked.

'I must leave,' he said, 'but I have no driver.'

'Father Paul is waiting outside,' Sanchez said. 'He is

279

going back to Lima immediately. You may ride with him if you wish.'

'Indeed I do,' Connor said.

'Wait, what if they run into those troops?' I asked.

'I don't think they would stop Father Paul,' Sanchez said. 'He is not well-known.'

At that moment Julia came back into the room and saw Sanchez. The two hugged warmly and, again, I introduced Connor. As I spoke, Connor seemed to grow even more fearful and after only a few minutes, Sanchez told him that it was time for Father Paul to start back. Connor left to get his belongings from his room and quickly returned. Both Sanchez and Julia escorted him outside, but I told him good-bye there and waited at the table. I wanted to think. I knew meeting Connor was significant somehow, and that Sanchez finding us here was important, but I couldn't quite figure it out.

Before long, Julia came back into the room and sat down beside me. 'I told you something was going to happen here,' she said. 'If we hadn't stopped we wouldn't have seen Sanchez, or Connor for that matter. By the way, what did you learn from Connor?'

'I'm not sure yet,' I said. 'Where is Father Sanchez?'

'He checked into a room to rest for a while. He hasn't slept in two days.'

I looked away. I knew that Sanchez was tired, but hearing that he was unavailable disappointed me. I wanted very much to talk with him, to see if he could add some perspective to what was happening, especially concerning the soldiers. I felt uneasy and part of me wanted to flee with Connor.

Julia picked up on my impatience. 'Take it easy,' she

said. 'Slow down and tell me what you think of the Eighth Insight so far.'

I looked at her and tried to center myself. 'I'm not sure where to start.'

'What do you think the Eighth Insight is saying?'

I thought back. 'It's about a way of relating to other people, to children and to adults. It's about naming control dramas and breaking through them and focusing on other people in a way that sends them energy.'

'And?' she asked.

I focused on her face and immediately saw what she was getting at. 'And if we are observant about who to talk with, then we get the answers we desire as a result.'

Julia smiled broadly.

'Have I grasped the Insight?' I asked.

'Almost,' she said. 'But there's one more thing. You understand how one person can uplift another. Now you're about to see what happens in a group when all of the participants know how to interact this way.'

I walked out to the porch and sat in one of the wrought-iron chairs. After a few minutes Julia came through the door and joined me. We had eaten a leisurely dinner without much talking and afterward had decided to sit outside in the night air. Three hours had gone by since Sanchez had gone to his room and I was beginning to feel impatient again. When Sanchez suddenly walked outside and sat down with us I was relieved.

'Have you heard anything about Wil?' I asked him.

When I spoke, he slid his chair around to face Julia and me. I noticed that he was carefully adjusting the position of his chair so that he was an equal distance from each of us.

'Yes,' he said finally. 'I have.'

He paused again and appeared to be in thought, so I asked, 'What did you hear?'

'Let me tell you everything that happened,' he said. 'When Father Carl and I left to go back to my mission, we expected to find Father Sebastian there, along with the military. We expected an inquisition. When we arrived we found that Father Sebastian and the soldiers had left abruptly several hours earlier, after receiving a message.

'For a whole day we didn't know what was going on, then yesterday we were visited by a Father Costous, whom I understand you have met. He told us that he was directed to my mission by Wil James. Apparently Wil remembered the name of my mission from his conversation earlier with Father Carl, and intuitively knew that we would need the information Father Costous was bringing. Father Costous has decided to support the Manuscript.'

'Why did Sebastian leave so suddenly?' I asked.

'Because,' Sanchez said, 'he wanted to speed up the implementation of his plans. The message he received told him that Father Costous was about to expose his intention to destroy the Ninth Insight.'

'Sebastian found it?'

'Not yet, but he expects to. They found another document that indicated where the Ninth is.'

'Where is it supposed to be?' Julia asked.

'At the Celestine ruins,' Sanchez replied.

'Where is that?' I inquired.

Julia looked at me. 'About sixty miles from here. It's a dig the Peruvian scientists have excavated exclusively and with quite a lot of secrecy. It consists of several layers of ancient temples, first Mayan, then Inca. Apparently both cultures believed there was something special about that location.'

I suddenly realized that Sanchez was concentrating on the conversation with unusual intensity. When I talked, he would focus totally on me, without breaking his gaze at all. When Julia spoke, Father Sanchez shifted his position to focus completely on her. He seemed to be acting very deliberately. I wondered what he was doing, and at that precise moment there occurred a lull in the conversation. They both looked at me expectantly.

'What?' I asked.

Sanchez smiled. 'It's your time to speak.'

'Are we taking turns?' I asked.

'No,' Julia said, 'we are having a conscious conversation. Each person speaks when the energy moves to him. We could tell it had moved to you.'

I didn't know what to say.

Sanchez looked at me warmly. 'Part of the Eighth Insight is learning to interact consciously when in a group. But don't get self-conscious. Just understand the process. As the members of a group talk, only one will have the most powerful idea at any one point in time. If they are alert, the others in the group can feel who is about to speak, and then they can consciously focus their energy on this person, helping to bring out his idea with the greatest clarity.

'Then, as the conversation proceeds, someone else will have the most powerful idea, then someone else and so forth. If you concentrate on what is being said, you can feel when it is your turn. The idea will come up into your mind.'

Sanchez shifted his eyes to Julia, who asked, 'What idea were you having that you didn't express?'

I tried to think. 'I was wondering,' I said finally, 'why Father Sanchez was looking intensely at whomever was speaking. I guess I was wondering what it meant.'

'The key to this process,' Sanchez said, 'is to speak up when it is your moment and to project energy when it is someone else's time.'

'Many things can go wrong,' Julia interjected. 'Some people get inflated when in a group. They feel the power of an idea and express it, then because that burst of energy feels so good, they keep on talking, long after the energy should have shifted to someone else. They try to monopolize the group.

'Others are pulled back and even when they feel the power of an idea, they won't risk saying it. When this happens, the group fragments and the members don't get the benefit of all the messages. The same thing happens when some members of the group are not accepted by some of the others. The rejected individuals are prevented from receiving the energy and so the group misses the benefit of their ideas.'

Julia paused and we both looked at Sanchez, who was taking a breath to speak. 'How people are excluded is important,' he said. 'When we dislike someone, or feel threatened by someone, the natural tendency is to focus on something we dislike about the person, something that irritates us. Unfortunately, when we do this – instead of seeing the deeper beauty of the person and giving them energy – we take energy away and actually do them harm. All they know is that they suddenly feel less beautiful and less confident, and it is because we sapped their energy.'

'That is why,' Julia said, 'this process is so important. Humans are aging each other at a tremendous rate out there with their violent competitions.'

'But remember,' Sanchez added, 'in a truly functional group, the idea is to do the opposite of this, the idea is for every member's energy and vibration to increase because of the energy sent by all of the others. When this occurs, everyone's individual energy field merges with everyone else's and makes one pool of energy. It is as if the group is just one body, but one with many heads. Sometimes one head speaks for the body. Sometimes another talks. But in a group functioning this way, each individual knows when to speak and what to say because he truly sees life more clearly. This is the Higher Person the Eighth Insight talked about in connection with a romantic relationship between a man and a woman. But other groups can form one as well.'

Father Sanchez's words made me think of Father Costous suddenly, and of Pablo. Had this young Indian finally changed Father Costous's mind, leading him to now want to preserve the Manuscript? Was Pablo able to do this because of the power of the Eighth Insight?

'Where is Father Costous now?' I asked.

Both individuals looked mildly surprised at my question, but Father Sanchez quickly replied, 'He and Father Carl decided to go to Lima to speak with our church leaders about what Cardinal Sebastian seems to have planned.'

'I guess that's why he was so adamant about going to

your mission with you. He knew there was something else he was supposed to do.'

'Exactly,' Sanchez said.

A lull developed in the conversation and we looked at one another, each of us waiting for the next idea.

'The question now,' Father Sanchez finally said, 'is what are *we* supposed to do?'

Julia spoke first. 'I've had thoughts all along about being involved with the Ninth Insight somehow, of getting hold of it long enough to do something . . . but I can't quite see it clearly.'

Sanchez and I gazed at her intensely.

'I see this happening at a particular place . . .' she continued. 'Wait a minute. The place I've been thinking about is at the ruins, at the Celestine ruins. There is a particular spot there between the temples. I'd almost forgotten.' She looked back at us. 'That's where I need to go; I need to go to the Celestine ruins.'

As Julia finished, both she and Sanchez shifted their gaze to me.

'I don't know,' I said. 'I've been interested in why Sebastian and his people are so against the Manuscript. I found out it's because they fear the idea of our inner evolution . . . but now I don't know where to go . . . those soldiers are coming . . . it appears that Sebastian is going to find the Ninth Insight first . . . I don't know; I've been thinking I'm involved somehow in convincing him not to destroy it.'

I stopped speaking. My thoughts went to Dobson again and then abruptly to the Ninth Insight. I suddenly realized that the Ninth Insight was going to reveal where we humans were going with this evolution. I had wondered how humans would be acting toward each other as a result of the Manuscript, and that question had been answered with the Eighth Insight, and now the logical next question was: where is it all going to lead, how will human society change? That had to be what the Ninth was about.

I knew somehow that this knowledge could also be used to ease Sebastian's fears about conscious evolution . . . If he would listen.

'I still think Cardinal Sebastian can be convinced to support the Manuscript!' I said with conviction.

'You see yourself convincing him?' Sanchez asked me.

'No . . . no, not really. I'm with someone else who can reach him, someone who knows him and can speak at his level.'

As I said that, Julia and I both spontaneously looked at Father Sanchez.

He struggled to smile and spoke with resignation. 'Cardinal Sebastian and I have avoided a confrontation over the Manuscript for a long time. He has always been my superior. He considered me his protégé and I must admit that I looked up to him. But I guess I always knew that it would come to this. The first time you mentioned it, I knew that the task of convincing him was mine. My whole life has set me up for it.'

He looked intensely at Julia and me, then continued, 'My mother was a Christian reformer. She hated the use of guilt and coercion when evangelizing. She felt that people should come to religion because of love, not out of fear. My father, on the other hand, was a disciplinarian who later became a priest, and like Sebastian, believed adamantly in tradition and authority. That left me wanting to work within church authority, but always seeking ways it should be amended so that higher religious experience is emphasized.

'Dealing with Sebastian is the next step for me. I've been resisting it, but I know I have to go to Sebastian's mission at Iquitos.'

'I'll ride with you,' I said.

The Emerging Culture

The road north wound through dense jungle and across several large streams – tributaries, Father Sanchez told me – of the Amazon. We had risen early and said a quick good-bye to Julia, then left in a vehicle Father Sanchez had borrowed, a truck with raised, oversized tires and four-wheel drive. As we traveled, the terrain rose slightly and the trees became more widely spaced and larger.

'This looks like the land around Viciente,' I told Sanchez.

He smiled at me and said, 'We've entered a fifty mile stretch of land about twenty miles wide that is different, more energized. It runs all the way to the Celestine ruins. On all sides of this area is pure jungle.'

Far to the right, at the edge of the jungle, I noticed a patch of cleared land. 'What is that?' I asked, pointing. 'That,' he said, 'is the government's idea of agricultural development.'

A wide stretch of trees had been bulldozed and pushed into piles, some partially burned. A herd of cattle grazed aimlessly amid the wild grasses and eroded topsoil. As we passed, several looked our way, distracted by the sound. I noticed another patch of freshly bulldozed land

and realized the development was moving toward the larger trees we were traveling through.

'That looks awful,' I said.

'It is,' Sanchez replied. 'Even Cardinal Sebastian is against it.'

I thought of Phil. Maybe this was the place he was trying to protect. What had happened to him? Suddenly, I thought of Dobson again. Connor had said Dobson intended to come to the inn. Why had Connor been there to tell me that? Where was Dobson now? Deported? Imprisoned? It did not escape my notice that I had spontaneously perceived an image of Dobson in connection with Phil.

'How far away is Sebastian's mission?' I asked.

'About an hour,' Sanchez replied. 'How are you feeling?'

'What do you mean?'

'I mean, how is your energy level?'

'I think it's high,' I said. 'Lots of beauty here.'

'What did you think of the talk we three had last night?' he asked.

'I thought it was amazing.'

'Did you understand what was happening?'

'You mean, the way ideas were bubbling up in each of us at different times?'

'Yes, but the greater meaning of that.'

'I don't know.'

'Well, I've been thinking about it. This way of consciously relating, in which everyone attempts to bring out the best in others rather than to have power over them, is a posture the entire human race will eventually adopt. Think of how everyone's energy level and pace of evolution will increase at that point!'

'Right,' I said, 'I've been wondering how human culture will change as the overall energy level rises.'

He looked at me as if I had hit on the exact question. 'That's what I want to know, too,' he said.

We looked at each other for an instant and I knew we were both waiting to see who would have the next idea. Finally he said, 'The answer to that question must be in the Ninth Insight. It must explain what will happen as the culture evolves forward.'

'That's what I think,' I said.

Sanchez slowed the truck. We were approaching a cross-roads and he seemed undecided about which route to take.

'Do we go anywhere near San Luis?' I asked.

He looked directly into my eyes. 'Only if we turn left at this intersection. Why?'

'Connor told me Dobson had been planning to come through San Luis on his way to the inn. I think it was a message.'

We continued to look at each other.

'You were already slowing down at this crossroads,' I said. 'Why?'

He shrugged. 'I don't know; the most direct route to Iquitos is straight ahead. I just felt hesitant for some reason.'

A chill shot through my body.

Sanchez raised one eyebrow and grinned. 'I guess we had better go through San Luis, huh?'

I nodded and felt a rush of energy. I knew that stopping at the inn and making contact with Connor was taking on more meaning. As Sanchez turned left and proceeded toward San Luis, I watched the roadside expectantly.

Thirty or forty minutes passed and nothing happened. We rode through San Luis and still nothing of note occurred. Then, suddenly, a horn blew and we turned to see a silver jeep roaring up behind us. The driver was frantically waving. He looked familiar.

'That's Phil!' I said.

We pulled to the side of the road and Phil jumped out and ran to my side of the truck, grabbing my hand and nodding at Sanchez.

'I don't know what you're doing here,' he said, 'but the road ahead is full of soldiers. You'd better come back and wait with us.'

'How did you know we were coming?' I asked.

'I didn't,' he said. 'I just looked up and saw you pass by. We're about a half mile back.' He looked around for a second, then added, 'We'd better get off this road!'

'We'll follow you,' Father Sanchez said.

We followed as Phil turned his jeep around and headed back the way we'd come. He turned east onto another road and quickly parked. From behind a group of trees, another man walked out to greet the vehicle. I couldn't believe my sight. It was Dobson!

I climbed out of the truck and walked toward him. He was equally surprised and hugged me warmly.

'It's great to see you!' he said.

'Same here,' I replied. 'I thought you were shot!'

Dobson patted my back and said, 'No, I guess I panicked; they simply detained me. Later, some officials sympathetic to the Manuscript let me go. I've been running ever since.'

He paused, smiling at me. 'I'm glad you're all right. When Phil told me he had met you at Viciente and then was arrested with you later, I didn't know what to think. But I should have known we would run into each other again. Where are you headed?'

'To see Cardinal Sebastian. We think he intends to destroy the last Insight.'

Dobson nodded and was about to say something, but Father Sanchez walked up.

I quickly introduced them.

'I think I heard your name mentioned in Lima,' Dobson said to Sanchez, 'in connection with a couple of priests that were being detained.'

'Father Carl and Father Costous?' I asked.

'I think those were their names, yes.'

Sanchez only shook his head slightly. I watched him for a moment, then Dobson and I spent several minutes describing our experiences since being separated. He told me he had studied all eight insights and seemed anxious to say something else, but I interrupted to tell him that we had met Connor and that he had returned to Lima.

'He'll probably be detained himself,' Dobson said. 'I regret I couldn't get to the inn in time, but I wanted to come to San Luis first to see another scientist. As it turned out I couldn't find him, but I did run into Phil and . . .'

'What is it?' Sanchez asked.

'Maybe we ought to sit down,' Dobson said. 'You won't believe this. Phil found a copy of part of the Ninth Insight!'

No one moved.

'He found a translated copy?' Father Sanchez asked.

'Yes.'

Phil had been doing something inside his vehicle and was now walking toward us.

293

'You found part of the Ninth?' I asked him.

'I didn't find it, really,' he said. 'It was given to me. After you and I were captured, I was taken to another town. I don't know where. After a while, Cardinal Sebastian showed up. He kept probing me about the work at Viciente and my efforts to save the forests. I didn't know why until a guard brought me a partial copy of the Ninth Insight. The guard had stolen it from some of Sebastian's people, who had apparently just translated it. It talks about the energy of old forests.'

'What did it say?' I asked Phil.

He paused, thinking, so Dobson asked again that we sit down. He led us to a spot where a tarpaulin was laid out in the center of a partial clearing. The place was beautiful. A dozen large trees formed a circle about thirty feet in diameter. Within the circle were highly fragrant tropical bushes and long-stemmed ferns of the brightest green I had ever seen. We sat facing each other.

Phil looked at Dobson. Then Dobson looked at Sanchez and me and said, 'The Ninth Insight explains how human culture will change in the next millennium as a result of conscious evolution. It describes a significantly different way of life. For instance, the Manuscript predicts that we humans will voluntarily decrease our population so that we all may live in the most powerful and beautiful places on the Earth. But remarkably, many more of these areas will exist in the future, because we will intentionally let the forests go uncut so that they can mature and build energy.

'According to the Ninth Insight, by the middle of the next millennium,' he continued, 'humans will typically live among five hundred year old trees and carefully tended gardens, yet within easy travel distance of an urban area of incredible technological wizardry. By then, the means of survival – foodstuffs and clothing and transportation – will all be totally automated and at everyone's disposal. Our needs will be completely met without the exchange of any currency, yet also without any overindulgence or laziness.

'Guided by their intuitions, everyone will know precisely what to do and when to do it, and this will fit harmoniously with the actions of others. No one will consume excessively because we will have let go of the need to possess and to control for security. In the next millennium, life will have become about something else.

'According to the Manuscript,' he went on, 'our sense of purpose will be satisfied by the thrill of our own evolution – by the elation of receiving intuitions and then watching closely as our destinies unfold. The Ninth depicts a human world where everyone has slowed down and become more alert, ever vigilant for the next meaningful encounter that comes along. We will know that it could occur anywhere: on a path that winds through a forest, for instance, or on a bridge that traverses some canyon.

'Can you visualize human encounters that have this much meaning and significance? Think how it would be for two people meeting for the first time. Each will first observe the other's energy field, exposing any manipulations. Once clear, they will consciously share life stories until, elatedly, messages are discovered. Afterward, each will go forward again on their individual journey, but they will be significantly altered. They will vibrate at a new level and will thereafter touch others in a way not possible before their meeting.'

As we gave him energy, Dobson became ever more eloquent and inspired with his description of the new human culture. And what he said rang true. I personally had no doubt that he was describing an achievable future. Yet I also knew that throughout history many visionaries had glimpsed such a world, Marx for example, yet no way had been found to create such a utopia. Communism had become a tragedy.

Even with the knowledge imparted in the first eight insights, I couldn't imagine how the human race could get to the place described by the Ninth, considering human behavior generally. When Dobson paused. I voiced my concern.

'The Manuscript says our natural pursuit of the truth will lead us there,' Dobson explained, smiling directly at me. 'But to grasp how this movement will occur, perhaps it is necessary to visualize the next millennium in the same manner you studied the current one with me on the airplane, remember? As though you were living through it in one lifetime?'

Dobson briefly informed the other men of the process and then continued, 'Think about what has occurred already in this millennium. During the Middle Ages we lived in a simple world of good and evil, defined by the churchmen. But during the Renaissance we broke free. We knew there had to be more to man's situation in the universe than the churchmen knew, and we wanted the full story.

'We then sent science out to discover our true situation, but when this effort didn't provide the answers we needed right away, we decided to settle in, and turned our modern work ethic into a preoccupation that secularized reality and squeezed the mystery out of the world. But now, we can see the truth of that preoccupation. We can see that the real reason we spent five centuries creating material supports for human life was to set the stage for something else, a way of life that returns the mystery to existence.

'That is what the information now returning from the scientific method indicates: mankind is on this planet to consciously evolve. And as we learn to evolve and pursue our particular path, truth by truth, the Ninth Insight says the overall culture will transform in a very predictable way.'

He paused, but no one said anything. Obviously we wanted to hear more.

'Once we reach the critical mass,' he continued, 'and the insights begin to come in on a global scale, the human race will first experience a period of intense introspection. We'll grasp how beautiful and spiritual the natural world really is. We'll see trees and rivers and mountains as temples of great power to be held in reverence and awe. We'll demand an end to any economic activity that threatens this treasure. And those closest to this situation will find alternative solutions to this pollution problem because someone will intuit these alternatives as they seek their own evolution.

'This will be part of the first great shift that will occur,' he continued, 'which will be a dramatic movement of individuals from one occupation to another because when people begin to receive clear intuitions of who they really are and what they're supposed to be doing, they very often discover they're in the wrong job and they have to jump to another type of work in order to continue to grow. The Manuscript says that during this period people will sometimes change careers several times during their lifetimes.

'The next cultural shift will be an automation of the production of goods. To the people who are doing the automating, the technicians, this will feel like a need to make the economy run more efficiently. But as their intuitions become clearer, they will see that what automation is actually doing is freeing up everyone's time, so that we can pursue other endeavors.

'The rest of us, meanwhile, will be following our own intuitions within our chosen occupations and wishing we had even more of this free time. We will realize that the truth we have to tell and the things we have to do are too unique to fit within a usual job setting. So we will find ways to cut our employment hours to pursue our own truth. Two or three people will hold what used to be one full-time job. This trend will make it easier for those displaced by the automation to find at least part-time jobs.'

'But what about money?' I asked. 'I can't believe people will voluntarily reduce their incomes.'

'Oh, we won't have to,' Dobson said. 'The Manuscript says our incomes will remain stable because of the people who are giving us money for the insights we provide.'

I almost laughed. 'What?'

He smiled and looked directly at me. 'The Manuscript says that as we discover more about the energy dynamics of the universe, we will see what really happens when we give someone something. Right now the only spiritual idea about giving is the narrow concept of religious tithing.'

He moved his gaze to Father Sanchez. 'As you know, the scriptural notion of tithing is interpreted most commonly as an injunction to give ten percent of one's income to a church. The idea behind this is that whatever we give will be returned many times. But the Ninth Insight explains that giving is really a universal principle of support, not just for churches, but for everyone. When we give, we receive in return because of the way energy interacts in the universe. Remember, when we project energy into someone this creates a void in ourselves which, if we are connected, fills up again. Money works exactly the same way. The Ninth Insight says that once we begin to give constantly, we will always have more coming in than we could possibly give away.

'And our gifts,' he went on, 'should go to the persons who have given us spiritual truth. When people come into our lives at just the right time to give us the answers we need, we should give them money. This is how we will begin to supplement our incomes and ease out of the occupations which limit us. As more people engage in this spiritual economy we will begin a real shift into the culture of the next millennium. We will have moved through the stage of evolving into our right occupation and will be entering the stage of getting paid for evolving freely and offering our unique truth to others.'

I looked at Sanchez; he was listening intensely and appeared radiant.

'Yes,' he said to Dobson. 'I see that clearly. If everyone were participating then we would be giving and receiving constantly and this interaction with others, this exchange of information, would become everyone's new work, our new economic orientation. We'd be paid by the people we touched. This situation would then allow the material supports of life to become fully automated, because we would be too busy to own those systems, or to operate them. We would want material production automated and run like a utility. We'd own stock in it, perhaps, but the situation would free us up to expand what is already the information age.

'But the important thing for us right now is that we can now understand where we are going. We could not save the environment and democratize the planet and feed the poor before because for so long we could not release our fear of scarcity and our need to control, so that we could give to others. We couldn't release it because we had no view of life that served as an alternative. Now we do!'

He looked at Phil. 'But wouldn't we need a cheap source of energy?'

'Fusion, superconductivity, artificial intelligence,' Phil said. 'The technology to automate is probably not that far away, now that we have the knowledge of why to do it.'

'That's right,' Dobson said. 'The most important thing is that we see the truth of this way of life. We're here on this planet not to build personal empires of control, but to evolve. Paying others for their insights will begin the transformation and then as more and more parts of the economy are automated, currency will disappear altogether. We won't need it. If we are correctly following our intuitive guidance then we will take only what we need.'

'And we'll understand,' Phil interjected, that the natural areas of the Earth have to be nurtured and

300

protected for the sources of incredible power that they are.'

As Phil spoke, our full attention went to him. He seemed surprised by the lift it provided.

'I haven't studied all of the insights,' he said, looking at me. 'In fact, after the guard helped me escape, I might not have kept this part of the Ninth at all if I hadn't run into you earlier. I remembered what you said about this Manuscript being important. But even though I haven't read the other insights, I do understand the importance of keeping the automation in harmony with the energy dynamics of the Earth!

'My interest has been forests and the part they play in the ecosphere,' he continued. 'I know now that it always has been, ever since I was a child. The Ninth Insight says that as the human race evolves spiritually, we will voluntarily decrease the population to a point sustainable by the Earth. We will be committed to living within the natural energy systems of the planet. Farming will be automated except for the plants one wants to energize personally and then consume. The trees necessary for construction will be grown in special, designated areas. This will free the remainder of the Earth's trees to grow and age and finally mature into powerful forests.

'Eventually, these forests will be the rule rather than the exception, and all human beings will live in close proximity to this kind of power. Think what an energy-filled world we will live in.'

'That ought to raise everyone's energy level,' I said.

'Yes, it would,' Sanchez said distractedly, as though he were thinking ahead about what the increase in energy would mean.

Everyone waited.

'It would accelerate,' he said finally, 'the pace of our evolution. The more readily we have energy flowing into us, the more mysteriously the universe responds by bringing people into our lives to answer our questions.' He looked thoughtful again. 'And every time we follow an intuition and some mysterious encounter leads us forward, our personal vibration increases.

'Onward and upward,' he continued, half to himself. 'If history continues, then . . .'

'We'll continue to achieve higher and higher levels of energy and vibration,' Dobson said, finishing his sentence.

'Yes,' Sanchez said. 'That's it. Excuse me for a minute.' He got up and walked several yards into the forest and sat down alone.

'What else does the Ninth Insight say?' I asked Dobson.

'We don't know,' he said. 'That's where the part we have ends. Would you like to see it?'

I told him I would, so he walked to his truck and came back with a manila folder. Inside were twenty typed pages. I read the manuscript, impressed with how thoroughly Dobson and Phil had captured its basic points. When I came to the last page I understood why they said it was only a part of the Ninth Insight. It ended abruptly, in the middle of a concept. Having just introduced the idea that the transformation of the planet would create a totally spiritual culture and would raise human beings to higher and higher vibrations, it suggested that this rise would lead to the occurrence of something else, but it didn't say what.

After an hour, Sanchez stood up and walked over to

me. I had been content to sit with the plants, observing their incredible energy fields. Dobson and Phil were standing behind their jeep talking. 'I think we should go on to Iquitos,' he said.

'What about those soldiers?' I asked.

'I think we should risk it. I've had a clear thought that we can make it through if we leave right now.'

I agreed to go with his intuition and we walked over and told Dobson and Phil our plans.

Both men supported the idea, then Dobson said, 'We've also been discussing what to do. We're going directly to the Celestine ruins, I think. Maybe we can help save the rest of the Ninth Insight.'

We bade them good-bye and drove north again.

'What are you thinking about?' I asked after a period of silence.

Father Sanchez slowed the truck and looked at me. 'I'm thinking about Cardinal Sebastian, about what you have said: that he would stop fighting the Manuscript if only he could be made to understand.'

As Father Sanchez made this statement, my mind wandered into a daydream of actually confronting Sebastian. He was standing in a courtly room looking down at us. At that moment he had the power to destroy the Ninth Insight and we were fighting to make him understand before it was too late.

When I finished the thought, I noticed Sanchez was smiling at me.

'What were you seeing?' he asked.

'I was just thinking of Sebastian.'

'What was happening?'

'The image of confronting Sebastian was clearer. He was about to destroy the last insight. We were trying to talk him out of it.'

Sanchez took a deep breath, 'It looks like whether the rest of the Ninth Insight becomes known will depend on us.'

My stomach drew into a knot at the idea. 'What should we say to him?'

'I don't know. But we must persuade him to see the positive, to understand that the Manuscript as a whole doesn't negate but clarifies the truth of the church. I'm sure the rest of the Ninth Insight does just that.'

We rode in silence for an hour, seeing no other traffic of any kind. My thoughts raced through the events which had transpired since I'd come to Peru. I knew the Manuscript's insights had finally merged in my mind into one consciousness. I was alert to the mysterious way my life evolved, as revealed by the First Insight. I knew that the whole culture was sensing this mystery again as well, and we were in the process of constructing a new world view, as pointed out by the Second. The Third and Fourth had showed me that the universe was in reality a vast system of energy and that human conflict was a shortage of and a manipulation for this energy.

The Fifth Insight revealed that we could end this conflict by receiving an inpouring of this energy from a higher source. For me, this ability had almost become habit. The Sixth, that we could clear our old repeated dramas, and find our true selves, was also permanently etched in my mind. And the Seventh had set in motion the evolution of these true selves: through question, intuition of what to do, and answer. Staying in this magic flow was truly the secret of happiness.

And the Eighth, knowing how to relate in a new way to others, bringing out in them the very best, was the key to keeping the mystery operating and the answers coming.

All the Insights had integrated into a consciousness that felt like a heightened sense of alertness and expectation. What was left, I knew, was the Ninth, which revealed where our evolution was taking us. We had discovered some of it. What about the rest?

Father Sanchez pulled the truck to the side of the road.

'We're within four miles of Cardinal Sebastian's mission,' he said. 'I think we should talk.'

'Okay.'

'I don't know what to expect but I presume all we can do is drive right in.'

'How large a place is this?'

'Large. He has developed this mission for twenty years. He selected this location to serve the rural Indians whom he felt had been neglected. But now students come from all over Peru. He has administrative duties with the church organization in Lima, but this is his special project. He is totally devoted to this mission.'

He looked directly into my eyes. 'Please stay alert. There may come a time when we need to help each other.'

After saying this, Sanchez drove ahead. For several miles we saw nothing, then we passed two military jeeps parked at the right side of the road. The soldiers inside looked at us intensely as we drove by.

'Well,' Father Sanchez said, 'they know we are here.' A mile further we came to the entrance to the mission. Large iron gates protected the paved drive. Although the gates were open, a jeep and four soldiers blocked our way and signaled us to stop. One of the military men talked into a short-wave radio.

Sanchez smiled as a soldier walked up. 'I'm Father Sanchez, here to see Cardinal Sebastian. '

The soldier scrutinized Sanchez, then me. He turned and walked back to the soldier with the radio. They talked without taking their eyes off us. After several minutes the soldier came back and said we should follow them.

The jeep led us up the tree-lined drive for several hundred yards until we came to the mission grounds. The church was built of cut stone and was massive, capable of seating, I guessed, over a thousand people. On both sides of the church were two other buildings which looked like classrooms. Both were four stories high.

'This place is impressive,' I said.

'Yes, but where are the people?' he asked.

I noticed the paths and walkways were empty.

'Sebastian runs a famous school here,' he said. 'Why are there no students?'

The soldiers led us to the entrance of the church and asked us politely but firmly to get out and follow them inside. As we walked up the cement steps, I could see several trucks parked behind an adjacent building. Thirty or forty soldiers stood at attention nearby. Once inside we were led through the sanctuary and asked to enter a small room. There we were searched thoroughly and told to wait. The soldiers left and the door was locked.

'Where is Sebastian's office?' I asked.

'Further back toward the rear of the church,' he said.

The door suddenly opened. Flanked by several

soldiers stood Sebastian. His posture was tall and erect.

'What are you doing here?' Sebastian asked Sanchez.

'I want to talk with you,' Sanchez said.

'About what?'

'The Ninth Insight of the Manuscript.'

'There's nothing to discuss. It will never be found.'

'We know you've already found it.'

Sebastian's eyes widened. 'I will not allow this insight to be disseminated,' he said. 'It is not the truth.'

'How do you know it's not the truth?' Sanchez asked. 'You could be wrong. Let me read it.'

Sebastian's face softened as he looked at Sanchez. 'You used to think I would make the correct decision in a matter of this kind.'

'I know,' Sanchez said. 'You were my mentor. My inspiration. I patterned my mission after yours.'

'You respected me until this Manuscript was discovered,' Sebastian said. 'Don't you see how divisive it is? I tried to let you go your own way. I even let you alone after I knew you were teaching the insights. But I will not let this document destroy everything our church has built.'

Another soldier walked up behind Sebastian and asked to see him. Sebastian glanced at Sanchez, then walked back into the hall. We could still see but could no longer hear the conversation. The message obviously alarmed Sebastian. As he turned to walk away, he signaled for all the soldiers to follow him except for one, whom he apparently told to wait with us.

The soldier walked into the room and leaned against the wall, a disturbed look on his face. He was only about twenty years old.

'What is wrong?' Sanchez asked him.

The soldier only shook his head.

'Is it about the Manuscript, the Ninth Insight?'

The soldier's face displayed surprise. 'What do you know of the Ninth Insight?' he asked timidly.

'We're here to save it,' Sanchez said.

'I too want it saved,' the soldier replied.

'Have you read it?' I asked.

'No,' he said. 'But I have heard the talk. It brings our religion alive.'

Suddenly, from outside the church came the sound of gunfire.

'What's going on?!' Sanchez asked.

The soldier stood motionless.

Sanchez gently touched his arm, 'Help us.'

The young soldier walked to the door and checked the hall, then said. 'Someone has broken into the church and stolen a copy of the Ninth Insight. They seem to still be here on the grounds somewhere.'

More gunfire broke out.

'We must try to help them,' Sanchez told the young man.

He looked horrified.

'We must do what's right,' Sanchez stressed. 'This is for the whole world.'

The soldier nodded and said we should move to another area of the church where there would be less activity, that perhaps he could find a way to help. He led us down the hall and up two flights of stairs to a larger corridor which spanned the full width of the church.

'Sebastian's office is right below us, two stories down,' the young man said.

Suddenly we could hear a group of people running down an adjacent corridor, heading our way. Sanchez and the soldier were ahead of me and ducked into a room to the right. I knew I couldn't reach that room so I ran into the one next to it and closed the door.

I was in a classroom. Desks, podium, closet. I ran to the closet, found it unlocked, and squeezed in amid boxes and several musty smelling jackets. I attempted to conceal myself as best I could, but I knew if anyone checked in the closet, I would be discovered. I tried not to move, not even to breathe. The door to the classroom squeaked open and I could hear several people enter and walk about the room. One seemed to be coming toward the closet, then stopped and headed in the other direction. They were talking loudly in Spanish. Then silence. No movement.

I waited ten minutes before I slowly cracked the closet door and looked out. The room was empty. I walked to the door. There was no indication of anyone outside. I quickly walked to the room where Sanchez and the soldier had hidden. To my surprise, I found it was not a room at all but a hallway. I listened but could hear nothing. I leaned against the wall, feeling anxiety in the pit of my stomach. I quietly called out Sanchez's name. No response. I was alone. I could feel a slight dizziness from the anxiety.

I took a deep breath and tried to talk to myself; I had to keep my wits about me and increase my energy. For several minutes, I struggled until the colors and shapes in the hallway had more presence. I tried to project love. Finally I felt better, and thought of Sebastian again. If he was in his office, Sanchez would go there.

Ahead, the hallway ended at another stairway, so I walked two flights down to the first level. Through the window of the stairway door, I looked down the corridor. No one was in view. I opened the door and walked ahead, not sure where I wanted to go.

Then I heard Sanchez's voice coming from a room in front of me. The door was cracked. Sebastian's voice boomed back at him. As I approached the door, a soldier inside opened it suddenly and pointed a rifle at my heart, forcing me inside and against the wall. Sanchez acknowledged me with a glance and put his hand on his solar plexus. Sebastian shook his head in disgust. The young soldier who had helped us was nowhere to be seen.

I knew that Sanchez's gesture to his stomach meant something. All I could think of was that he needed energy. As he spoke, I focused on his face, trying to see his higher self. His energy field widened.

'You can't stop the truth,' Sanchez said. 'People have a right to know.'

Sebastian looked condescendingly at Sanchez. 'These insights violate the scriptures. They could not be true.'

'But do they really violate the scriptures, or do they just show us what the scriptures mean?'

'We know what they mean,' Sebastian said. 'We've known for centuries. Have you forgotten your training, your years of study?'

'No, I haven't,' Sanchez said. 'But I also know that the insights expand our spirituality. They . . .'

'According to whom?' Sebastian shouted. 'Who wrote this Manuscript anyway? Some pagan Mayan who learned somewhere how to speak Aramaic? What did these people know? They believed in magic places and mysterious energy. They were primitives. The ruins where the Ninth was found is called the Celestine Temples, the *Heavenly* Temples. What could this culture possibly know about heaven?

'Did their culture endure?' he continued. 'No. No one knows what happened to the Mayans. They just disappeared without a trace. And you want us to believe this Manuscript? This document makes it sound as though humans are in control, as though we are in charge of change in the world. We are not. God is. The only issue humans face is whether to accept the scriptural teachings and thereby win our own salvation.'

'But think about that,' Sanchez replied, 'What does accepting the teachings and winning salvation really mean? What is the process through which this happens? Doesn't the Manuscript show us the exact process of becoming more spiritual, connected, saved – the way it actually feels? And don't the Eighth and Ninth show us what would happen if everyone were acting this way?'

Sebastian shook his head and walked away, then turned and looked at Sanchez piercingly. 'You haven't even seen the Ninth Insight.'

'Yes. I have. Part of it.'

'How?'

'Part of it was described to me before we arrived here. I read another section a few minutes ago.'

'What?! How?'

Sanchez walked closer to the older priest. 'Cardinal Sebastian, people everywhere want this last insight revealed. It places the other insights into perspective. It shows us our destiny. What spiritual consciousness really is!'

'We know what spirituality is, Father Sanchez.'

'Do we? I think not. We've spent centuries talking about it, visualizing it, professing our belief in it. But we've always characterized this connection as something abstract, something we believe in intellectually. And we've always cast this connection as something an individual must do to avoid something bad happening, rather than to acquire something good and tremendous. The Manuscript describes the inspiration that comes when we are truly loving others and evolving our lives forward.'

'Evolve! Evolve! Listen to yourself, Father, you have always fought against the influence of evolution. What has happened to you?'

Sanchez collected himself. 'Yes, I fought against the idea of evolution as a replacement for God, as a way to explain the universe without reference to God. But now I see that the truth is a synthesis of the scientific and religious world views. The truth is that evolution is the way God created, and is still creating.'

'But there is no evolution,' Sebastian protested. 'God created this world and that's it.'

Sanchez glanced at me but I had no ideas to express.

'Cardinal Sebastian,' he continued, 'the Manuscript describes the progress of succeeding generations as an evolution of understanding, an evolution toward a higher spirituality and vibration. Each generation incorporates more energy and accumulates more truth and then passes that status on to the people of the next generation, who extend it further.'

'That's nonsense,' Sebastian said. 'There is only one way to become more spiritual and that's by following the examples in the scriptures.'

312

'Exactly!' Sanchez said. 'But again, what are the examples? Isn't the story of the scriptures a story of people learning to receive God's energy and will within? Isn't that what the early prophets led the people to do in the Old Testament? And isn't that receptivity to God's energy within what culminated in the life of a carpenter's son, to the extent that we say God, himself, descended to Earth?

'Isn't the story of the New Testament,' he continued, 'the story of a group of people being filled with some kind of energy that transformed them? Didn't Jesus, himself, say that what he did, we could do also, and more? We've never really taken that idea seriously, not until now. We're only now grasping what Jesus was talking about, where he was leading us. The Manuscript clarifies what he meant! How to do it!'

Sebastian looked away, his face red with anger.

During the pause in the conversation, a high ranking officer burst into the room and told Sebastian that the intruders had been seen.

'Look!' the officer said, pointing out the window. 'There they are!'

Three or four hundred yards away we could see two figures running through an open field headed toward the forest. A number of soldiers at the edge of the clearing seemed ready to open fire.

The officer turned from the window and looked at Sebastian, his radio raised.

'If they get to the wooded area,' he said, 'they will be hard to find. Do I have your permission to open fire?'

As I watched the two running, I suddenly recognized who they were.

'That's Wil and Julia!' I shouted.

Sanchez walked even closer to Sebastian. 'In the name of God, you cannot commit murder over this!'

The officer persisted. 'Cardinal Sebastian, if you want this Manuscript contained, I must give the order now.'

I was frozen.

'Father, trust me,' Sanchez was saying. 'The Manuscript will not erode all you have built, all you have stood for. You cannot kill these people.'

Sebastian shook his head. 'Trust you . . .?' Then he sat down on his desk and looked at the officer. 'We will shoot no one. Tell your troops to capture them alive.'

The officer nodded and walked out of the room. Sanchez said, 'Thank you, you made the right choice.'

'Not to kill, yes,' Sebastian said. 'But I will not change my mind. This Manuscript is a curse. It would undermine our basic structure of spiritual authority. It would entice people to think they are in control of their spiritual destiny. It would undermine the discipline needed to bring everyone on the planet into the church, and people would be caught wanting when the rapture comes.' He looked hard at Sanchez. 'At this moment, thousands of troops are arriving. It doesn't matter what you or anyone else does. The Ninth Insight will never leave Peru. Now get out of my mission.'

As we sped away, we could hear dozens of trucks approaching in the distance.

'Why did he let us go?' I asked.

'I suppose because he thinks it makes no difference,'

314

Sanchez replied, 'that there's nothing we can do. I really don't know what to think.' His eyes met mine. 'We didn't convince him, you know.'

I too, was confused. What did it mean? Perhaps we hadn't been there to convince Sebastian after all. Perhaps we were just supposed to delay him.

I glanced back at Sanchez. He was concentrating on driving and searching the roadside for any sign of Wil and Julia. We had decided that we would double back in the direction they had been running, but so far we had seen nothing. As we rode, my mind wandered to the Celestine ruins. I imagined what the site looked like: the tiered excavations, the scientist's tents, the looming pyramidal structures in the background.

'They don't seem to be in these woods,' Sanchez said. 'They must have had a vehicle. We must decide what to do.'

'I think we should go to the ruins,' I said.

He looked at me. 'We might as well. There's nowhere else to go.'

Sanchez made a turn to the west.

'What do you know of these ruins?' I asked.

'They were built by two different cultures, as Julia said. The first, the Mayans, had a thriving civilization there, though most of their temples were further north in the Yucatan. Mysteriously, all signs of their civilization suddenly vanished about 600 BC without apparent cause. The Incas developed another civilization afterward at the same location.'

'What do you think happened to the Mayans?'

Sanchez glanced at me. 'I don't know.'

We rode for several minutes in silence, then I suddenly

315

remembered that Father Sanchez had told Sebastian he had read more of the Ninth Insight.

'How did you see more of the Ninth Insight?' I asked.

'The young soldier who helped us knew where another part was being hidden. After you and I were separated, he took me to another room and showed it to me. It added only a few more concepts to what Phil and Dobson told us, but it gave me the points I used with Sebastian.'

'What did it say specifically?'

'That the Manuscript would clarify many religions. And would help them fulfill their promise. All religion, it says, is about humankind finding relationship to one higher source. And all religions speak of a perception of God within, a perception that fills us, makes us more than we were. Religions become corrupted when leaders are assigned to explain God's will to the people instead of showing them how to find this direction within themselves.

'The Manuscript says that sometime in history one individual would grasp the exact way of connecting with God's source of energy and direction and would thus become a lasting example that this connection is possible.' Sanchez looked at me. 'Isn't that what Jesus really did? Didn't he increase his energy and vibration until he was light enough to...?' Sanchez ended his sentence without finishing it and seemed to be deep in thought.

'What are you thinking?' I asked.

Sanchez looked perplexed. 'I don't know. The soldier's copy ended right there. It said that this individual would blaze a path that the whole human race was destined to follow. But it didn't say where this path led.'

For fifteen minutes we rode in silence. I attempted to receive some indication of what would happen next, but I could think of nothing. I seemed to be trying too hard.

'There are the ruins,' Sanchez said.

Ahead, through the forest to the left of the road, I could make out three large pyramidal shaped structures. After we parked and walked closer, I could tell the pyramids were constructed of cut stone and were spaced an equal distance apart, about a hundred feet. Between them was an area paved with a smoother stone. Several excavation sites were dug into the base of the pyramids.

'Look, there!' Sanchez said, pointing toward the more distant pyramid.

A lone figure was sitting in front of the structure. As we walked that way, I noticed an increase in my energy level. By the time we reached the center of the paved area I felt incredibly energized. I looked at Sanchez and he raised an eyebrow. When we got closer I recognized the person by the pyramid to be Julia. She sat cross-legged and held several papers in her lap.

'Julia,' Sanchez called.

Julia turned and stood up. Her face seemed iridescent.

'Where is Wil?' I asked.

Julia pointed to her right. There, perhaps a hundred yards away was Wil. He seemed to be glowing in the fading twilight.

'What is he doing?' I asked.

'The Ninth,' Julia replied, holding the papers toward us. Sanchez told Julia that we had seen some of the insight, the part which foretold of a human world transformed by conscious evolution.

'But where does this evolution take us?' Sanchez asked.

Julia didn't answer. She just held up the papers in her hand, as though she expected us to read her mind.

'What?' I asked.

Sanchez reached over and touched my forearm. His look reminded me to stay alert and to wait.

'The Ninth reveals our ultimate destiny,' Julia said. 'It makes it all crystal clear. It reiterates that as humans, we are the culmination of the whole of evolution. It talks about matter beginning in a weak form and increasing in complexity, element by element, then species by species, always evolving into a higher state of vibration.

'When primitive humans came along, we continued this evolution unconsciously by conquering others and gaining energy and moving forward a little bit, and then being conquered ourselves by someone else and losing our energy. This physical conflict continued until we invented democracy, a system that didn't end the conflict but shifted it from a physical to a mental level.

'Now,' Julia went on, 'we're bringing this whole process into consciousness. We can see that all of human history has prepared us to achieve conscious evolution. Now, we can increase our energy and experience the coincidences consciously. This carries evolution onward at a faster pace, lifting our vibrations even higher.'

She hesitated for a moment, looking at each of us, then repeated what she had said, 'Our destiny is to continue to increase our energy level. And as our energy level increases, the level of vibration in the atoms of our bodies increases.'

She hesitated again.

'What does that mean?' I asked.

318

'It means,' Julia said, 'that we are getting lighter, more purely spiritual.'

I looked at Sanchez. He was focused intensely on Julia.

'The Ninth Insight,' Julia continued, 'says that as we humans continue to increase our vibration, an amazing thing will begin to happen. Whole groups of people, once they reach a certain level, will suddenly become invisible to those who are still vibrating at a lower level. It will appear to the people on this lower level that the others just disappeared, but the group themselves will feel as though they are still right here – only they will feel lighter.'

As Julia talked I noticed her face and body changing somewhat. Her body was taking on the characteristics of her energy field. Her features were still clear and distinct but it was no longer muscles and skin at which I was looking. She looked as though she were made of pure light, glowing from within.

I looked at Sanchez. He appeared the same way. To my amazement, everything appeared this way: the pyramids, the stone under our feet, the surrounding forest, my hands. The beauty I was able to perceive had increased beyond anything I had experienced before, even when on the ridge top.

'When humans begin to raise their vibrations to a level where others cannot see them,' Julia continued, 'it will signal that we are crossing the barrier between this life and the other world from which we came and to which we go after death. This conscious crossing over is the path shown by the Christ. He opened up to the energy until he was so light he could walk on water. He transcended death right here on Earth, and was the first to cross over, to expand the physical world into the spiritual. His life demonstrated how to do this, and if we connect with the same source we can head the same way, step by step. At some point everyone will vibrate highly enough so that we can walk into Heaven, in our same form.'

I noticed Wil was walking slowly toward us. His movements seemed unusually graceful, as though he was gliding.

'The Insight says,' Julia went on, 'that most individuals will reach this level of vibration during the third millennium, and in groups consisting of the people with whom they are most connected. But some cultures in history have already achieved the vibration. According to the Ninth Insight, the Mayans crossed over together.'

Julia abruptly stopped talking. From behind us, we heard muffled voices in Spanish. Dozens of soldiers were entering the ruins, coming right for us. To my surprise I was unafraid. The soldiers continued to walk in our general direction but strangely not directly toward us.

'They can't see us!' Sanchez said. 'We're vibrating too highly!'

I looked again at the soldiers. He was right. They were walking twenty or thirty feet to our left, completely ignoring us.

Suddenly we heard loud shouts in Spanish by the pyramid to our left. The soldiers closest to us stopped and ran in that direction.

I strained to see what was happening. Another group of soldiers were emerging from the forest holding the arms of two other men. Dobson and Phil. The sight of their capture jolted me, and I could feel my energy level

320

plummet. I looked at Sanchez and Julia. Both were staring intently toward the soldiers and appearing equally disturbed.

'Wait!' Wil seemed to shout from the opposite direction. 'Don't lose your energy!' I felt the words as well as heard them. They were slightly garbled.

We turned to see Wil walking quickly toward us. As we watched he seemed to say something else, but this time the words were completely unintelligible. I realized I was having trouble focusing. His image was becoming hazy, distorted. Gradually, as I stared in disbelief, he disappeared altogether.

Julia turned to face, Sanchez and me. Her energy level seemed lower but she was completely undaunted, as though whatever just happened clarified something.

'We weren't able to maintain the vibration,' she said. 'Fear lowers one's vibration tremendously.' She looked toward the spot where Wil had faded from view. 'The Ninth Insight says that while some individuals may cross over sporadically, a general rapture will not occur until we have abolished fear, until we can maintain a sufficient vibration in all situations.'

Julia's excitement grew. 'Don't you see? We can't do it yet but the role of the Ninth Insight is to help create that confidence. The Ninth Insight is the insight of knowing where we are headed. All the other insights create a picture of the world as one of incredible beauty and energy, and of ourselves as increasing our connection with and thus seeing this beauty.

'The more beauty we can see, the more we evolve. The more we evolve, the higher we vibrate. The Ninth Insight shows us that ultimately our increased perception and vibration will open us up to a Heaven that is already before us. We just can't see it yet.

'Whenever we doubt our own path, or lose sight of the process, we must remember what we are evolving toward, what the process of living is all about. Reaching heaven on Earth is why we are here. And now we know how it can be done . . . how it will be done.'

She paused momentarily, 'The Ninth mentions that a Tenth Insight exists. I think it must reveal . . .'

Before she could finish, a burst of machine-gun fire ripped up the stone tiles by our feet. We all dived to the ground, our hands raised. No one spoke as the soldiers came and confiscated the papers and took each of us in a different direction.

The first weeks after my capture were spent in constant terror. My energy level fell dramatically as one military officer after another questioned me threateningly about the Manuscript.

I played the dumb tourist and claimed ignorance. After all, it was true that I had no idea who among the other priests had copies, or how widespread public acceptance of the document had become. Gradually, my tactic worked. Over time the soldiers seemed to grow tired of me and passed me on to a group of civilian authorities, who took a different approach.

These officials sought to convince me that my trip to Peru had been crazy from the beginning, crazy because according to them the Manuscript never really existed. They argued that the insights had in fact been invented by a small group of priests with the intent to foster rebellion. I had been duped, these officials told me, and I let them talk.

After a while, the conversations became almost cordial. Everyone began to treat me as a guiltless victim of this plot, as a gullible Yankee who had read too many adventure tales and found himself lost in a foreign country.

And because my energy was so low, I possibly would have become vulnerable to this brainwashing, had something else not occurred. I was suddenly transferred from the military base where I was being held to a governmental compound near the airport in Lima – a compound in which Father Carl was also being detained. The coincidence brought back some of my lost confidence.

I was walking in the open courtyard when I first saw him sitting on a bench, reading. I strolled over, restraining my exuberance and hoping I wouldn't attract attention from the officials inside the building. When I sat down, he looked up at me and grinned.

'I've been expecting you,' he said.

'You have?'

He put down his book, and I could see the delight in his eyes.

'After Father Costous and I came to Lima,' he explained, 'we were immediately detained and separated, and I've been here in custody ever since. I couldn't understand why, nothing seemed to be happening. Then I began to think repeatedly of you.' He gave me a knowing look. 'So, I figured you would show up.'

'I'm grateful you're here,' I said. 'Did anyone tell you what happened at the Celestine ruins?'

'Yes,' Father Carl replied. 'I spoke briefly with Father Sanchez. He was held here for a day before being taken away.'

'Is he all right? Did he know what happened to the others? And what about him? Were they going to imprison him?'

'He had no information about the others, and as for Father Sanchez, I don't know. The government's strategy is to methodically search out and destroy all copies of the Manuscript. Then to treat the whole affair as a grand hoax. We'll all be thoroughly discredited, I imagine, but who knows what they will ultimately do with us.'

'What about Dobson's copies,' I said, 'the First and Second Insights he left in the States?'

'They already have them,' Father Carl replied. 'Father Sanchez told me that agents of the government found out where they were hidden and stole them. Apparently Peruvian agents have been everywhere. They knew about Dobson from the beginning, and about your friend, Charlene.'

'And you think when the government is through, no copies will remain?'

'I think it will be a miracle if any survive.'

I turned away, feeling my new-found energy diminish.

'You know what this means, don't you?' Father Carl asked.

I looked at him but said nothing.

'This means,' he continued, 'that each of us must remember exactly what the Manuscript said. You and Sanchez didn't convince Cardinal Sebastian to release the Manuscript, but you delayed him long enough for the Ninth Insight to be understood. Now it has to be communicated. You have to be involved in communicating it.'

His statement made me feel pressured and my aloof

drama activated inside me. I leaned against the back of the bench and looked away, which made Father Carl laugh. Then, at just that moment, we both realized several embassy officials were watching us from an office window.

'Listen,' Father Carl said quickly. 'From now on the insights will have to be shared between people. Each person, once they hear the message and realize that the insights are real, must pass on the message to everyone who is ready for it. Connecting with energy is something humans have to be open to and talking about and expecting, otherwise the whole human race can go back to pretending that life is about having power over others and exploiting the planet. If we go back to doing this, then we won't survive. Each of us must do what we can to get this message out.'

I noticed that the two officials were out of the building, walking toward us.

'One more thing,' Father Carl said, speaking lowly.

'What?' I asked.

'Father Sanchez told me Julia had spoken of a Tenth Insight. It hasn't yet been found and no one knows where it might be.'

The officials were almost on us.

'I've been thinking,' Father Carl continued, 'that they're going to release you. You may be the only one that can look for it.'

The men suddenly interrupted our conversation and escorted me toward the building. Father Carl smiled and waved and said something else but I could only half pay attention. As soon as Father Carl had mentioned a Tenth Insight, I had been consumed by a thought of Charlene.

Why was I thinking of her? How was she connected to a Tenth Insight?

The two men insisted that I pack the few things I had left and follow them to the front of the Embassy and into a state vehicle. From there I was taken directly to the airport and up to a boarding concourse, where one of them smiled faintly and looked at me from behind thick glasses.

His smile faded as he handed me a passport and a ticket for a flight to the United States . . . then told me in a heavy Peruvian accent to never, never return.

THE END

The Celestine Prophecy

The story behind the phenomenal international bestseller

In 1995 and 1996, James Redfield's *The Celestine Prophecy* was the bestselling book in the world – a phenomenal novel which spent over three years on the *New York Times* bestseller list, appeared on the *Sunday Times* list and featured on numerous other lists throughout the world. In 1996 the eagerly awaited sequel, *The Tenth Insight: Holding The Vision*, also became an instant international bestseller.

Born in March 1950, James Redfield grew up in a rural area near Birmingham, Alabama and from an early age he was motivated by a need for clarity in spiritual matters. He was brought up in a Methodist tradition that was loving and community-oriented, but James was frustrated by a lack of answers to the many questions he had about the true nature of spiritual experience.

As a young man he studied Eastern philosophies, including Taoism and Zen, while majoring in sociology at Auburn University. He later received a Master's degree in counselling and spent more than fifteen years as a therapist to abused adolescents.

During this time, James was drawn into the Human Potential Movement and turned to it for theories about intuitions and psychic phenomena that would help him to treat his troubled clients. All along he was forming ideas that would eventually find their way into *The Celestine Prophecy* and in 1989 he left his job as a therapist to write full-time, synthesizing his interest in interactive psychology, Eastern and Western philosophies, science, futurism, ecology, history and mysticism.

Using an adventure parable approach that has been called 'part Indiana Jones, part Scott Peck,' *The Celestine Prophecy* created a model for spiritual perception and actualization that resonated with millions of people and focused on the mysterious coincidences that occur in each of our lives.

In *The Celestine Vision*, his non-fiction title published in 1997, Redfield says, 'The actual writing of *The Celestine Prophecy* occurred from January 1989 through to April 1991 and was characterized by a sort of trial-and-error process. Quite amazingly, as I remembered earlier experiences and wrote about them, lacing them into an adventure tale, striking coincidences would occur to emphasize the particular points I wanted to make. Books would show up mysteriously, or I would have timely encounters with the exact sort of individuals I was attempting to describe. Sometimes strangers would open up to me for no apparent reason and tell me about their spiritual experiences.'

Feeling 'kind of stuck' at one point, Redfield went to the high-energy vortexes of Sedona, Arizona – an area that he and many others regard as a sacred place. As he recounts in an interview in *Body, Mind, Spirit* magazine: 'I was sitting on a ridge near the Chapel Vortex and trying to work with the notes for the book. It was not coming easily. All of a sudden, a crow flew out of the canyon and right over my head and then flew back into the canyon. I continued to make notes. I was having some trouble getting the story to flow out. The crow came out of the canyon again and flew over me, then back into the canyon, so I went into the canyon, and when I sat down the book just came pouring out.'

The flow halted, however, when Redfield began sending *The Celestine Prophecy* to publishers in 1992. He received a few offers, but they did not seem right. 'The companies all wanted to take between a year and eighteen months to get the book out. I felt the book was timely and that we should get it out right away.

'All the coincidences stopped, and I felt dead in the water. I was interpreting the complete lack of publishing opportunity as a failure, a negative event, and that was the interpretation that had stopped the coincidences that I felt had been leading me forward. When I realized what was happening, I snapped to attention and made more revisions to the book, emphasizing this point.'

Within days, Redfield heard about a publishing consultant from New York who had just moved into the area. The two met, and the coincidences began again. Redfield quickly decided to self-publish the book and just as he began printing, he met Salle Merrill, who brought with her a timely emphasis on the importance of giving.

Now husband and wife, James and Salle filled the trunk of their car with copies of *The Celestine Prophecy* and drove to bookshops, meeting readers and talking about the book. 'Of the first 3,000 copies we printed, we mailed or personally gave away 1,500 to small bookshops and individuals in Alabama, Florida, North Carolina and Virginia.

As James recalls in *The Celestine Vision*, 'Word of mouth recommendations took care of everything else.' In six months, there were over 100,000 copies in print, the book was available in all fifty states and it was appearing in countries around the world. 'It sold not because of any publicity I did, but because others began to give it to their friends everywhere.'

After a perceptive sales rep brought the self-published book to the attention of Warner Books, Warner bought the rights and published the hardcover edition in March 1994. The book quickly climbed to the No. 1 position on the *New York Times* bestseller list, where it remained for more than three years. It was joined by *The Tenth Insight*, which built upon the nine insights revealed in the first novel. The book was also published in the UK in 1994 by Bantam Books and became a major *Sunday Times* bestseller.

The Celestine series of adventure parables continued in 1999 with the publication of *The Secret of Shambhala: In Search of the Eleventh Insight* (Bantam Books). Set in modern-day Tibet, Redfield's next novel continued the inspiring journey of *The Celestine Prophecy* and *The Tenth Insight* – carrying readers to a new adventure in a sacred place where truths that can affect all of humanity await.

James Redfield was awarded the prestigious Medal of the Presidency of the Italian Senate at the XXIII Pio Manzu International Conference in Italy, and has also been widely involved in saving America's last wilderness

THE TENTH INSIGHT
HOLDING THE VISION
JAMES REDFIELD

The journey continues in this superb sequel to *The Celestine Prophecy*.

The Celestine Prophecy and its companion *The Celestine Prophecy: An Experiential Guide*, took the world by storm – capturing the spiritual moment and focusing on the quest for knowledge and enlightenment.

With *The Tenth Insight* James Redfield continues the compelling spiritual adventure and carries his readers further into a new spiritual understanding that is emerging in human culture throughout the world. As he travels beyond the here and now, he explores what might be called the Fourth Spatial Dimension, or the Afterlife Dimension, where Near Death Experiences occur. Through the insights we gain during these spiritual journeys we reach a greater understanding of the way we live our lives and the path of evolution as it relates to us today.

'*The Tenth Insight* is about compassion, forgiveness and tenacity'
Larry Dossey, author of *Healing Words*

'Spellbinding...a worthy sequel to his *Celestine* masterpiece, James Redfield packs thrills, suspense and spiritual wisdom into a book you cannot put down. You must read *The Tenth Insight*!' Brian Weiss, M.D., author of *Many Lives, Many Masters*

A Bantam Paperback
9780553815733

THE CELESTINE VISION
LIVING THE NEW SPIRITUAL AWARENESS

JAMES REDFIELD

In this step-by-step guide James Redfield begins his exploration of the emerging interest in spirituality around the globe. Beginning with a survey of the most common synchronistic experiences, he shows how those interested in broadening their spiritual perception can actually experience for themselves the shifts in consciousness that are changing the world.

Described as the most direct explanation of the new world vision presented in the phenomenally successful *Celestine* fiction series, and based on James Redfield's own experiences and those reported to him from every corner of the world since the writing of *The Celestine Prophecy* and *The Tenth Insight*, this book describes the first-hand growth techniques *Celestine* fans everywhere are looking for.

'The godfather of gurus is back... his style is clear and engaging'
Express

'The world-changing results sound like dreams come true'
Los Angeles Times

A Bantam Paperback
9780553506372

THE SECRET OF SHAMBHALA
IN SEARCH OF THE ELEVENTH INSIGHT

JAMES REDFIELD

The Insights found in *The Celestine Prophecy* and *The Tenth Insight* have touched the lives of many millions of people.

Now, in *The Secret of Shambhala*, James Redfield takes us on an exciting spiritual adventure through Tibet and to Shambhala, a secret, mysterious village set high in the Himalayan mountains. Here exists a community of people who live according to the Insights revealed in *The Celestine Prophecy* and *The Tenth Insight*. But as this inspiring adventure unfolds, it is clear that Shambhala is in danger, threatened by foreign forces who seek to destroy its higher spiritual plane of existence.

'The best yet from James Redfield' Marianne Williamson, author of *A Return to Love*

'Great storytelling... read this book to get in touch with the mysteries of great masters' Deepak Chopra, author of *The Seven Spiritual Laws of Success*

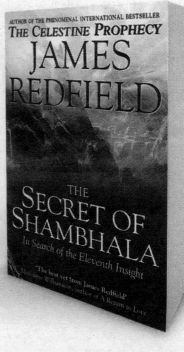

A Bantam Paperback
9780553506389

GOD AND THE EVOLVING UNIVERSE
THE NEXT STEP IN PERSONAL EVOLUTION

JAMES REDFIELD
MICHAEL MURPHY AND SYLVIA TIMBERS

From James Redfield, the author of the phenomenal international bestseller, *The Celestine Prophecy*, and Michael Murphy, the author of the bestselling *Golf in the Kingdom*, with documentary filmmaker Sylvia Timbers, comes the story of the past, present and future of human potential – and a journey that can take contemporary seekers to the next level of spiritual evolution.

Written with the insight of the *The Celestine Prophecy* and representing a unique collaboration of global visionaries, *God and the Evolving Universe* is a book that deepens our knowledge of personal growth and shows how each of us can begin to integrate our extraordinary experiences into a heightened synchronistic flow – allowing us to participate consciously in an unfolding evolutionary adventure.

'Informative, thought-provoking and challenging' *Library Journal*

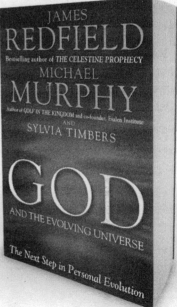

A Bantam Paperback
9780553814811